D0986363

Perfect Babies' Names

Rosalind Fergusson, a former teacher, is a freelance writer and editor with a wide range of reference books to her name. She lives in Kent with her husband David and occupies her leisure time with walking, sailing, literature, and music.

Other titles in the *Perfect* series

Perfect Answers to Interview Questions – Max Eggert
Perfect Best Man – George Davidson
Perfect CV – Max Eggert
Perfect Interview – Max Eggert
Perfect Numerical Test Results – Joanna Moutafi and Ian Newcombe
Perfect Personality Profiles – Helen Baron
Perfect Psychometric Test Results – Joanna Moutafi and Ian Newcombe
Perfect Pub Quiz – David Pickering
Perfect Punctuation – Stephen Curtis
Perfect Readings for Weddings – Jonathan Law
Perfect Wedding Speeches and Toasts – George Davidson

Perfect
Babies' Names

Rosalind Fergusson

BOOKS

Published by Random House Books 2007

2 4 6 8 10 9 7 5 3

Copyright © Rosalind Fergusson 2007

Rosalind Fergusson has asserted her right under the Copyright, Designs
and Patents Act 1988 to be identified as the author of this work

This book is sold subject to the condition that it shall not, by way of trade or
otherwise, be lent, resold, hired out, or otherwise circulated without the
publisher's prior consent in any form of binding or cover other than that in
which it is published and without a similar condition, including this condition,
being imposed on the subsequent purchaser

First published in the United Kingdom in 2007 by Random House Books

Random House Books
Random House, 20 Vauxhall Bridge Road,
London SW1V 2SA

www.randomhouse.co.uk

Addresses for companies within The Random House Group Limited can be
found at: www.randomhouse.co.uk/offices.htm

The Random House Group Limited Reg. No. 954009

A CIP catalogue record for this book
is available from the British Library

ISBN 9781905211661

The Random House Group Limited makes every effort to ensure that the
papers used in its books are made from trees that have been legally sourced
from well-managed and credibly certified forests. Our paper procurement
policy can be found at: www.randomhouse.co.uk/paper.htm

Typeset by Palimpsest Book Production Limited,
Grangemouth, Stirlingshire

Printed in the UK by CPI Bookmarque, Croydon CR0 4TD.

Contents

Introduction   vii

Using the book   ix

Top ten tips   x

A–Z   1

Appendix: The most popular names in the UK   240

Introduction

Choosing a name for your new baby can be a difficult task. Only when your child grows up will you know whether you made the right choice. If you have already decided to name your daughter or son after a particular person – a beloved relative, perhaps, or a current celebrity – you will probably not be reading this book. However, if you remain undecided, or if you want to make sure that your chosen name has a pleasant meaning and no undesirable associations, then *Perfect Babies' Names* will give you useful guidance and plenty of new ideas.

The range of names that people give their babies is constantly expanding. Fifty years ago, children given one of the top ten names for their year of birth were sure to have at least one classmate with the same name (and sometimes two or more). This still happens, but less often. Not only are there new additions from other cultures and countries, but there is also a growing tendency to convert surnames (such as Mason or Paige) into forenames and to use short forms (such as Freddie or Millie) as names in their own right.

In this book you will find more than 3,000 names used in the English-speaking world, including a selection of Welsh, Scottish, Irish, Jewish, Indian, and Arabic names. The meaning of each name is given (where known), usually followed by further information that may influence your decision, such as famous bearers or other associations of the name. Whether you choose to read the book from A to Z, or simply open it at random and pick a name from that page, is entirely up to you!

Using the book

- The names are listed in alphabetical order, labelled (M) for boys and (F) for girls. Unisex names that have the same origin are labelled (M/F) if the name is more commonly given to boys and (F/M) if the name is more commonly given to girls.

- Names that have accents (such as Chloë or René) are increasingly written without them in modern times, partly because of the difficulty of producing accented letters on a computer. So the main form of these names is given as **Chloe, Rene**, etc., but the accents are shown in an 'ALTERNATIVE FORM' at the end of the entry.

- A pronunciation guide is given for some of the more difficult names, such as **Sinead** [shi-NAID]. These are spelt out to make them readable without using special symbols for particular sounds, with two exceptions: [zh] for the sound in the middle of the word *measure* and [dh] for the sound in the middle of the word *mother*.

- At the end of some entries you will find lists of 'RELATED NAMES'. These include short forms that have become established as names in their own right (e.g. **Abby** and **Gail** for **Abigail**), alternative forms of the name that are very different, often because they come from other languages (e.g. **Sean** and **Ian** for **John**), and names that basically have the same meaning (e.g. **Margaret** and **Pearl**).

- At the end of the book there are lists of the most popular names in the UK for various years since 1974. The most recent lists will show you which names are currently in and out of fashion, and whether the name you have chosen is as unusual as you think it is.

Top ten tips

1. Choose a set of names that sound good together, but beware of initials that spell a word, such as Frederick Adam Thomas.

2. Read the chosen first name and surname aloud, to avoid a combination that sounds like a common word or phrase (such as Isla White, Paige Turner, Joe King, or Robin Banks).

3. Do not spell a common name in an unusual way just to be different (such as Dayzi for Daisy). Your child will soon get tired of having to spell it out to everybody.

4. If you do not know how to pronounce a particular name (such as the Irish boys' name Oisin), do not choose it. Other people will have the same problem.

5. Consider how the name could be shortened by your child's friends. You may think that Dorcas is a nice, unusual name for a girl, but would you want to hear your daughter called 'Dork'?

6. Many popular babies' names are short forms of other names. However, if you want to call your little girl Charlie, for example, it may be better to put the full form on her birth certificate. That way, if she tires of her unisex name in later life, she can reinvent herself as Charlotte or even Lottie.

7. If you choose an unusual first name for your child, it is a good idea to add a more conventional middle name, which can be used instead if your child does not want to stand out from the crowd. And vice versa.

8. It is useful to have a middle name, but do not give your child too many forenames. Remember that space is limited on forms that ask for a person's full name.

9. Many people are proud to bear a name that has been in the family for generations, but if it sounds particularly old-fashioned, consider using a related name instead.

10. Each of your children is an individual. Do not choose a younger child's name simply because it 'goes with' the name of his or her elder brother or sister. And if all of your children have the same initial, they may end up opening one another's mail by accident.

A

Aaliyah (F) the feminine form of the Arabic name **Ali** ('sublime'). It was borne by a US singer who died in a plane crash in 2001 at the age of 22.
ALTERNATIVE FORM: **Aliyah**.

Aaron [AIR-un] (M) a biblical name, possibly meaning 'high mountain'. In the Bible, Aaron is the brother of Moses and first high priest of the Israelites. Famous modern bearers include the US composer Aaron Copland. Aaron was the middle name of the US singer Elvis Presley.
ALTERNATIVE FORMS: **Aron, Arran, Arn**.
RELATED NAMES: **Aharon, Harun**.

Ab (M) short for **Abner**.

Abbas (M) 'austere, stern'. An Arabic name borne in the 6th century by Muhammad's uncle and later by various Muslim rulers, notably a 17th-century shah of Persia.

Abbie (F) a short form of **Abigail**, now sometimes given as a name in its own right.
ALTERNATIVE FORMS: **Abby, Abi, Abbi, Abbey**.
RELATED NAME: **Gail**.

Abdullah (M) 'servant of Allah'. An Arabic name borne in the 6th century by Muhammad's father.
SHORT FORM: **Abdul**.
ALTERNATIVE FORM: **Abdallah**.

Abe (M) short for **Abraham, Abel**, or **Abner**.

Abel (M) a biblical name, possibly meaning 'breath', 'worthlessness', or 'son'. In the Bible, Abel is the second son of Adam and Eve, killed by his brother Cain. A famous fictional bearer is the convict Abel Magwitch in Charles Dickens' novel *Great Expectations* (1861).
SHORT FORM: **Abe**.

Abigail (F) 'father's joy'. A biblical name, borne by one of the wives of King David. Abigail referred to herself as her husband's handmaid, and perhaps for this reason the name was often given to ladies' maids in literature.
RELATED NAMES: **Abbie, Gail**.

Abilene (F) from a place name of biblical origin, possibly meaning 'grass', or a compound of **Abbie** and the name-ending -*lene*.

Abla (F) 'full-figured'. An Arabic name borne by a beautiful woman who featured in several 6th-century love poems.

Abner (M) 'father of light'. A biblical name, borne by the commander of King Saul's army. More popular in the USA than elsewhere, the name was given to the cartoon character Li'l Abner by his creator, A1 Capp, in the 1930s.
SHORT FORMS: **Ab, Abe**.
RELATED NAME: **Avner**.

Abraham (M) 'father of a multitude'. A biblical name, given by God to the first Jewish patriarch, formerly called Abram. Famous bearers include the 19th-century US president Abraham Lincoln.
SHORT FORMS: **Abe, Ham, Bram**.
RELATED NAMES: **Abram, Avram, Ibrahim**.

Abram (M) 'high father'. The original name of the biblical character **Abraham**, and sometimes regarded as another form of that name.
RELATED NAME: **Avram**.

Absalom (M) 'father of peace'. A biblical name, borne by one of the sons of King David, whose rebellion and death caused his father great sorrow.
ALTERNATIVE FORM: **Absolon**.
RELATED NAME: **Axel**.

Acacia (F) from the plant name, sometimes associated with immortality or warding off evil.

Achilles [a-KIL-eez] (M) the name of a hero in Greek mythology. All parts of Achilles' body were invulnerable to injury except his heel, and it is for this weak point (rather than his military exploits) that he is best remembered.

Ada (F) 'noble'. The name was borne by a 19th-century mathematician (Lord Byron's daughter, the Countess of Lovelace) and given in her honour to a computer-programming language. A fictional bearer of the name is Aunt Ada Doom, a character in Stella Gibbons' novel *Cold Comfort Farm* (1932) who famously 'saw something nasty in the woodshed'.
RELATED NAME: **Adela**.

Adah (F) 'adornment'. A biblical name, borne by the wife of Esau.

Adam (M) 'earth' or 'man'. In the Bible, Adam is the first man, created by God from the dust of the earth. The name has been fashionable since the late 1960s, when it may have been popularized by the British singer Adam Faith.
SHORT FORMS: **Addie, Adie**.

Adan (M) another spelling of **Aidan** ('fire').

Addie (F) short for **Adelaide, Adela, Adele, Adelina**, or **Adeline**.
ALTERNATIVE FORMS: **Addy, Addi**.

Ade (M) short for **Adrian** or **Aidan**.

Adela (F) 'noble'. In the 11th century the name was borne by the youngest daughter of William the Conqueror.
SHORT FORM: **Addie**.
ALTERNATIVE FORMS: **Adella, Adele, Adelina, Adeline**.
RELATED NAMES: **Ada, Della**.

Adelaide (F) 'of noble kind'. From the German name *Adelheid*. The city of Adelaide in Australia is named after Queen Adelaide, the German-born wife of William IV, who popularized the name in the 19th century.
SHORT FORM: **Addie**.
RELATED NAMES: **Alice, Ailish, Ally, Alison, Heidi**.

Adele (F) another form of **Adela**, of French origin.
SHORT FORM: **Addie**.
ALTERNATIVE FORMS: **Adèle, Adel, Adelle**.

Adelina (F) another form of **Adela**, of Italian origin. It was popularized in the late 19th century by the opera singer Adelina Patti.
SHORT FORM: **Addie**.

Adeline (F) another form of **Adela**, of French origin.
SHORT FORM: **Addie**.
ALTERNATIVE FORM: **Aline**.

Adella (F) another spelling of **Adela**.

Adelle (F) another spelling of **Adele**.

Aden (M) another spelling of **Aidan** ('fire').

Adie (M) short for **Adam, Adrian**, or **Aidan**.

Adil (M) an Arabic name meaning 'just, fair'.

Adlai [AD-lay] (M) 'God is just' or 'my ornament'. The name of a minor biblical character. More recent famous bearers include the 19th-century US statesman Adlai Stevenson and his grandson of the same name.

Adnan (M) an Arabic name meaning 'settler'.

Adolph (M) 'noble wolf'. The name is chiefly associated with the German dictator Adolf Hitler, for which reason it is rarely given in modern times.
SHORT FORMS: **Dolly, Dolph**.
ALTERNATIVE FORMS: **Adolf, Adolphus**.

Adonis (M) 'lord'. The name of a beautiful youth in Greek mythology.

Adria (F) a feminine form of **Adrian**.
RELATED NAMES: **Adriana, Adrienne**.

Adrian (M) the English form of **Hadrian** ('person from Hadria in Italy'), borne in the 12th century by the only English pope, Adrian IV. It came back into fashion in the latter half of the 20th century, and in 1982 the writer Sue Townsend gave the

name to a fictional teenage diarist,
Adrian Mole.
SHORT FORMS: **Ade, Adie.**
FEMININE FORMS: **Adriana,
    Adrienne, Adria.**

Adriana (F) a feminine form of
Adrian.
ALTERNATIVE FORMS: **Adrianna,
    Adriane, Adrianne.**
RELATED NAMES: **Adrienne, Adria.**

Adrienne (F) a feminine form of
Adrian, of French origin.
RELATED NAMES: **Adriana, Adria.**

Aeneas [ee-NEE-us] (M) the name of
a hero of classical mythology,
possibly meaning 'praise'. The story
of Aeneas is told in Virgil's *Aeneid*.

Aeronwen [ire-RON-wen] (F) a
Welsh name meaning 'fair berry'.

Africa (F) from the name of the
continent. It is chiefly used in the
USA by African Americans.
ALTERNATIVE FORM: **Afrika.**

Agatha (F) 'good, honourable'.
Famous bearers of the name include
St Agatha, a 3rd-century martyr, and
the 20th-century British novelist
Agatha Christie, creator of the
fictional detectives Hercule Poirot
and Miss Marple.
SHORT FORM: **Aggie.**

Agnes (F) 'pure, holy'. The name was
borne by St Agnes, martyred in the
early 4th century.
SHORT FORMS: **Aggie, Nessie.**
RELATED NAMES: **Annis, Ines, Nesta.**

Aharon (M) a Jewish form of **Aaron**
(possibly meaning 'high mountain').

Ahmed (M) 'very praiseworthy'. An
Arabic name borne in its alternative
forms by several Muslim rulers,
including the founder of
Afghanistan and three sultans of
Turkey.
ALTERNATIVE FORMS: **Ahmad,
    Ahmet.**

Aidan (M) 'fire'. Of Irish origin, from
the name of a Celtic sun god. St
Aidan founded the monastery on
the island of Lindisfarne, off the
north-east coast of England, in the
7th century. The name came back
into fashion in the late 20th century.
SHORT FORMS: **Ade, Adie.**
ALTERNATIVE FORMS: **Aiden, Aden,
    Adan.**

Ailbhe [AL-bay] (M/F) 'white'. An
Irish name borne by a 6th-century
male saint and a legendary female
warrior.
RELATED NAMES: **Albie, Alby, Alva.**

Aileen [AY-leen, EYE-leen] (F) the
Scottish form of an Irish name that
is probably another form of **Aveline.**
SHORT FORM: **Ailie.**
ALTERNATIVE FORM: **Aline.**
RELATED NAMES: **Eileen, Evelyn.**

Ailie (F) short for **Aileen** or **Ailsa**, or
another spelling of **Eilidh** (a Scottish
form of **Ellie**).

Ailish [AY-lish] (F) the Irish form of
Alice ('of noble kind').

ALTERNATIVE FORM: **Ailis**.
RELATED NAMES: **Ally, Alison, Adelaide, Heidi**.

Ailsa (F) from the place name Ailsa Craig, a rocky islet off the west coast of Scotland.
SHORT FORM: **Ailie**.

Aimee [AY-may] (F) 'beloved'. Of French origin, the name is now popular in the English-speaking world, often pronounced like **Amy** (which is an older English form of the same name).
ALTERNATIVE FORMS: **Aimée, Aimi, Aimie**.

Aine [AHN-ya, AWN-ya] (F) 'brightness'. An Irish name borne in legend by a goddess of fruitfulness and prosperity and by a fairy queen.

Ainsley (M/F) from a Scottish surname and English place name. Although the name may also be given to girls, its best-known bearer in modern times is the male television chef Ainsley Harriott.
ALTERNATIVE FORMS: **Ainslie, Ainslee**.

Aisha [eye-EE-sha] (F) 'alive'. An Arabic name borne in the 7th century by Muhammad's third and favourite wife. Another form of the name is part of the title of H. Rider Haggard's novel *Ayesha: The Return of She* (1905).
ALTERNATIVE FORMS: **Ayesha, Aishah, Ashia**.

Aisling [ASH-ling] (F) 'dream, vision'. An Irish name that became particularly popular in the late 20th century.
ALTERNATIVE FORMS: **Ashling, Aislin, Aislinn, Ashlyn**.

Aithne [ETH-nee, EN-ya] (F) another spelling of **Eithne** ('kernel').

Ajay (M) an Indian name meaning 'unconquerable'.

Akash (M) an Indian name meaning 'sky'.

Al (M) short for various boys' names beginning with these letters, especially **Alan, Albert, Alfred,** or **Alistair**. Famous 20th-century bearers include the US singer Al Jolson, the US gangster Al Capone, and the US actor Al Pacino, whose real names were Asa, Alphonse, and Alfred respectively.

Alaina (F) a feminine form of **Alan**.
ALTERNATIVE FORMS: **Alayna, Alaine**.
RELATED NAME: **Alana**.

Alaine (F) another form of **Alaina** or **Elaine**.

Alan (M) a name of Celtic origin, possibly meaning 'rock'. Famous modern bearers include the British playwrights Alan Bennett and Alan Ayckbourn.
SHORT FORM: **Al**.
ALTERNATIVE FORMS: **Allan, Allen, Alun**.
FEMININE FORMS: **Alana, Alaina**.

Alana (F) a feminine form of **Alan**, or another spelling of **Alannah**.
ALTERNATIVE FORMS: **Alanna, Alannah**.
RELATED NAME: **Alaina**.

Alannah (F) an Irish name meaning 'O child', or another spelling of **Alana**.
ALTERNATIVE FORMS: **Alanna, Alana**.

Alaric (M) 'ruler of all'. The name was borne by two kings of the Visigoths in the 5th century.

Alasdair (M) the Scottish spelling of **Alistair**, another form of **Alexander** ('defender of men').
ALTERNATIVE FORMS: **Alastair, Alaster**.

Alban (M) 'white' or 'rock'. St Alban was the first Christian martyr in Britain, executed in the 3rd century in what is now the city of St Albans.
SHORT FORM: **Albie**.
ALTERNATIVE FORM: **Albin**.

Alberic (M) 'elf ruler'. In Germanic mythology, Alberic was the king of the elves. The name has never been common in this form in English-speaking countries.
RELATED NAME: **Aubrey**.

Albert (M) 'noble and illustrious'. The name was popularized in the 19th century by Prince Albert, beloved husband of Queen Victoria, but gradually fell from favour during the first half of the 20th century. Other famous bearers include the British actor Albert Finney, born in 1936.
SHORT FORMS: **Al, Albie**.
FEMININE FORMS: **Alberta, Albertina, Albertine**.
RELATED NAMES: **Bert, Bertie**.

Alberta (F) a feminine form of **Albert**. Queen Victoria and Prince Albert gave the name to one of their daughters, after whom the Canadian province of Alberta was named.
ALTERNATIVE FORMS: **Albertina, Albertine**.

Albie (M) short for **Albert** or **Alban**, or an English form of the Irish name **Ailbhe** ('white').
ALTERNATIVE FORM: **Alby**.

Albin (M) another form of **Alban**.

Albina (F) 'white'. St Albina was a Christian martyr of the 3rd century.
SHORT FORM: **Bina**.
ALTERNATIVE FORM: **Albinia**.

Aldous [AWL-dus] (M) 'old'. The British novelist Aldous Huxley is the best-known modern bearer of this rare and ancient name.
ALTERNATIVE FORM: **Aldus**.

Alec (M) a short form of **Alexander**, sometimes given as a name in its own right, as in the case of the 20th-century British actor Sir Alec Guinness. It also occurs in the phrase *smart Alec(k)*, referring to somebody whose cleverness causes irritation.
ALTERNATIVE FORMS: **Alick, Aleck**.

RELATED NAMES: **Alex, Lex, Lexie, Xander, Alistair, Sasha**.

Aled (M) 'child, offspring'. A Welsh name popularized in the late 20th century by the singer Aled Jones.

Alethea (F) 'truth'. Like many other names representing virtues, it was popular with the Puritans in the 17th century.
RELATED NAME: **Verity**.

Alex (M/F) a short form of **Alexander, Alexandra**, or **Alexis**, now sometimes given as a name in its own right.
ALTERNATIVE FORM: **Alix** (F).
RELATED NAMES: **Lexie, Sasha, Alec** (M), **Lex** (M), **Xander** (M), **Alistair** (M), **Sandy** (F), **Sandra** (F), **Zandra** (F).

Alexa (F) another form of **Alexandra** or **Alexis**.

Alexander (M) 'defender of men'. The enduring popularity of the name has been attributed to Alexander the Great, a powerful ruler of the 4th century BC. Other famous bearers include several Scottish kings, Russian emperors, and popes, not to mention the inventor Alexander Graham Bell and the bacteriologist Alexander Fleming. It was also the middle name of the children's writer A. A. Milne, who gave it to a pet beetle in one of his poems.
SHORT FORMS: **Al, Sandy**.

FEMININE FORMS: **Alexandra**.
RELATED NAMES: **Alex, Alec, Lex, Lexie, Xander, Alistair, Sasha**.

Alexandra (F) a feminine form of **Alexander**. The name was popularized in the late 19th and early 20th centuries by Queen Alexandra, wife of Edward VII, and Princess Alexandra, cousin of Elizabeth II.
ALTERNATIVE FORMS: **Alexa, Alexandria, Alexandrina**.
RELATED NAMES: **Alex, Lexie, Sandy, Sandra, Zandra, Sasha**.

Alexandria (F) another form of **Alexandra**, possibly influenced by the Egyptian city of this name, founded by Alexander the Great.

Alexandrina (F) another form of **Alexandra**. The first name of Queen Victoria, it was briefly popular in the 19th century.

Alexis (M/F) 'defender'. The name of a 5th-century male saint, it was chiefly given to boys until the late 20th century, when the character played by Joan Collins in the soap opera *Dynasty* made it a fashionable girls' name.
ALTERNATIVE FORMS: **Alexa** (F), **Alexia** (F).
RELATED NAMES: **Alex, Lexie, Lex** (M).

Alfa (M/F) another spelling of **Alpha**.

Alfie (M) a short form of **Alfred**, sometimes given as a name in its own right. It was popularized by the film *Alfie* (1966), starring Michael Caine in the title role of a cockney ladies' man.

Alfred (M) 'elf counsel'. Alfred the Great, King of Wessex in the 9th century, is probably the best-known bearer of the name.
SHORT FORMS: Al, Alf.
FEMININE FORM: Alfreda.
RELATED NAMES: Alfie, Fred, Avery.

Alfreda (F) a feminine form of Alfred or another form of Elfreda ('elf strength').
RELATED NAME: Freda.

Alger (M) 'elf spear'. A rare name, perhaps most famously borne by US government official Alger Hiss, accused in 1949 of spying for the USSR.

Algernon (M) 'with a moustache'. Originally a nickname for a man who was not clean-shaven, it was adopted by various aristocratic families. Oscar Wilde gave the name to a character in his comedy *The Importance of Being Earnest* (1895).
SHORT FORMS: Algy, Algie.

Ali (M) 'sublime'. An Arabic name borne by Muhammad's cousin and son-in-law, an important figure in the history of Islam.
FEMININE FORM: Aaliyah.

Ali (M/F) short for Alistair, or another spelling of Ally.

Alice (F) 'of noble kind'. From

Adalheidis, another form of the German name *Adelheid*. Its best-known bearer is the fictional heroine of two children's books by Lewis Carroll, *Alice's Adventures in Wonderland* (1865) and *Through the Looking-Glass* (1872).
ALTERNATIVE FORMS: Alys, Alis, Alicia, Alyssa.
RELATED NAMES: Ailish, Ally, Alison, Adelaide, Heidi.

Alicia (F) another form of Alice. Famous modern bearers include the British ballerina Dame Alicia Markova.
ALTERNATIVE FORMS: Alisha, Alisia.

Alick (M) another spelling of Alec.

Aline (F) another form of Adeline ('of noble kind') or Aileen.

Alis (F) another spelling of Alice.

Alisa (F) another spelling of Alyssa.

Alisdair (M) another spelling of Alistair.

Alisha (F) another spelling of Alicia.
ALTERNATIVE FORM: Alisia.

Alison (F) another form of Alice, of French origin. It was particularly popular in the mid-20th century, when the British actress Alison Steadman and the British singer Alison Moyet were born.
ALTERNATIVE FORMS: Allison, Allyson, Alyson.
RELATED NAMES: Ailish, Ally, Adelaide, Heidi.

Alissa (F) another spelling of **Alyssa**. SHORT FORM: **Lissa**.

Alistair (M) another form of **Alexander** ('defender of men'), of Scottish origin. Famous modern bearers of the name include the Scottish actor Alastair Sim and the English-born broadcaster Alistair Cooke.
SHORT FORMS: **Al, Ali**.
ALTERNATIVE FORMS: **Alasdair, Alastair, Alaster, Alisdair, Alister**.
RELATED NAMES: **Alex, Alec, Lex, Lexie, Xander, Sasha**.

Alix (F) another spelling of **Alex**.

Aliyah (F) another spelling of **Aaliyah**.

Allan (M) another spelling of **Alan**, more frequently used as a surname.
ALTERNATIVE FORM: **Allen**.

Allegra (F) 'happy, lively'. The poet Lord Byron apparently coined the name (from an Italian adjective) in 1817 for his illegitimate daughter, who died five years later.

Allison (F) another spelling of **Alison**.

Ally (F) a short form of various names beginning with *Al-* or *Ali-*, especially **Alice** or **Alison**, sometimes given as a name in its own right. It was popularized in the late 1990s by the US television series *Ally McBeal*, starring Calista Flockhart in the title role as a young lawyer.
ALTERNATIVE FORMS: **Allie, Ali, Aly**.

Allyson (F) another spelling of **Alison**.

Alma (F) 'kind, nurturing'. The name became fashionable after the British victory at the Battle of Alma (1854) in the Crimean War. Famous 20th-century bearers include the British singer Alma Cogan.

Aloysia [al-oh-ISH-a, a-LOY-sha] (F) the feminine form of **Aloysius**.
RELATED NAMES: **Louise, Louisa, Luisa, Lulu**.

Aloysius [al-oh-ISH-us] (M) another form of **Louis** ('famous warrior'), borne by the 16th-century Jesuit St Aloysius Gonzaga. Evelyn Waugh gave the name to a teddy bear owned by one of the main characters in his novel *Brideshead Revisited* (1945).
FEMININE FORM: **Aloysia**.
RELATED NAMES: **Lewis, Luis, Ludovic, Clovis**.

Alpha (M/F) from the first letter of the Greek alphabet, regarded as a symbol of excellence or high rank.
ALTERNATIVE FORM: **Alfa**.

Alphonse (M) 'noble and ready'. Alphonse was the full name of the 20th-century US gangster Al Capone.
SHORT FORMS: **Al, Fonsie, Fonzie**.
FEMININE FORM: **Alphonsine**.

Alphonsine (F) feminine form of **Alphonse**.

Althea (F) 'wholesome'. The name of

a character in Greek mythology, the mother of the Argonaut Meleager. The poet Richard Lovelace gave this name to his beloved in the poem 'To Althea, from Prison' (1642).

Altman (M) 'old man'. A Jewish name, traditionally given to protect the child from early death.

Alton (M) from a surname and place name meaning 'settlement at the source of a river'. It was the first name of the 20th-century US bandleader Glenn Miller.

Alun (M) another spelling of **Alan**, of Welsh origin. Famous modern bearers of the name in this form include the British actor Alun Armstrong.

Alva (M/F) an English form of the Irish name **Ailbhe** ('white'). It is sometimes given to girls as a feminine form of **Alvin**. As a boys' name it may also be another form of a biblical name meaning 'height'. Its best-known bearer is the US scientist Thomas Alva Edison, whose many inventions of the late 19th century included the electric light bulb.

Alvar (M) 'elf army'. Famous bearers include the British radio announcer Alvar Liddell, whose voice was very familiar to listeners in the 1930s and 1940s.

Alvin (M) 'elf friend'. In the latter half of the 20th century the name was borne by a mischievous singing

chipmunk in a US television cartoon series. Alvin Stardust is the stage name of a British singer (born Bernard Jewry in 1942).
SHORT FORMS: **Al, Alvie.**
ALTERNATIVE FORMS: **Alwyn, Aylwin.**
FEMININE FORMS: **Alva, Elvina.**

Aly (F) another spelling of **Ally**.

Alys (F) another spelling of **Alice**.

Alyson (F) another spelling of **Alison**.

Alyssa (F) another form of **Alice**.
SHORT FORM: **Lyssa.**
ALTERNATIVE FORMS: **Alissa, Alisa.**

Amabel (F) 'lovable, lovely'. It comes from the same origin as the better-known name **Mabel**. It may also have influenced the coining of the name **Annabel**.
ALTERNATIVE FORM: **Amabelle.**

Amadeus [am-a-DAY-us] (M) 'loving God' or 'loved by God'. The middle name of the 18th-century composer Wolfgang Amadeus Mozart, it was used as the title of a play and film about his life.
RELATED NAME: **Theophilus.**

Amal (M/F) an Arabic name meaning 'hope, expectation'.

Amalia (F) 'work'. The name is rarely used in the English-speaking world, but it may have influenced the coining of the more familiar name **Amelia**.
ALTERNATIVE FORM: **Amalie.**

Amanda (F) 'lovable'. Borne by various literary characters from the late 17th century onwards, the name was fashionable in the 1960s and 1970s, when it was given to the British actresses Amanda Donohoe and Amanda Holden, among others.
SHORT FORM: **Manda**.
RELATED NAME: **Mandy**.

Amaryllis (F) 'sparkling'. In literature the name was typically given to shepherdesses and other country girls. It is now most familiar as a flower name, dating from the 19th century.

Amber (F) from the name of the fossil resin that is used to make jewellery and ornaments. It was popularized as a girls' name by Kathleen Winsor's novel *Forever Amber* (1944).

Ambrose (M) 'immortal'. The name was borne by several saints and by the 19th-century US satirist Ambrose Bierce.
RELATED NAME: **Emrys**.

Amelia (F) 'hard-working'. It is thought to be a blend of **Amalia** and **Emily**. The name was popularized in the 19th century by two royal bearers and the title character of a novel by Henry Fielding. In the early 20th century it was borne by the US pilot Amelia Earhart.
ALTERNATIVE FORMS: **Emelia, Emilia, Amelie**.

Amelie (F) another form of **Amelia**, of French origin. It is borne by the warm-hearted heroine of the film *Le Fabuleux Destin d'Amélie Poulain* (2001).
ALTERNATIVE FORM: **Amélie**.

Amery (M) another spelling of **Amory**.

Ami (F) another spelling of **Amy**.

Amice (F) 'friendship'.
ALTERNATIVE FORM: **Amicia**.
RELATED NAME: **Amity**.

Amie (F) another spelling of **Amy**.

Amin (M) an Arabic name meaning 'honest, trustworthy'.
FEMININE FORM: **Amina**.

Amina (F) the feminine form of **Amin**.

Amity (F) 'friendship'.
ALTERNATIVE FORM: **Amita**.
RELATED NAME: **Amice**.

Amory (M) from a surname meaning 'brave ruler'.
ALTERNATIVE FORMS: **Amery, Emery**.

Amos (M) a biblical name, possibly meaning 'borne by God'. Amos was a Hebrew prophet, whose sayings are to be found in the book that bears his name. It has often been given to rustic characters in literature.

Amrit (M) 'immortal'. An Indian name borne by a Hindu god.

Amy (F) 'beloved'. Famous bearers of the name include Amy March, one of the heroines of Louisa M. Alcott's novel *Little Women* (1868), and the British pilot Amy Johnson, who made pioneering solo flights in the 1930s.
ALTERNATIVE FORMS: **Ami, Amie, Aimie.**
RELATED NAME: **Aimee.**

Anais [an-eye-EESS] (F) another form of **Hannah** ('favour' or 'grace'), of French origin. The name was borne by the 20th-century US writer Anaïs Nin. It is also part of the name of an expensive brand of perfume.
ALTERNATIVE FORM: **Anaïs.**
RELATED NAMES: **Anna, Anya, Anita, Anne, Annie, Annette, Anneka, Anoushka, Nancy, Nanette.**

Anand (M) 'joy'. An Indian name borne by a Hindu god.
FEMININE FORM: **Ananda.**

Ananda (F) feminine form of **Anand**.

Anastasia (F) 'resurrection'. St Anastasia was a Christian martyr of the 4th century. The name was also borne by one of the daughters of the ill-fated last tsar of Russia, Nicholas II, who was rumoured to have survived the massacre of her family in 1918.
RELATED NAME: **Stacey.**

Anatole (M) 'sunrise'. A French name that is not common in the English-speaking world. Its best-known bearer is probably the French writer Anatole France, who won the Nobel Prize for literature in 1921.

Andie (F) short for **Andrea** or any other feminine form of **Andrew**. In the case of the US actress Andie MacDowell, it is short for her middle name, Anderson.
ALTERNATIVE FORM: **Andi.**

Andra (F) a feminine form of **Andrew**.
RELATED NAMES: **Andrea, Andriana, Andrine.**

Andre [AHN-dray] (M) another form of **Andrew**, of French origin. Famous modern bearers include the US conductor André Previn and the US tennis player Andre Agassi.
ALTERNATIVE FORM: **André.**
RELATED NAMES: **Andreas, Drew.**

Andrea [AN-dri-a] (F) the usual feminine form of **Andrew**. The 20th-century feminist Andrea Dworkin was a well-known bearer of the name. (It is found with different pronunciation as a boys' name in Italy, where it is borne by the singer Andrea Bocelli.)
SHORT FORM: **Andie.**
RELATED NAMES: **Andra, Andriana, Andrine.**

Andreas [an-DRAY-us] (M) another form of **Andrew**, of Greek origin.

Andrew (M) 'man, warrior'. St Andrew, one of Jesus Christ's apostles, is the patron saint of Scotland. In 1960 Elizabeth II gave the name to her second son, who later became the Duke of York. The short form was used by the 20th-century US artist Andy Warhol.
SHORT FORM: Andy.
FEMININE FORMS: Andrea, Andra, Andriana, Andrine.
RELATED NAMES: Andre, Andreas, Drew.

Andriana (F) a feminine form of Andrew, or a blend of **Andrea** and **Adriana**.
ALTERNATIVE FORM: Andreana.
RELATED NAMES: Andrea, Andra, Andrine.

Andrine (F) a feminine form of Andrew.
RELATED NAMES: Andrea, Andra, Andriana.

Aneka (F) another spelling of **Anneka**.
ALTERNATIVE FORM: Aneke.

Aneurin [a-NYE-rin] (M) a Welsh name, possibly meaning 'precious one' or 'noble'. It was borne by a Welsh poet who lived around AD 600. However, the name is most familiar in modern times as that of the 20th-century Welsh politician Aneurin Bevan.
SHORT FORM: Nye.
ALTERNATIVE FORM: Aneirin.

Angel (M/F) 'messenger of God'. A famous fictional bearer of the boys' name is Angel Clare, a character in Thomas Hardy's novel *Tess of the D'Urbervilles* (1891).

Angela (F) 'angel'. St Angela founded the Ursuline order of nuns in the 16th century. The British actress Angela Lansbury is a famous modern bearer of the name.
SHORT FORMS: Angie, Ange.
ALTERNATIVE FORMS: Angelina, Angeline.

Angelica (F) 'angelic'. The name is borne (in an alternative form) by the US actress Anjelica Huston, who played Morticia in the *Addams Family* films. The word *angelica* also refers to a plant whose candied stems are used to decorate cakes.
ALTERNATIVE FORMS: Anjelica, Angelique.

Angelina (F) another form of **Angela**. Famous bearers include the US actress Angelina Jolie and the dancing mouse Angelina Ballerina in a series of children's books and television cartoons.
ALTERNATIVE FORM: Angeline.

Angharad [ang-HARR-ad] (F) 'much loved'. A Welsh name, it was introduced to other parts of the UK in the 1970s when the Welsh actress Angharad Rees played the leading role of Demelza in the popular television drama series *Poldark*.

Angie (F) short for **Angela** or any other name beginning with *Angel-*. The US actress Angie Dickinson was born Angeline Brown.

Angus (M) 'the only choice'. Of Gaelic origin, the name is chiefly associated with Scotland, where it was given to a breed of beef cattle, the Aberdeen Angus. Human bearers include the television presenter Angus Deayton.
SHORT FORM: **Gus**.
RELATED NAME: **Innes**.

Anika (F) another spelling of **Anneka**.

Anil (M) 'air, wind'. An Indian name borne by a Hindu god.
FEMININE FORM: **Anila**.

Anila (F) the feminine form of **Anil**.

Anita (F) another form of **Hannah** ('favour' or 'grace'), of Spanish origin. The name is borne in the UK by various actresses, including Anita Harris and Anita Dobson, as well as the businesswoman Anita Roddick.
SHORT FORM: **Nita**.
RELATED NAMES: **Anna, Anya, Anne, Annie, Annette, Anneka, Anoushka, Anais, Nancy, Nanette**.

Anitra (F) a name apparently coined by the Norwegian dramatist Henrik Ibsen for an Arabic princess in his play *Peer Gynt* (1867). It is also an Italian word meaning 'duck'.

Anjelica (F) another spelling of **Angelica**.

Ann (F) another spelling of **Anne**.

Anna (F) another form of **Hannah** ('favour' or 'grace'). Famous bearers include the British novelist Anna Sewell, author of *Black Beauty* (1877), and the fictional heroine of Tolstoy's novel *Anna Karenina* (1877).
RELATED NAMES: *see list at* **Anne**.

Annabel (F) a compound of **Anna** and the name-ending *-bel* ('beautiful'), possibly influenced by **Amabel**.
SHORT FORM: **Bel**.
ALTERNATIVE FORMS: **Annabelle, Annabella**.
RELATED NAME: **Arabella**.

Annalisa (F) a compound of **Anna** and **Lisa**, coined as an English form of the German name *Anneliese*.

Anne (F) another form of **Hannah** ('favour' or 'grace'). Anne (or Ann) was the usual form of the name in English-speaking countries until the late 20th century, when Hannah became more popular. There have been various royal bearers of the name, including two of the wives of Henry VIII in the 16th century, Queen Anne in the 18th century, and the daughter of Elizabeth II in more recent times.
ALTERNATIVE FORM: **Ann**.
RELATED NAMES: **Annie, Annette,**

Anna, Anya, Anita, Anneka, Anouska, Anais, Hannah, Nancy, Nanette.

Anneka (F) another form of **Anne**, of Swedish or Dutch origin. The best-known bearer of the name in the UK is the television presenter Anneka Rice.
ALTERNATIVE FORMS: **Anneka, Annika, Anika, Aneka, Aneke.**
RELATED NAMES: *see list at* **Anne**.

Annette (F) another form of **Anne**, of French origin. The British actress Annette Crosbie is a famous modern bearer of the name.
SHORT FORMS: **Netta, Nettie.**
ALTERNATIVE FORM: **Annetta.**
RELATED NAMES: *see list at* **Anne**.

Annie (F) a pet form of **Anne**, sometimes given as a name in its own right. It was popularized in the 19th century by the Scottish song 'Annie Laurie' and in the 20th century by *Little Orphan Annie*, a cartoon strip that became a successful musical.
ALTERNATIVE FORM: **Anni.**
RELATED NAMES: *see list at* **Anne**.

Annika (F) another spelling of **Anneka**.

Annis (F) another form of **Agnes** ('pure, holy'), sometimes preferred because it lacks the hard sound of the letter 'g'. It is also used as a surname.

ALTERNATIVE FORMS: **Annys, Annice.**
RELATED NAMES: **Ines, Nesta.**

Anona (F) a name apparently coined in the 1920s as a blend of **Anne** and **Nona** (or some other name ending in *-ona*, such as **Fiona**). It was borne by the radio personality Anona Winn, a familiar voice on panel games in the middle decades of the 20th century.

Anouska [a-NOOSH-ka] (F) another form of **Hannah** ('favour' or 'grace'), of Russian origin. Its best-known bearer in the UK is the actress Anouska Hempel.
ALTERNATIVE FORMS: **Anoushka, Anushka.**
RELATED NAMES: **Anne, Annette, Annie, Anna, Anya, Anita, Anneka, Anais, Nancy, Nanette.**

Anselm (M) 'protected by God'. St Anselm became Archbishop of Canterbury in the 11th century.

Anthea (F) 'flowery'. The name occurs in Greek mythology and 17th-century poetry. Famous modern bearers include the television presenter Anthea Turner.

Anthony (M) from a Roman family name borne by Mark Antony, a politician and soldier of the 1st century BC. There were several saints of this name, such as St Anthony of Padua. More recent bearers include the actors Anthony Perkins and

Anthony Hopkins and the television presenter Ant McPartlin.
SHORT FORM: **Ant**.
ALTERNATIVE FORM: **Antony**.
FEMININE FORMS: **Antonia, Antoinette, Antonella**.
RELATED NAMES: **Tony, Anton, Antoine, Antonio**.

Antoine (M) another form of **Anthony**, of French origin.
FEMININE FORM: **Antoinette**.
RELATED NAMES: **Anton, Antonio, Tony**.

Antoinette (F) a feminine form of **Antoine** or **Anthony**. It was borne by Marie Antoinette, Queen of France, who was executed in 1793 during the French Revolution.
SHORT FORM: **Toinette**.
RELATED NAMES: **Antonia, Toni, Tonia, Antonella**.

Anton (M) another form of **Anthony**, of German or Russian origin. Famous bearers include the 19th-century Russian writer Anton Chekhov and the 20th-century British actor Anton Rodgers.
FEMININE FORM: **Antonella**.
RELATED NAMES: **Antoine, Antonio, Tony**.

Antonella (F) a feminine form of **Anton** or **Anthony**.
RELATED NAMES: **Antonia, Toni, Tonia, Antoinette, Antonella**.

Antonia (F) a feminine form of **Antonio** or **Anthony**. The British writer Lady Antonia Fraser is a well-known bearer of the name.
ALTERNATIVE FORMS: **Antonina, Antonietta**.
RELATED NAMES: **Toni, Tonia, Antoinette, Antonella**.

Antonio (M) another form of **Anthony**, of Spanish or Italian origin. The name is borne by various characters in Shakespeare's plays, notably the title character of *The Merchant of Venice*.
FEMININE FORM: **Antonia**.
RELATED NAMES: **Anton, Antoine, Tony**.

Antony (M) another spelling of **Anthony**.

Anushka (F) another spelling of **Anoushka**.

Anwar (M) 'bright, clear'. An Arabic name borne in the 20th century by the Egyptian president Anwar el-Sadat.

Anwen (F) a Welsh name meaning 'very beautiful'.

Anya (F) another form of **Hannah** ('favour' or 'grace'), from the Spanish form of the name. Famous bearers include Anya Seton, a 20th-century US writer of historical romances.

Aoife [EE-fa] (F) 'beautiful'. An Irish name borne by several legendary heroines.
RELATED NAME: **Eva**.

Aphra (F) 'woman with dark skin' or 'dust'. Its best-known bearer is the 17th-century author Aphra Behn, who may have been the first Englishwoman to earn her living in this way.

Apollonia (F) 'of the sun god Apollo'. St Apollonia was a Christian martyr of the 3rd century.

April (F) from the name of the month. It was chosen by the British transsexual April Ashley, born George Jamieson in April 1935, when she became a woman.
RELATED NAME: **Avril**.

Arabella (F) probably another form of **Annabel**. Famous modern bearers include the British comedian Arabella Weir.
ALTERNATIVE FORMS: **Arabel, Arabelle**.
RELATED NAME: **Bella**.

Aram (M) 'height'. A biblical name borne by a grandson of Noah.

Araminta (F) possibly a blend of **Arabella** and an old name meaning 'protector'. It occurs in literature of the 17th and 18th centuries.
SHORT FORMS: **Minta, Minty**.

Archibald (M) 'truly brave'. It has been particularly popular in Scotland, though it is not of Gaelic origin.
ALTERNATIVE FORM: **Archibold**.
RELATED NAME: **Archie**.

Archie (M) a short form of

Archibald, now sometimes given as a name in its own right. Fictional bearers include Archie Rice, the title character of John Osborne's play *The Entertainer* (1957). In the early 20th century the US writer Don Marquis gave the name to a cockroach in *archy and mehitabel* (1927) and other works.
ALTERNATIVE FORM: **Archy**.

Ardal (M) 'high valour'. An Irish name that has recently been popularized by the Irish comedian Ardal O'Hanlon.

Aretha (F) 'excellence'. Its most famous modern bearer is the US singer Aretha Franklin.

Ariadne [a-ri-AD-ni] (F) 'very holy'. The name of a character in Greek mythology. The daughter of King Minos, Ariadne helped Theseus to find his way out of the Labyrinth after killing the Minotaur.
ALTERNATIVE FORMS: **Ariana, Arianna, Arianne**.

Ariel [AIR-i-ul, A-ri-el] (M/F) 'lion of God'. A biblical name, traditionally given to boys, a notable bearer being the 20th-century Israeli statesman Ariel Sharon. In Shakespeare's play *The Tempest*, Ariel is a supernatural being. The name is now sometimes given to girls, especially in the USA.
ALTERNATIVE FORMS: **Arielle** (F), **Ariella** (F).

Arjun (M) 'white'. An Indian name

associated with the Hindu god of the dawn.

Arlene (F) possibly a blend of **Arlette** and **Charlene** or **Marlene**. It was popularized in the 1950s by the US actress Arlene Dahl.
ALTERNATIVE FORMS: **Arleen, Arline**.

Arlette (F) 'little eagle'. Of French origin, it was borne in the 11th century by the mother of William the Conqueror, his father's mistress.
ALTERNATIVE FORM: **Arletta**.

Armand (M) another form of **Herman,** of French origin. It was popularized in the 1950s by Armand Denis, a Belgian-born wildlife photographer and presenter who appeared with his wife Michaela in a number of television series filmed on safari in Africa and Asia.

Arn (M) another form of **Aaron** (possibly meaning 'high mountain'), or short for **Arnold**.
SHORT FORM: **Arnie**.

Arnold (M) 'eagle ruler'. It was popular in the late 19th and early 20th centuries, when it was borne by the British novelist Arnold Bennett. Famous modern bearers include the Austrian-born US actor and politician Arnold Schwarzenegger.
SHORT FORMS: **Arnie, Arn**.

Aron (M) another form of **Aaron** (possibly meaning 'high mountain').

Arran (M) from the place name, an island off the west coast of Scotland,

or another form of **Aaron** (possibly meaning 'high mountain').

Artemas (M) 'of Artemis'. The name occurs in the Bible, in St Paul's letter to Titus. The 19th-century US humorist Charles Farrar Browne used the alternative form in his pen-name, Artemus Ward.
ALTERNATIVE FORM: **Artemus**.

Artemis (F) the name of the goddess of hunting in Greek mythology.
ALTERNATIVE FORM: **Artemisia**.
RELATED NAMES: **Cynthia, Delia**.

Arthur (M) a name of Celtic origin, possibly meaning 'bear' or 'stone'. As well as the semi-legendary King Arthur, the name has been borne by various princes (including sons of Henry VII and Queen Victoria) and other prominent figures, notably the Duke of Wellington, who popularized it in the early 19th century. Some modern bearers are better known by short forms of the name, such as the US singer Art Garfunkel and the US jazz musician Artie Shaw.
SHORT FORMS: **Art, Artie**.

Arun (M) 'reddish-brown'. An Indian name associated with the Hindu god of the dawn.

Asa [AY-sa, AY-za] (M) 'doctor, healer'. A biblical name borne by a king of Judah. Famous modern bearers include the British historian Asa Briggs.

Asaph [ASS-af] (M) 'collector'. A biblical name borne by various minor characters. St Asaph was a 6th-century Welsh bishop.

Ash (F/M) short for any name beginning with these letters, especially **Ashley** or **Ashling**.

Asha (F) an Indian name meaning 'hope'.

Ashanti (F) from the name of an African people.

Asher (M) 'fortunate, happy'. A biblical name borne by a son of Jacob and Leah. The US writer Chaim Potok gave the name to the central character of his novel *My Name is Asher Lev* (1972).

Ashia (F) another form of **Asia** or **Aisha** ('alive').

Ashley (F/M) from a surname and place name meaning 'ash wood'. It was popularized as a boys' name by a character in Margaret Mitchell's best-selling novel *Gone with the Wind* (1936) but is now more often given to girls.
SHORT FORM: **Ash**.
ALTERNATIVE FORMS: **Ashleigh** (F), **Ashlee** (F), **Ashlea** (F).

Ashling (F) another form of **Aisling** ('dream, vision'), spelt as it sounds.
SHORT FORM: **Ash**.

Ashlyn (F) another form of **Aisling** ('dream, vision'), or a blend of **Ashley** and **Lynn**.

ALTERNATIVE FORMS: **Ashlynn**, **Ashlynne**.

Ashok (M) 'not causing or feeling sorrow'. An Indian name borne by an emperor of the 3rd century BC (better known as Ashoka or Asoka) who established Buddhism as the state religion.

Ashton (M/F) from a surname and place name meaning 'ash-tree settlement'. It became popular, particularly as a boys' name, in the early 21st century.

Asia (F) from the name of the continent.
ALTERNATIVE FORMS: **Ashia, Aysha**.

Aspasia (F) 'welcome one'. The name was borne in the 5th century BC by a Greek intellectual who became the mistress of the Athenian statesman Pericles.
ALTERNATIVE FORMS: **Aspatia**.

Astra (F) 'star'.
RELATED NAMES: **Stella, Estelle, Esther**.

Astrid (F) 'fair god'. Of Scandinavian origin, the name has had various royal bearers, including in recent times a Belgian queen and a Norwegian princess.
SHORT FORM: **Asta**.

Atalanta (F) the name of a character in Greek mythology who promised to marry any man who could outrun her.

Atarah (F) a biblical name meaning 'crown'.
ALTERNATIVE FORM: **Atara**.

Athanasius (M) 'immortal'. The name was borne in the 4th century by the Greek theologian and bishop St Athanasius.

Athena [a-THEEN-a] (F) the name of the goddess of war and wisdom in Greek mythology.
ALTERNATIVE FORM: **Athene**.

Auberon (M) 'noble bear'. In this form the name was borne by the 20th-century British writer and journalist Auberon Waugh.
SHORT FORM: **Bron**.
ALTERNATIVE FORM: **Oberon**.

Aubrey (M/F) another form of **Alberic** ('elf ruler') that is the usual form of the name in English-speaking countries. Famous bearers include the 19th-century artist Aubrey Beardsley. Its use as a girls' name is relatively recent and largely confined to the USA.
SHORT FORM: **Aub**.
ALTERNATIVE FORM: **Aubree** (F).

Audrey (F) from an Old English name meaning 'noble strength'. St Audrey, also known as St Etheldreda, was a 6th-century abbess and former princess. Her name gave rise to the adjective *tawdry* in the Middle Ages, and for this reason it fell from favour for 500 years. It became fashionable again in the 20th century, popularized by the Belgian-born actress Audrey Hepburn (whose real name was Edda).
SHORT FORM: **Aud**.
ALTERNATIVE FORMS: **Audrie, Audry, Audra, Audrina**.
RELATED NAMES: **Etheldreda, Dreda**.

Augusta (F) the feminine form of **Augustus**. It was popularized in the 18th century by Princess Augusta, whose son became George III. There have been two notable fictional characters called Aunt Augusta: Lady Bracknell in Oscar Wilde's comedy *The Importance of Being Earnest* (1895) and the title character of Graham Greene's novel *Travels with My Aunt* (1969).
SHORT FORM: **Gussie**.

Augustina (F) the feminine form of **Augustine**.
SHORT FORM: **Gussie**.

Augustine (M) another form of **Augustus**. The name was borne by two saints, one of whom became the first Archbishop of Canterbury in the late 6th century.
SHORT FORMS: **Gus, Gussie**.
ALTERNATIVE FORM: **Augustin**.
FEMININE FORM: **Augustina**.
RELATED NAME: **Austin**.

Augustus (M) 'great, magnificent'. It was the title of various Roman emperors, notably Octavian, who adopted it in 27 BC. More recent

famous bearers include the Welsh-born painter Augustus John.
SHORT FORMS: **Gus, Gussie**.
ALTERNATIVE FORM: **Augustine**.
FEMININE FORM: **Augusta**.

Aurelia (F) 'golden'. From a Roman family name. It has been borne by various literary characters from the 17th century onwards.
ALTERNATIVE FORMS: **Auriel, Auriol**.

Aurora (F) 'dawn'. The name of the Roman goddess of the dawn. Fictional bearers include the title characters of Charles Perrault's fairy tale 'The Sleeping Beauty' (1697) and Elizabeth Barrett Browning's poem *Aurora Leigh* (1856). The word *aurora* also refers to a spectacular display of coloured light seen in the northern or southern sky.
RELATED NAME: **Dawn**.

Austin (M) another form of **Augustine**, better known as a surname than as a forename. Famous bearers include the British politician Sir Austen Chamberlain, joint winner of the Nobel Peace Prize in 1925.
ALTERNATIVE FORMS: **Austen, Austyn**.

Autumn (F) from the name of the season.

Ava [AY-va] (F) another form of **Eva** ('living'), from the pronunciation of the name in some European languages, or a short form of an ancient name beginning with *Av-*. Popularized in the mid-20th century by the US actress Ava Gardner, it came back into fashion in the early 21st century.

Aveline [AV-a-line] (F) probably another form of **Avila** or **Ava**. The television comedy writer Carla Lane gave the name to the only daughter of the Boswell family in *Bread*, a popular sitcom of the 1980s.
ALTERNATIVE FORM: **Avelina**.
RELATED NAMES: **Aileen, Eileen, Evelyn**.

Averil (F) another form of **Avril**.

Avery (M/F) from a surname that originated as another form of **Alfred**.

Avila (F) possibly from an ancient name beginning with *Av-*, but now often associated with the 16th-century mystic St Teresa of Avila (a city in Spain).

Avis (F) possibly from an ancient name beginning with *Av-*, but now often associated with the Latin word *avis*, meaning 'bird'. It is also the name of a car hire company.
ALTERNATIVE FORM: **Avice**.

Avner (M) a Jewish form of **Abner** ('father of light').

Avram (M) a Jewish form of **Abram** ('high father') or **Abraham** ('father of a multitude').

Avril (F) from the French word for April, or from an Old English name meaning 'like a boar in battle'.
ALTERNATIVE FORM: **Averil**.
RELATED NAME: **April**.

Axel (M) another form of **Absalom** ('father of peace'), of Scandinavian origin.

Ayesha (F) another spelling of **Aisha** ('alive').

Aylmer (M) another form of **Elmer** ('noble and famous').

Aylwin (M) another form of **Alvin** ('elf friend').

Aysha (F) another form of **Asia** or **Aisha** ('alive').

Azalea (F) from the plant name (which simply means 'dry', because it does not need much water). The spelling of the alternative form may have been influenced by *Azaliah*, the name of a minor male character in the Bible.
ALTERNATIVE FORM: **Azalia**.

Azaria (F) probably another spelling of **Azariah**, adopted as a girls' name because it looks and sounds feminine.

Azariah (M) 'helped by God'. A biblical name borne by a prophet, a king of Judah, and various other male characters.

Aziz (M) an Arabic name meaning 'invincible' or 'cherished'.
FEMININE FORM: **Aziza**.

Aziza (F) the feminine form of **Aziz**.

Azriel (M) 'God helps'. The name of a minor biblical character. In its alternative form it is borne by Lord Asriel, a major figure in Philip Pullman's trilogy *His Dark Materials* (1995–2000).
ALTERNATIVE FORM: **Asriel**.

place name meaning 'barley enclosure'.

RELATED NAME: **Bart**.

Baruch (M) a biblical name meaning 'blessed'.

Bas (M) short for **Basil** or **Barry**.

Basil (M) 'royal'. The name was borne by several saints, notably the 4th-century theologian and bishop St Basil the Great. More recent famous bearers include the British actor Basil Rathbone and the fictional character Basil Fawlty, a manic hotel proprietor in the television sitcom *Fawlty Towers*.

SHORT FORMS: **Baz, Bazza**.

Bathsheba (F) 'daughter of the oath'. A biblical name, borne by one of the wives of King David, who became the mother of King Solomon. Its best-known bearer is Bathsheba Everdene, the heroine of Thomas Hardy's novel *Far from the Madding Crowd* (1874).

SHORT FORM: **Sheba**.

Baylee (F) another spelling of **Bailey**.

Baz (M) short for **Basil** or **Barry**.

ALTERNATIVE FORM: **Bazza**.

Beata (F) 'blessed'. The name was borne by St Beata, an early Christian who was martyred in Africa.

Beatrice [BEER-triss] (F) another form of **Beatrix**, of French or Italian origin. The Italian poet Dante Alighieri fell in love with a girl

called Beatrice in 1274, and she features prominently in his *Divine Comedy* and other works. The name was given by the Duke and Duchess of York to their first daughter, born in 1988.

SHORT FORMS: **Bea, Bee, Beattie**.

Beatrix [BEER-triks] (F) 'blessed' or 'voyager'. St Beatrix was martyred in Rome in the early 4th century. The best-known British bearer of the name is the children's author and illustrator Beatrix Potter, creator of such characters as Peter Rabbit and Squirrel Nutkin.

SHORT FORMS: **Bea, Bee, Beattie**.

ALTERNATIVE FORM: **Beatrice**.

RELATED NAME: **Trixie**.

Beau [boe] (M) 'handsome'. Originally a nickname, borne by the British dandy Beau Brummell (whose real name was George), a leader of fashion in the early 19th century. It was popularized by the hero of P. C. Wren's novel *Beau Geste* (1924) and a character in Margaret Mitchell's best-selling novel *Gone with the Wind* (1936).

Becca (F) short for **Rebecca**.

Becky (F) a short form of **Rebecca** (possibly meaning 'binding'), sometimes given as a name in its own right. As a short form it was used by the unscrupulous Becky Sharp in William Makepeace Thackeray's novel *Vanity Fair* (1848).

Bee (F) short for **Beatrix** or **Beatrice**.

Beena (F) an Indian name of uncertain origin.
ALTERNATIVE FORM: **Bina**.

Bel (F) short for any name beginning or ending with these letters, such as **Belinda, Annabel**, or **Isabel**.

Belinda (F) a name of uncertain origin, possibly meaning 'beautiful', 'cunning', or 'wise'. It was first used in literary works of the late 17th and early 18th centuries.
SHORT FORM: **Bel**.
RELATED NAMES: **Linda, Lindy**.

Bella (F) 'beautiful'. A short form of any name ending with these letters, such as **Arabella** or **Isabella**, sometimes given as a name in its own right.
ALTERNATIVE FORM: **Belle**.

Bellamy (M) from the surname, meaning 'handsome friend'.

Ben (M) a short form of various names beginning with these letters, especially **Benjamin**, often given as a name in its own right. The 17th-century dramatist Ben Jonson is known by this short form, as is the comedian and writer Ben Elton, born in 1959. Other famous modern bearers include the actor Ben Kingsley (whose real name is Krishna Bhanji).
RELATED NAMES: **Benny, Binyamin**.

Benedict (M) 'blessed'. The name was borne in the 6th century by St

Benedict, founder of the Benedictine order of monks. Shakespeare gave the alternative form Benedick to one of the principal characters in his play *Much Ado About Nothing*.
ALTERNATIVE FORM: **Benedick**.
FEMININE FORM: **Benedicta**.
RELATED NAME: **Bennett**.

Benedicta (F) the feminine form of Benedict.
RELATED NAME: **Benita**.

Benita (F) another form of **Benedicta**, of Spanish origin. Its masculine equivalent *Benito*, chiefly associated with the 20th-century Italian dictator Benito Mussolini, is not found in English-speaking countries.

Benjamin (M) 'son of the south' or 'son of my old age'. A biblical name, given by Jacob to his youngest son. Famous bearers include the 19th-century British statesman Benjamin Disraeli. The name was popularized in the latter half of the 20th century by the title character of the film *The Graduate* (1967), played by Dustin Hoffman.
SHORT FORMS: **Benjy, Benjie**.
RELATED NAMES: **Ben, Benny, Binyamin**.

Bennett (M) another form of **Benedict**, now more often found as a surname.

Benny (M) a short form of various

names beginning with *Ben-*, especially **Benjamin**, sometimes given as a name in its own right. Famous bearers include the 20th-century British comedian Benny Hill (whose real name was Alfred).
ALTERNATIVE FORM: **Bennie**.
RELATED NAMES: **Ben, Binyamin**.

Benson (M) from the surname, meaning 'son of Ben'.

Bentley (M) from a surname and place name meaning 'bent-grass meadow'. The use of Bentley as a forename may be influenced by its association with large expensive cars.

Berenice (F) 'bringer of victory'. The name had various royal bearers in ancient times, including a queen of Egypt in the 3rd century BC and a Jewish princess in the 1st century AD.
ALTERNATIVE FORM: **Bernice**.
RELATED NAME: **Veronica**.

Beresford (M) from a surname and place name meaning 'beaver ford'.

Berkeley [BARK-li] (M) another spelling of **Barclay**.

Bernadette (F) a feminine form of **Bernard**, of French origin. It is chiefly associated with St Bernadette, whose visions of the Virgin Mary at Lourdes in 1858 established it as a place of pilgrimage.
SHORT FORM: **Bernie**.

ALTERNATIVE FORM: **Bernardette**.
RELATED NAME: **Bernardine**.

Bernadine (F) a feminine form of **Bernard**.
ALTERNATIVE FORM: **Bernardine**.
RELATED NAME: **Bernardette**.

Bernard (M) 'as strong or brave as a bear'. The name was borne by two medieval saints, one of whom indirectly gave it to a large breed of dog used in mountain rescue. More recent famous bearers include the Irish-born dramatist George Bernard Shaw.
SHORT FORM: **Bernie**.
FEMININE FORMS: **Bernadette, Bernadine**.

Bernice (F) another form of **Berenice**. It is the more common form of the name in the English-speaking world.
SHORT FORM: **Bernie**.
RELATED NAME: **Binnie**.

Bernie (M/F) short for any name beginning with *Bern-*, especially **Bernard, Bernadette**, or **Bernice**.

Berry (F) from the name of the fruit.

Bert (M) 'illustrious'. A short form of **Bertram** or various names ending with these letters (such as **Albert, Herbert, Egbert**, or **Hubert**), sometimes given as a name in its own right.
ALTERNATIVE FORMS: **Bertie, Burt**.

Bertha (F) 'illustrious'. In the early 20th century it became associated

with 'Big Bertha', the nickname of a large gun used by the Germans during the First World War, and consequently fell from favour.
ALTERNATIVE FORMS: **Berta, Bertina**.

Bertice (F) probably a blend of **Bertha** and **Bernice**. Famous bearers include the US singer and actress Bertice Reading.

Bertie (M) another form of **Bert**. It was popular in the first half of the 20th century as the pet name of George VI, whose first name was Albert, and the fictional character Bertram Wooster, created by P. G. Wodehouse.

Bertram (M) 'illustrious raven' or 'illustrious and wise'. In its alternative form, of French origin, the name was borne by the 20th-century British philosopher Bertrand Russell.
ALTERNATIVE FORM: **Bertrand**.
RELATED NAMES: **Bert, Bertie**.

Beryl (F) from the name of the gemstone. The name was particularly popular in the UK in the 1920s and 1930s, when the actress Beryl Reid and the writer Beryl Bainbridge were born.

Bess (F) a short form of **Elizabeth** ('oath of God'), sometimes given as a name in its own right. It was used as a nickname for Elizabeth I in the 16th century. The alternative form was borne by the fictional character

Bessie Bunter, a plump schoolgirl in a children's magazine of the 1920s and 1930s.
ALTERNATIVE FORM: **Bessie**.
RELATED NAMES: *see list at* **Beth**.

Bet (F) short for **Betty**.

Beth (F) a short form of **Elizabeth** ('oath of God') or **Bethany**, often given as a name in its own right. It was popularized by Beth March, one of the heroines of Louisa M. Alcott's novel *Little Women* (1868).
RELATED NAMES: **Betty, Betsy, Bess, Bethan, Babette, Lizbeth, Elspeth, Eliza, Elsa, Elsie, Elise, Eilis, Liza, Lisa, Lizzie, Libby, Lili, Lisette, Buffy, Isabel**.

Bethan (F) a short form of **Elizabeth** ('oath of God'), of Welsh origin.
RELATED NAMES: *see list at* **Beth**.

Bethany (F) from the biblical place name, possibly meaning 'house of figs'.
RELATED NAME: **Beth**.

Betsy (F) a short form of **Elizabeth** ('oath of God'), sometimes given as a name in its own right. It is borne by the character Betsey Trotwood in Charles Dickens' novel *David Copperfield* (1850).
ALTERNATIVE FORM: **Betsey**.
RELATED NAMES: *see list at* **Betty**.

Bette [BET-i, bet] (F) another form of **Betty**, made famous in the English-speaking world by the 20th-century US actress Bette Davis (born Ruth Elizabeth Davis), who used the two-syllable pronunciation of the name. The US actress and comedian Bette Midler pronounces her name as one syllable.

Betty (F) a short form of **Elizabeth** ('oath of God'), sometimes given as a name in its own right. Famous bearers include the 20th-century US actress Betty Grable.
SHORT FORM: Bet.
ALTERNATIVE FORMS: Bette, Bettina.
RELATED NAMES: Betsy, Bess, Beth, Bethan, Babette, Eliza, Elsa, Elsie, Elspeth, Elise, Eilis, Liza, Lisa, Lizzie, Libby, Lizbeth, Lili, Lisette, Buffy, Isabel.

Beulah [BEW-la] (F) 'married'. A biblical name, it was borne by the 20th-century US actress Beulah Bondi. It is well known in the context of a line spoken by Mae West in the film *I'm No Angel* (1933): 'Beulah, peel me a grape.'

Bevan (M) from the Welsh surname, which means 'son of Evan'.
SHORT FORM: Bev.

Beverley (F) from the surname and place name, which means 'beaver stream'. The alternative spelling is more popular in the USA, where the name may be associated with Beverly Hills in Los Angeles.
SHORT FORM: Bev.
ALTERNATIVE FORM: Beverly.

Bharat (M) 'being maintained'. An Indian name sometimes given to the god of fire or to India itself.
FEMININE FORM: Bharati.

Bhaskar (M) an Indian name meaning 'bright light'. Bhaskara was a famous Indian mathematician and astronomer of the 12th century.

Bianca (F) 'white' or 'pure'. Of Italian origin, the name is borne by the political activist Bianca Jagger, former wife of the British rock singer Mick Jagger.
RELATED NAMES: Blanche, Candida.

Bibi (F) a Muslim name meaning 'lady of the house'.

Biddy (F) short for **Bridget**.

Bilal (M) 'wetting'. An Arabic name borne by an early convert to Islam.

Bill (M) short for **William** or **Billy**.

Billie (F) a feminine form of **Billy** or **William** ('resolute protector'). It is sometimes combined with another name, as in the case of the US tennis player Billie Jean King.
RELATED NAMES: Wilhelmina, Wilma, Willa, Mina, Minnie.

Billy (M) a short form of **William** ('resolute protector'), sometimes given as a name in its own right. Famous bearers include the 20th-century US film director Billy Wilder (whose real name was Samuel).
SHORT FORM: Bill.
FEMININE FORM: Billie.

RELATED NAMES: **Will, Liam, Gwilym, Wilkie.**

Bina (F) short for any name ending with these letters, such as **Albina, Robina,** or **Sabina.** Bina is also a Jewish name, meaning 'bee' or 'understanding', and another spelling of the Indian name **Beena.**

Bindi (F) an Australian name, possibly from an Aboriginal word meaning 'little girl' or referring to a type of plant. It is borne by the daughters of the artist and entertainer Rolf Harris and the naturalist and television presenter Steve Irwin. Bindi is also an Indian name meaning 'a drop'.

Binnie (F) a short form of **Bernice** ('bringer of victory'), sometimes given as a name in its own right. It is also short for various other names containing the letters -*bin*- or -*ben*-.
ALTERNATIVE FORM: **Binny.**

Binyamin (M) the Jewish form of **Benjamin.** Famous modern bearers include the Israeli politician Binyamin Netanyahu.
RELATED NAME: **Ben.**

Blaine (M) 'yellow'. An alternative form of the name was borne by St Blane, a 6th-century Scottish bishop.
ALTERNATIVE FORMS: **Blain, Blane.**

Blair (M/F) from a surname and place name meaning 'field'. It is a popular boys' name in Scotland and is sometimes given to girls elsewhere.

Blaise (M/F) 'lisping'. Famous male bearers include an early Christian martyr and the 17th-century French mathematician and philosopher Blaise Pascal.

Blake (M) from the surname, which can mean either 'black' or 'white' and was originally a nickname for people with dark or light hair or skin. Famous bearers include the US film director Blake Edwards.

Blanche (F) 'white' or 'pure'. Of French origin, the name was popularized in the English-speaking world by Blanche DuBois, the heroine of Tennessee Williams' play *A Streetcar Named Desire* (1947).
RELATED NAMES: **Blanca, Candida.**

Blane (M) another form of **Blaine.**

Blodwen (F) a Welsh name meaning 'white flowers'.
ALTERNATIVE FORM: **Blodwyn.**

Blossom (F) from the word *blossom*, referring to the flowers of a fruit tree.

Blythe (F) from the surname, which is another spelling of the word *blithe*, meaning 'cheerful'.

Boaz (M) a biblical name, possibly meaning 'swiftness'. In the Bible, Boaz is the second husband of Ruth.

Bob (M) short for **Robert** or **Bobby.**

Bobbie (F) a short form of **Roberta** ('great fame'), sometimes given as a name in its own right. The US singer Bobbie Gentry uses this short form of her name.

RELATED NAMES: **Robbie, Robin**.

Bobby (M) a short form of **Robert** ('great fame'), sometimes given as a name in its own right. Famous bearers include the British footballers Bobby Charlton and Bobby Moore.

SHORT FORM: **Bob**.

RELATED NAMES: **Robbie, Robin, Rupert**.

Boniface (M) 'good fate' or 'doer of good deeds'. The name was borne by a number of saints and popes.

Bonita (F) 'pretty'. Coined from a Spanish adjective, it is the full name of the British actress and entertainer known as Bonnie Langford.

SHORT FORM: **Bonnie**.

Bonnie (F) 'attractive'. Originally a nickname, from the word *bonny*, it is also a short form of **Bonita**. It was popularized by the film *Bonnie and Clyde* (1967), which glamorized the story of two real-life criminals, Bonnie Parker and Clyde Barrow.

Booker (M) from the surname, possibly meaning 'scribe' or 'bookbinder'. The 19th-century African-American educationist Booker T. Washington was a famous bearer of the name.

Booth (M) from the surname, meaning 'hut'.

Boris (M) 'small' or 'battle'. A name of Russian origin, borne in the 20th century by the writer Boris Pasternak and the statesman Boris Yeltsin. It may also be associated with the British actor Boris Karloff, who starred in many horror films and whose real name was William Pratt.

Boyce (M) from the surname, meaning 'wood'.

Boyd (M) from the surname, possibly meaning 'yellow-haired' or referring to somebody from the Scottish island of Bute.

Braden (M) from the Irish surname, which ultimately comes from a word meaning 'salmon'.

Bradford (M) from a surname and place name meaning 'broad ford'.

SHORT FORM: **Brad**.

Bradley (M) from a surname and place name meaning 'broad meadow'. It is the middle name of the US actor known as Brad Pitt.

SHORT FORM: **Brad**.

Brady (M) from the surname, possibly meaning 'large-chested'.

Bram (M) short for **Abraham**. This short form was used by Bram Stoker, author of *Dracula* (1897).

Brandon (M) from a surname and place name meaning 'gorse hill'. Its

adoption as a forename may have been influenced by **Brendan**.
ALTERNATIVE FORMS: **Branden, Brandyn**.

Brandy (F) probably from the name of the alcoholic spirit, influenced by the boys' name **Brandon**. It has recently been popularized by the US actress and singer whose full name is Brandy Norwood.

Brant (M) from a surname meaning 'sword', or another form of **Brent**.

Branwell (M) probably from the surname *Bramwell*. It was borne by Branwell Brontë, brother of the writers Charlotte, Emily, and Anne.

Branwen (F) a Welsh name meaning 'fair raven'.

Braxton (M) from a surname and place name of uncertain origin.

Breda (F) a short form of **Brigid**, given as a name in its own right.
RELATED NAMES: **Bridget, Brigitte, Bridie, Bree, Britt**.

Bree (F) a short form of **Brigid**, given as a name in its own right.
ALTERNATIVE FORM: **Brie**.
RELATED NAMES: **Bridie, Bridget, Brigitte, Britt**.

Brenda (F) 'sword'. The name was particularly popular in the mid-20th century, when the US singer Brenda Lee and the Irish actress Brenda Fricker were born.
SHORT FORM: **Bren**.

Brendan (M) 'prince'. Of Irish origin, the name was borne by two saints and the 20th-century dramatist Brendan Behan.

Brenna (F) another form of **Brennan**, given only to girls.

Brennan (M/F) from the Irish surname, meaning 'little drop of water'.
ALTERNATIVE FORM: **Brenna** (F).

Brent (M) from a surname and place name meaning 'hill'.
ALTERNATIVE FORM: **Brant**.

Brett (M) from the surname, meaning 'Breton'. The 19th-century US writer William Brett Harte used the alternative spelling for his pen-name, Bret Harte.
ALTERNATIVE FORM: **Bret**.

Brian [BRY-un, BREE-un] (M) 'noble, strong'. Of Irish origin, the name was borne by Brian Boru, who became High King of Ireland in the early 11th century.
ALTERNATIVE FORM: **Bryan**.
FEMININE FORMS: **Brianna, Brianne, Brina**.
RELATED NAME: **Bryant**.

Brianna (F) a feminine form of **Brian**.
ALTERNATIVE FORM: **Brianne**.
RELATED NAME: **Brina**.

Brice (M) another spelling of **Bryce**.

Bridget (F) another form of **Brigid**. It is the usual form of the name outside Ireland. Famous modern

bearers include the US actress Bridget Fonda and the fictional diarist Bridget Jones, created by Helen Fielding in the 1990s.
SHORT FORM: **Biddy**.
ALTERNATIVE FORM: **Brigit**.
RELATED NAMES: **Brigitte, Bridie, Bree, Breda, Britt**.

Bridie (F) a short form of **Brigid**, sometimes given as a name in its own right.
RELATED NAMES: **Bridget, Brigitte, Bree, Breda, Britt**.

Brie [bree] (F) another spelling of **Bree**, influenced by the name of a French region and its cheese.

Brigham (M) from a surname and place name meaning 'homestead by a bridge'. The 19th-century US Mormon leader Brigham Young is the best-known bearer of the name.

Brigid (F) 'exalted' or 'strong and powerful'. From the Irish name of a Celtic goddess. Famous bearers include St Brigid, also known as St Bride, an Irish abbess of the 5th and 6th centuries who is regarded as one of the patron saints of Ireland.
ALTERNATIVE FORM: **Brigit**.
RELATED NAMES: **Bridget, Brigitte, Bridie, Bree, Breda, Britt**.

Brigitte [BRIZH-it, brizh-EET] (F) another form of **Brigid**, of French origin. It was popularized in the English-speaking world in the mid-20th century by the French actress Brigitte Bardot.

RELATED NAMES: **Bridget, Britt, Bridie, Bree, Breda**.

Brina (F) short for **Sabrina**, or a feminine form of **Brian**.

Brinley (M/F) from a surname and place name meaning 'burnt wood or clearing'.
ALTERNATIVE FORM: **Brynley**.

Briony (F) another spelling of **Bryony**.

Britt (F) another form of **Brigid**, of Swedish origin. It was popularized in the English-speaking world in the latter half of the 20th century by the Swedish actress Britt Ekland.
RELATED NAMES: **Bridget, Brigitte, Bridie, Bree, Breda**.

Brittany (F) from the name of a French region, so called because its original inhabitants came from Britain. Its adoption as a forename may have been influenced by **Britt**. The US singer Britney Spears has recently popularized its alternative spelling.
ALTERNATIVE FORM: **Britney**.

Brock (M) from the surname, meaning 'badger'.

Broderick (M) from the surname, meaning 'son of Roderick'. The US actor Broderick Crawford is a famous bearer of the name.

Brodie (M/F) from the Scottish surname, meaning 'muddy place'.
ALTERNATIVE FORM: **Brody**.

Brogan (M/F) 'little shoe'. Originally an Irish boys' name, it became a surname and was later readopted as a forename for either sex.

Bron (M/F) short for **Auberon** or **Bronwen**.

Bronte [BRON-ti] (F) from the surname of the 19th-century British novelists Charlotte, Emily, and Anne Brontë. It is the name of a village in Sicily, and also a Greek word meaning 'thunder'. Bronte was popularized as a forename by the fictional heroine of the film *Green Card* (1990).
ALTERNATIVE FORM: **Brontë**.

Bronwen (F) a Welsh name meaning 'fair bosom'.
SHORT FORM: **Bron**.
ALTERNATIVE FORM: **Bronwyn**.

Brooke (F/M) from the surname, meaning 'person who lives by a stream'. It was popularized as a girls' name in the late 20th century by the US actress Brooke Shields. The name is only occasionally given to boys, usually in its alternative form.
ALTERNATIVE FORM: **Brook**.

Brooklyn (M/F) from the US place name. The British footballer David Beckham and his wife Victoria gave it to their firstborn son in 1999.

Bruce (M) from the Scottish surname. It is commonly regarded as a typical Australian forename. Famous modern bearers in other parts of the English-speaking world include the British entertainer Bruce Forsyth and the US actor Bruce Willis.

Brunella (F) a feminine form of Bruno.

Bruno (M) 'brown'. Of German origin, it was popularized in the 19th century by Lewis Carroll's novel *Sylvie and Bruno* (1889).
FEMININE FORM: **Brunella**.

Brutus (M) from a Roman family name meaning 'stupid'. It is chiefly associated with Julius Caesar's assassin, whose full name was Marcus Junius Brutus.

Bryan (M) another spelling of **Brian**.

Bryant (M) from the surname, which is another form of **Brian**.

Bryce (M) from the surname, possibly meaning 'speckled'.
ALTERNATIVE FORM: **Brice**.

Bryn (M/F) 'hill'. A Welsh boys' name that is now sometimes given to girls, usually in its alternative form. Famous male bearers include the Welsh singer Bryn Terfel.
ALTERNATIVE FORM: **Brynn**.

Brynley (M/F) another spelling of **Brinley**.

Brynmor (M) from a Welsh place name meaning 'large hill'.

Bryony (F) from the plant name. The British writer Ian McEwan gave the alternative form of the name to the heroine of his novel *Atonement* (2001).

ALTERNATIVE FORM: **Briony**.

Bryson (M) from the surname, meaning 'son of Bryce'.

Buck (M) from the word *buck*, meaning 'male deer', given as a nickname to a lively or virile young man. Chiefly found in the USA, it was popularized in early 20th century by the cartoon hero Buck Rogers.

Buddy (M) from the word *buddy*, meaning 'friend', given as a nickname. Famous 20th-century bearers include the US singer Buddy Holly (whose real name was Charles) and the US comedian Bud Abbott (whose real name was William).

SHORT FORM: **Bud**.

Budur (F) another form of **Badr**.

Buffy (F) a short form of **Elizabeth** ('oath of God'), sometimes given as a name in its own right. It is now chiefly associated with Buffy the Vampire Slayer, a fictional character created by Joss Whedon in the 1990s.

RELATED NAMES: **Eliza, Elsa, Elsie, Elspeth, Elise, Eilis, Liza, Lisa, Lizzie, Libby, Lizbeth, Lili, Lisette, Beth, Bethan, Betty, Betsy, Bess, Babette, Isabel**.

Bunty (F) possibly from a nickname for a pet lamb. It was popularized in the 20th century as the title of a comic for girls.

ALTERNATIVE FORM: **Buntie**.

Burl (M) 'cup-bearer'. The name was borne by the 20th-century US actor and singer Burl Ives.

Burt (M) another spelling of **Bert** ('illustrious') or a short form of **Burton**. Famous modern bearers include the US songwriter Burt Bacharach (whose father's name was Bert) and the US actors Burt Lancaster and Burt Reynolds (whose full names were Burton).

Burton (M) from a surname and place name meaning 'fortified enclosure'.

SHORT FORM: **Burt**.

Buster (M) from a nickname meaning 'person who breaks things'. Its best-known bearer is the US silent film comedian Buster Keaton (whose real name was Joseph).

Byron (M) from the surname of the 19th-century British poet Lord Byron, which means 'person who looks after cattle'.

C

Caddy (F) short for **Caroline** or **Catherine**.

Cade (M) from the surname, which was originally a nickname meaning 'round'.
ALTERNATIVE FORM: **Kade**.

Cadell (M) a Welsh name meaning 'battle'.

Caden (M) from a surname of Scottish or Irish origin.
ALTERNATIVE FORM: **Kaden**.

Cadfael [KAD-file, KAD-vile] (M) 'battle prince'. A Welsh name, it is now chiefly associated with Brother Cadfael, a medieval detective created in the late 1970s by the British novelist Ellis Peters.

Cadogan [ka-DUG-un] (M) the English form of a Welsh name meaning 'battle glory'.

Caerwyn (M) another form of **Carwyn** ('fair love').

Caesar (M) 'emperor'. Originally a Roman family name, borne by the dictator Caius Julius Caesar in the 1st century BC, it was subsequently adopted as an imperial title.

Cai [kye] (M) a short form of **Caius**, sometimes given as a name in its own right, or another spelling of **Kai**.

Cain (M) 'acquired'. A biblical name, borne by the eldest son of Adam and Eve, who killed his brother Abel. The name **Kane**, which sounds the same but is of different origin, is generally preferred.

Caitlin [KATE-lin, kath-LEEN] (F) the Irish form of **Catherine** ('pure').
ALTERNATIVE FORMS: **Caitlyn, Kaitlyn, Katelyn**.
RELATED NAMES: **Kate, Katie, Kathleen, Cathy, Catriona, Katrina, Karen, Kitty, Kay, Katha, Katya**.

Caius [KYE-us] (M) a name of Roman origin, possibly meaning 'rejoice'. It was borne by the dictator Caius (or Gaius) Julius Caesar in the 1st century BC.
ALTERNATIVE FORM: **Gaius**.
RELATED NAME: **Cai**.

Cal (M) short for **Calvin** or **Callum**, or another form of **Cathal** ('mighty in battle').

Caleb [KAY-leb] (M) 'dog'. A biblical name, borne by one of the companions of Moses on his journey from Egypt to the Promised Land.

Calista (F) 'most beautiful'. The name was popularized in the late 1990s by the US actress Calista Flockhart, who starred in the television series *Ally McBeal*.
SHORT FORMS: **Cali, Callie, Cally**.
ALTERNATIVE FORM: **Callista**.

Calliope [ka-LYE-a-pi] (F) 'beautiful face'. The name of the Greek muse of epic poetry.
SHORT FORMS: **Callie, Cally**.

Callum (M) the usual English spelling of **Calum**, which is the Scottish form of **Columba** ('dove').
SHORT FORM: **Cal**.
RELATED NAMES: **Colm, Colman**.

Calvin (M) 'little bald one'. Originally a surname (borne by the 16th-century French theologian Jean Calvin), it was the middle name of the US president known as Calvin Coolidge and was popularized by the US fashion designer Calvin Klein.
SHORT FORM: **Cal**.

Cameron (M/F) from the Scottish surname, which may mean 'crooked nose'. Famous modern bearers include the British theatrical director Cameron Mackintosh (male) and the US actress Cameron Diaz (female).

Camilla (F) from a Roman family name, possibly meaning 'attendant at a pagan ceremony'. It is borne by the second wife of Prince Charles, formerly known as Camilla Parker Bowles.
ALTERNATIVE FORM: **Camille**.
RELATED NAMES: **Millie, Milla**.

Campbell (M) from the Scottish surname, meaning 'crooked mouth'.

Candace [KAN-diss, kan-DAY-si] (F) the name of a queen of Ethiopia mentioned in the Bible.
ALTERNATIVE FORM: **Candice**.
RELATED NAME: **Candy**.

Candice [KAN-diss] (F) another form of **Candace**, more frequent in modern times. The US actress Candice Bergen is a famous bearer.
RELATED NAME: **Candy**.

Candida (F) 'white' or 'pure'. George Bernard Shaw gave the name to the heroine of his play *Candida* (1898). It is also the name of a yeast-like fungus, which causes the infection known as thrush.
RELATED NAME: **Candy**.

Candy (F) a short form of **Candice**, **Candace**, or **Candida**, sometimes given as a name in its own right. It may also be associated with the word *candy*, referring to sweets.

ALTERNATIVE FORMS: **Candi, Candie.**

Caoimhe [KEE-va] (F) an Irish name meaning 'gentle, beautiful'. It is related to the boys' name **Kevin**.
ALTERNATIVE FORMS: **Keeva, Keva.**

Caolan [KEE-lun, KAY-lun] (M) an Irish name meaning 'slender'.
ALTERNATIVE FORMS: **Keelan, Kelan.**

Caprice (F) from the word *caprice*, meaning 'whim'. It has recently been popularized by the US model whose full name is Caprice Bourret.

Cara (F) 'beloved' or 'friend'. The name is borne by a character in Evelyn Waugh's novel *Brideshead Revisited* (1945).
ALTERNATIVE FORM: **Kara.**
RELATED NAMES: **Carina, Carita.**

Carenza (F) another spelling of **Karenza** ('loving').

Carey [KAIR-i] (F/M) another form of **Cary**. It is the usual form of the name for girls.

Carina (F) another form of **Cara**, possibly influenced by **Karen** ('pure').
SHORT FORM: **Rina.**
ALTERNATIVE FORM: **Karina.**
RELATED NAME: **Carita.**

Caris (F) another form of **Charis** ('grace').

Carissa (F) another form of **Charis** ('grace').

Carita (F) another form of **Cara**, possibly influenced by a Latin word meaning 'charity, love'.
RELATED NAME: **Carina.**

Carl (M) the usual English spelling of **Karl**, which is a German form of **Charles** ('free man'). Famous modern bearers include the US astronomer Carl Sagan. It is also used as a short form of **Carlton**.
RELATED NAMES: **Carlo, Carlos, Charlie, Chay, Chuck, Carol.**

Carla (F) a feminine form of **Charles** ('free man'). Famous modern bearers include the British television writer Carla Lane.
RELATED NAMES: *see list at* **Carlotta.**

Carlo (M) another form of **Charles**, of Italian origin.
RELATED NAMES: **Carl, Carlos, Charlie, Chay, Chuck, Carol.**

Carlos (M) another form of **Charles**, of Spanish origin.
RELATED NAMES: **Carl, Carlo, Charlie, Chay, Chuck, Carol.**

Carlotta (F) a feminine form of **Charles**, of Italian origin.
RELATED NAMES: **Charlotte, Charlie, Lottie, Charlene, Carla, Carly, Carol, Caroline, Carolina, Carrie.**

Carlton (M) from a surname and place name meaning 'settlement of free men'. It is the middle name of the US athlete known as Carl Lewis.
SHORT FORM: **Carl.**
RELATED NAME: **Charlton.**

Carly (F) a feminine form of **Charles**. Famous modern bearers include the US singer Carly Simon.
RELATED NAMES: *see list at* **Carlotta**.

Carmel (F) 'garden'. The name of a mountain in the Holy Land, where the Carmelite order of monks was founded.
ALTERNATIVE FORMS: **Carmela, Carmella, Carmelina, Carmelita, Carmen**.

Carmen (F) another form of **Carmel**, of Spanish origin, also associated with the Latin word *carmen*, meaning 'song'. Its best-known bearer is the heroine of Bizet's opera *Carmen* (1875).
ALTERNATIVE FORM: **Carmine**.

Carol (F/M) another form of **Charles** ('free man'), from the Latin form of the name. Since the early 20th century it has been chiefly given to girls, the British film director Sir Carol Reed being a notable exception.
ALTERNATIVE FORMS: **Carroll, Carole** (F), **Carola** (F), **Caryl** (F).
RELATED NAMES: **Charlie, Carl** (M), **Carlo** (M), **Carlos** (M), **Chay** (M), **Chuck** (M), **Caroline** (F), **Carolina** (F), **Carrie** (F), **Charlotte** (F), **Lottie** (F), **Charlene** (F), **Carlotta** (F), **Carla** (F), **Carly** (F).

Carolina (F) a feminine form of **Charles** ('free man'), of Italian origin. The area of the USA that contains the states of North and South Carolina was named by Charles II in honour of his father, Charles I.
RELATED NAMES: *see list at* **Caroline**.

Caroline (F) a feminine form of **Charles** ('free man'), of French origin. Famous bearers include Lady Caroline Lamb, who was Lord Byron's lover in the early 19th century.
SHORT FORMS: **Caro, Caddy**.
ALTERNATIVE FORM: **Carolyn**.
RELATED NAMES: **Carol, Carolina, Carrie, Charlotte, Charlie, Lottie, Charlene, Carlotta, Carla, Carly**.

Caron (F) 'love'. A Welsh name, it is sometimes used in other parts of the English-speaking world as a blend of **Carol** and **Karen**.

Carrie (F) a short form of **Caroline**, sometimes given as a name in its own right. It is borne by the heroine of Stephen King's horror novel *Carrie* (1974), filmed in 1976.
RELATED NAMES: *see list at* **Caroline**.

Carroll (M/F) another spelling of **Carol**. As a boys' name it may also be the English form of an Irish name meaning 'fierce in battle'.

Carson (M/F) from a surname of uncertain origin. It is chiefly given to boys, a notable exception being the 20th-century US novelist Carson McCullers.

Carter (M) from the surname, meaning 'person who transports goods by cart'.

Carwyn (M) a Welsh name meaning 'fair love'.
ALTERNATIVE FORM: **Caerwyn**.

Cary [KARR-i, KAIR-i] (M/F) from a surname that comes from a river name. It is chiefly given to boys in this form, popularized in the mid-20th century by the British-born actor Cary Grant (whose real name was Archibald Leach).
ALTERNATIVE FORM: **Carey**.

Caryl (F) another form of **Carol**. Famous modern bearers include the British dramatist Caryl Churchill.
RELATED NAMES: **Caroline, Carolina, Carrie, Charlotte, Charlie, Lottie, Charlene, Carlotta, Carla, Carly**.

Caryn (F) another spelling of **Karen**, which is a form of **Catherine** ('pure').

Carys (F) a Welsh name meaning 'love'.
ALTERNATIVE FORM: **Cerys**.

Casey (M/F) possibly from an Irish surname meaning 'watchful in battle'. As a boys' name it may be associated with the 19th-century US engine driver and folk hero Casey Jones (who gained this nickname from his home town of Cayce). As a

girls' name it may be regarded as another form of **Cassie**.
ALTERNATIVE FORMS: **Kasey, Kacey**.

Caspar (M) another form of **Jasper** ('treasurer'), of Dutch origin. Caspar was one of the three Magi who brought gifts to the young Jesus. More recently the name has been borne by the US statesman Caspar Weinberger and by the cartoon character Casper the Friendly Ghost.
ALTERNATIVE FORM: **Casper**.

Cass (F/M) short for **Cassandra, Cassie, Cassia**, or **Cassidy**.

Cassandra (F) the name of a prophetess in Greek mythology whom nobody ever believed. It was popularized in the 20th century as the pseudonym of a *Daily Mirror* columnist and by a character in the television sitcom *Only Fools and Horses*.
SHORT FORM: **Cass**.
RELATED NAMES: **Cassie, Sandra**.

Cassia (F) another form of **Kezia**, or a feminine form of **Cassius**.
SHORT FORM: **Cass**.

Cassidy (M/F) from an Irish surname meaning 'curly-haired'.
SHORT FORM: **Cass**.

Cassie (F) a short form of **Cassandra**, sometimes given as a name in its own right.
SHORT FORM: **Cass**.
ALTERNATIVE FORM: **Casey**.
RELATED NAME: **Sandra**.

Cassius (M) from a Roman family name, possibly meaning 'empty'. It was borne in the 1st century BC by one of Julius Caesar's assassins and in the 20th century by the US boxer Cassius Clay, better known as Muhammad Ali.
FEMININE FORM: **Cassia**.

Cate (F) short for **Catherine** (or any of its alternative forms). It is sometimes used instead of **Kate** by people whose full name is spelt with a C, notably the Australian actress Cate Blanchett.

Cathal [KA-hal] (M) 'mighty in battle'. An Irish name borne by a 7th-century saint who served as a bishop in Italy.
ALTERNATIVE FORM: **Cal**.

Catherine (F) 'pure'. The name was borne by various saints, notably an early Christian martyr who was tortured on a spiked wheel, and by three of the wives of Henry VIII. More recent bearers include the English writer Catherine Cookson and the Welsh actress Catherine Zeta-Jones.
SHORT FORMS: **Cath, Cat, Cate, Caddy**.
ALTERNATIVE FORMS: **Katherine, Katharine, Catharine, Kathryn, Cathryn**.
RELATED NAMES: **Cathy, Kate, Katie, Kathleen, Caitlin, Catriona, Katrina, Karen, Kitty, Kay, Katha, Katya**.

Cathleen (F) another form of **Catherine**, of Irish origin. The alternative spelling **Kathleen** is more frequent.
SHORT FORM: **Cath**.
RELATED NAMES: *see list at* **Catherine**.

Cathy (F) a short form of **Catherine**, sometimes given as a name in its own right. It was borne by the central character in the television play *Cathy Come Home* (1966), about a homeless family.
ALTERNATIVE FORM: **Kathy**.
RELATED NAMES: *see list at* **Catherine**.

Catrina (F) another form of **Catherine**. It may be a shortening of **Catriona** or of *Caterina* or *Catarina* (used in various European countries). The alternative spelling **Katrina** is more frequent.
SHORT FORM: **Trina**.
RELATED NAMES: *see list at* **Catherine**.

Catriona [ka-TREE-na] (F) another form of **Catherine**, of Scottish or Irish origin. It was popularized by Robert Louis Stevenson's novel *Catriona* (1893), the sequel to *Kidnapped* (1886).
RELATED NAMES: *see list at* **Catherine**.

Cecil [SESS-il, SISS-il, SEE-sil] (M) from a Roman family name meaning 'blind' or a Welsh name meaning 'sixth'. (The aristocratic

English surname comes from the latter.) Famous bearers include the 19th-century British statesman Cecil Rhodes and the 20th-century US film producer Cecil B. De Mille.

FEMININE FORMS: Cecilia, Cecile, Cecily.

Cecile [si-SEEL, SESS-eel] (F) another form of **Cecilia**, of French origin.
ALTERNATIVE FORM: Cécile.
RELATED NAMES: Cecily, Cicely, Cissie, Celia, Sheila.

Cecilia [si-SIL-i-a] (F) from a Roman family name meaning 'blind'. It was borne by the early Christian martyr St Cecilia, patron saint of music.
RELATED NAMES: Cecile, Cecily, Cicely, Cissie, Celia, Sheila.

Cecily [SESS-i-li] (F) another form of Cecilia. Oscar Wilde gave the name to a character in his comedy *The Importance of Being Earnest* (1895).
RELATED NAMES: Cecile, Cicely, Cissie, Celia, Sheila.

Cedric (M) a name given by Sir Walter Scott to a character in his novel *Ivanhoe* (1819). It may be from *Cerdic*, the name of a 6th-century Saxon leader who founded the kingdom of Wessex, or from the Welsh name *Cedrych*, meaning 'generous'.

Ceinwen [KANE-wen, KINE-wen] (F) 'beautiful'. A Welsh name borne by a 5th-century saint.

Celeste (F) 'heavenly'. It was originally a boys' name, and the alternative form Celestine was borne by five popes.
ALTERNATIVE FORMS: Céleste, Celestine, Celestina.

Celia (F) from a Roman name, probably meaning 'heaven', or a short form of **Cecilia**. Famous bearers include a character in Shakespeare's play *As You Like It* and, more recently, the British actresses Celia Johnson and Celia Imrie.
RELATED NAMES: Celina, Celine, Cecile, Cicely, Cissie, Sheila.

Celina (F) another form of **Celine** or **Selina**.

Celine [say-LEEN, SAY-leen] (F) from a Roman name, probably meaning 'heaven'. Of French origin, the name was popularized in the late 20th century by the Canadian singer Céline Dion.
ALTERNATIVE FORMS: Céline, Celina.
RELATED NAME: Celia.

Ceri [KERR-i] (F) another form of **Cerys**, a short form of **Ceridwen**, or another spelling of **Kerry**.

Ceridwen [ke-RID-wen] (F) the name of the Welsh goddess of poetic inspiration.
SHORT FORM: Ceri.

Cerys [KERR-iss] (F) another form of the Welsh name **Carys** ('love').
ALTERNATIVE FORM: Ceri.

Chad (M) from an Old English name, possibly meaning 'warrior'. St Chad was Archbishop of York in the 7th century. More recent bearers include the British churchman Chad Varah, who founded the Samaritans organization in 1953.

Chaim [hyme, HY-im] (M) another form of the Jewish name **Hyam** ('life'). Famous bearers include Chaim Herzog, President of Israel from 1983 to 1993.

Chandan (M) an Indian name meaning 'sandalwood' (referring to a substance used in Hindu ceremonies).

Chandler (M/F) from the surname, meaning 'maker or seller of candles'. The boys' name has recently been popularized by a character in the US television series *Friends*.

Chandra (M/F) in Indian name meaning 'moon'.

Chanel [sha-NEL] (F) from the surname of the 20th-century French fashion designer and perfumier Coco Chanel.
ALTERNATIVE FORMS: **Chanelle, Shanelle, Shanel.**

Chantal [shahn-TAL] (F) from the title of a 17th-century French saint, which was originally a French place name meaning 'stone'.
ALTERNATIVE FORM: **Chantelle.**

Chantelle [shahn-TEL] (F) another form of **Chantal**, or a name coined from the French word *chant* (meaning 'song') and the name-ending *-elle*.

Chapman (M) from the surname, meaning 'merchant, pedlar'. It is the middle name of the British journalist and novelist known as Chapman Pincher.

Chardonnay [SHAR-da-nay] (F) from the name of the wine. It has recently been popularized by a character in the British television series *Footballers' Wives*.

Charis [KARR-iss] (F) 'grace'.
ALTERNATIVE FORMS: **Caris, Karis, Charissa, Carissa.**

Charity (F) 'love'. From the word *charity* in its original meaning. Charles Dickens gave the name to a character in his novel *Martin Chuzzlewit* (1844).
SHORT FORM: **Cherry.**

Charlene [SHAR-leen, shar-LEEN] (F) a feminine form of **Charles**. It was popularized in the 1980s by a character in the Australian soap opera *Neighbours*, played by Kylie Minogue.
RELATED NAMES: *see list at* **Charlotte.**

Charles (M) 'free man'. The name has had many royal bearers, including two 17th-century British kings and the eldest son of Elizabeth II.

SHORT FORM: **Chas.**

FEMININE FORMS: **Charlotte, Charlie, Lottie, Charlene, Carla, Carly, Carlotta, Carol, Caroline, Carolina, Carrie.**

RELATED NAMES: **Charlie, Chay, Chuck, Carl, Carlo, Carlos, Carol.**

Charlie (M/F) a short form of **Charles, Charlotte,** or **Charlene,** now sometimes given as a name in its own right. As a short form it has been used by the 20th-century US actor Charlie Chaplin (male) and the British television gardener Charlie Dimmock (female).
ALTERNATIVE FORM: **Charley.**
RELATED NAMES: *see lists at* **Charles** *and* **Charlotte.**

Charlotte [SHAR-lut] (F) a feminine form of **Charles.** Famous bearers include the 19th-century British novelist Charlotte Brontë and the spider heroine of the children's novel *Charlotte's Web* (1952) by E. B. White.
RELATED NAMES: **Charlie, Lottie, Charlene, Carlotta, Carla, Carly, Carol, Caroline, Carolina, Carrie.**

Charlton (M) from a surname and place name meaning 'settlement of free men'. Its best-known bearer is the US actor Charlton Heston, famous for heroic screen roles such as the title character of *Ben-Hur* (1959).

RELATED NAME: **Carlton.**

Charmaine (F) another form of **Charmian,** or a name coined from the word *charm* and the name-ending *-aine*. It was the title of a popular song written in the 1920s.

Charmian (F) 'delight'. The name is borne by one of Cleopatra's attendants in Shakespeare's play *Antony and Cleopatra*.
ALTERNATIVE FORM: **Charmaine.**

Chas (M) short for **Charles.** It was originally a written abbreviation of the name.
ALTERNATIVE FORM: **Chaz.**

Chase (M) from the surname, which originated as a nickname for a hunter.

Chastity (F) from the word *chastity*, meaning 'purity'. The US actress and singer Cher played the title role in the film *Chastity* (1969) and gave the name to her daughter, born the same year.

Chauncey (M) from a surname that is more common in the USA than in the UK.
ALTERNATIVE FORM: **Chauncy.**

Chay (M) a Scottish pet form of **Charles,** sometimes given as a name in its own right. Its best-known bearer is the British yachtsman Chay Blyth (whose real name is Charles).
RELATED NAMES: **Charlie, Chuck, Carl, Carlo, Carlos, Carol.**

Chaya [HY-a] (F) a Jewish name meaning 'alive'.
ALTERNATIVE FORM: Haya.
RELATED NAME: Eve.

Chaz (M) another spelling of Chas.

Chelle [shell] (F) short for Michelle.

Chelsea (F) from the name of a fashionable district of London or its football club. It was popularized in the late 20th century by Chelsea Clinton, daughter of the US president Bill Clinton.
ALTERNATIVE FORMS: Chelsey, Chelsie.

Cher [shair] (F) a short form of any name beginning with these letters, sometimes given as a name in its own right, in which case it may also be associated with the French word *cher*, meaning 'dear'. The best-known bearer of the name is the US singer and actress Cher (whose full name is Cherilyn).

Cherie [she-REE] (F) 'darling'. Famous modern bearers of the name include the British actress Cherie Lunghi and the wife of the British politician Tony Blair.
ALTERNATIVE FORMS: Chérie, Cheri, Sherry, Cherry.

Cherilyn (F) a blend of Cheryl and Lynn.
ALTERNATIVE FORM: Sherilyn.

Cherry (F) probably from the name of the fruit. It may also be regarded as another form of Cherie or a short form of Charity.

Cheryl [SHEER-il, CHERR-il] (F) a blend of Cherry (or Cherie) and Beryl.
ALTERNATIVE FORMS: Sheryl, Cheryll, Cherryl.

Chesney (M) from a surname and place name meaning 'oak grove'. Famous bearers include the British comedian Chesney Allen.
SHORT FORMS: Ches, Chet.

Chester (M) from a surname and place name meaning 'military camp'.
SHORT FORM: Chet.

Chevonne (F) an English form of the Irish name Siobhan ('God is gracious').
ALTERNATIVE FORM: Shevaun.

Cheyenne (F) from the name of an American Indian people.
ALTERNATIVE FORM: Shyanne.

Chiara [ki-AR-a] (F) another form of Clara ('bright, clear'), of Italian origin.
ALTERNATIVE FORM: Kiara.
RELATED NAMES: Claire, Clare, Clarice, Clarissa.

Chip (M) short for Christopher.

Chloe [KLOE-ee] (F) from a name given to Demeter, the Greek goddess of agriculture and fertility. It is borne by one of the young lovers in the legend of Daphnis and Chloe.

The name was particularly popular in the early 21st century.
ALTERNATIVE FORM: **Chloë**.

Chris (M/F) short for any name beginning with these letters or this sound, especially **Christopher**, **Christian**, or **Christine**.

Chrissie (F) short for any girls' name beginning with *Chris-*, especially **Christine**.
ALTERNATIVE FORM: **Chrissy**.

Christa (F) a short form of various girls' names beginning with *Christ-*, such as **Christina** or **Christabel**, often given as a name in its own right.
RELATED NAMES: **Christie, Christiana, Tiana, Christine, Christelle, Tina, Kristen, Kirsten, Kirsty**.

Christabel (F) a blend of **Christian** and the name-ending *-bel* ('beautiful'). It was borne in the early 20th century by the British suffragette Christabel Pankhurst.
SHORT FORMS: **Chris, Chrissie**.
ALTERNATIVE FORMS: **Christabelle, Christabella**.
RELATED NAMES: **Christa, Christie**.

Christelle (F) a blend of **Christian** and the name-ending *-elle*, or another form of **Crystal**.
SHORT FORMS: **Chris, Chrissie**.
RELATED NAMES: **Christa, Christie**.

Christian (M/F) from the word *Christian*, meaning 'follower of

Christ'. It has chiefly been a boys' name since the late 17th century, when John Bunyan gave it to the title character of *The Pilgrim's Progress* (1678, 1684).
SHORT FORM: **Chris**.
ALTERNATIVE FORM: **Kristian**.
RELATED NAMES: **Christie**; *see list at* **Christina**.

Christiana (F) another form of **Christian**, from the feminine form of the Latin adjective with this meaning.
SHORT FORMS: **Chris, Chrissie**.
ALTERNATIVE FORMS: **Christianna, Christianne, Christiane**.
RELATED NAMES: *see list at* **Christina**.

Christie (M/F) a short form of various names beginning with *Christ-*, especially **Christine** or **Christopher**, sometimes given as a name in its own right.
ALTERNATIVE FORMS: **Christy, Kristy** (F), **Kristie** (F).
RELATED NAMES: **Christian, Kester** (M); *see list at* **Christina**.

Christina (F) another form of **Christian**. Famous bearers include the 19th-century British poet Christina Rossetti.
SHORT FORMS: **Chris, Chrissie**.
ALTERNATIVE FORMS: **Kristina**.
RELATED NAMES: **Christine, Christiana, Tiana, Christie, Christa, Tina, Kristen, Kirsten, Kirsty**.

Christine (F) another form of

Christian, of French origin. It was the usual feminine form of the name in the 20th century, when it was borne by two famous tennis players, Christine Truman and Chris Evert.

SHORT FORMS: **Chris, Chrissie**.

ALTERNATIVE FORMS: **Kristine**.

RELATED NAMES: *see list at* **Christina**.

Christopher (M) 'carrier of Christ'. Famous bearers of the name include St Christopher (patron saint of travellers), the 15th-century explorer Christopher Columbus, and A. A. Milne's son Christopher Robin (whose toy bear became famous in the 1920s as Winnie-the-Pooh).

SHORT FORMS: **Chris, Kris, Kit, Kip, Chip**.

RELATED NAMES: **Christie, Kester**.

Christy (M/F) another spelling of **Christie**.

Chrystal (F) another spelling of **Crystal**.

Chuck (M) a US pet form of **Charles**, sometimes given as a name in its own right. Famous bearers include the US singer Chuck Berry (whose real name is Charles).

RELATED NAMES: **Charlie, Chay, Carl, Carlo, Carlos, Carol**.

Cian [KEE-un] (M) 'ancient'. An Irish name borne by the son-in-law of Brian Boru, High King of Ireland.

ALTERNATIVE FORM: **Kian**.

RELATED NAMES: **Keane, Keenan**.

Ciara [KEER-a] (F) the feminine form of **Ciaran**.

ALTERNATIVE FORMS: **Kiera, Keira, Kira**.

Ciaran [KEER-un, KEER-ahn] (M) 'little dark-haired one'. An Irish name borne by a number of saints.

ALTERNATIVE FORMS: **Ciarán, Kieran, Kieron, Keiran**.

FEMININE FORM: **Ciara**.

Cicely [SISS-i-li] (F) another form of **Cecilia**. Famous bearers of the name include the 20th-century British actress Cicely Courtneidge.

RELATED NAMES: **Cecile, Cecily, Cissie, Celia, Sheila**.

Cilla (F) a short form of **Priscilla**, sometimes given as a name in its own right. Its best-known bearer is the British singer and television presenter Cilla Black (born Priscilla White).

Cindy (F) a short form of **Cynthia** or **Lucinda**, often given as a name in its own right.

ALTERNATIVE FORMS: **Cindi, Cyndi, Sindy**.

Cissie (F) a short form of **Cecilia** or **Cicely**, sometimes given as a name in its own right. It may be associated with the word *sissy* (or *cissy*), referring to somebody who is effeminate, weak, or cowardly.

ALTERNATIVE FORMS: **Cissy, Sissy, Sissie**.

RELATED NAMES: Cecile, Cecily, Celia, Sheila.

Claire (F) another form of **Clara**, of French origin. It became popular in the latter half of the 20th century, along with the less frequent English spelling **Clare**.
RELATED NAMES: Chiara, Clarice, Clarissa.

Clancy (M) from the surname, possibly meaning 'son of the ruddy warrior'.
ALTERNATIVE FORM: Clancey.

Clara [KLAIR-a, KLAR-a] (F) 'bright, clear'. The US actress Clara Bow popularized the name in the 1920s, when she was hailed as the 'It' girl.
SHORT FORM: Clarrie.
RELATED NAMES: Clare, Claire, Chiara, Clarice, Clarissa.

Clarabelle (F) another form of Claribel.

Clare (F) another form of **Clara**. St Clare founded an order of nuns known as the Poor Clares in the 12th century. Although Clare is the traditional English form of the name, the French spelling **Claire** is now more often used.
RELATED NAMES: Chiara, Clarice, Clarissa.

Clarence (M) from a title bestowed on the first Duke of Clarence in the 14th century. More recent famous bearers include the US lawyer

Clarence Darrow and a cross-eyed lion in the television series *Daktari*.

Claribel (F) a blend of **Clara** and the name-ending -*bel* ('beautiful').
SHORT FORM: Clarrie.
ALTERNATIVE FORM: Clarabelle.

Clarice (F) from a Latin name meaning 'fame', or another form of **Clara**. Famous modern bearers include the British ceramic artist Clarice Cliff.
SHORT FORM: Clarrie.
ALTERNATIVE FORM: Claris.
RELATED NAMES: Clarissa, Clare, Claire, Chiara.

Clarinda (F) a blend of **Clara** and the name-ending -*inda*. It occurs in literature, notably in a set of poems by the 18th-century Scottish poet Robert Burns.
SHORT FORM: Clarrie.

Clarissa (F) another form of **Clarice**. Famous fictional bearers include the title characters of Samuel Richardson's novel *Clarissa* (1748) and Virginia Woolf's novel *Mrs Dalloway* (1925).
SHORT FORM: Clarrie.
RELATED NAMES: Clara, Clare, Claire, Chiara.

Clark (M) from the surname, meaning 'clerk'. It was popularized in the 20th century by the US actor Clark Gable and the fictional character Clark Kent, alias Superman.
ALTERNATIVE FORM: Clarke.

Clarrie (F) short for **Clara, Clarice, Claribel, Clarinda,** or **Clarissa.**

Claude (M) another form of **Claudius,** of French origin. Famous bearers include the 19th-century French artist Claude Monet and the 20th-century British actor Claude Rains.
ALTERNATIVE FORM: **Claud.**
FEMININE FORMS: **Claudette, Claudine.**

Claudette (F) a feminine form of **Claude,** of French origin. It was popularized in the 20th century by the US actress Claudette Colbert.
RELATED NAMES: **Claudine, Claudia.**

Claudia (F) a feminine form of **Claudius.** It has recently been popularized by the German model Claudia Schiffer.
RELATED NAMES: **Claudette, Claudine.**

Claudine (F) a feminine form of **Claude,** of French origin. The French writer Colette gave the name to the heroine of a series of novels published in the early 20th century.
RELATED NAMES: **Claudette, Claudia.**

Claudius (M) 'lame'. The name of a 1st-century Roman emperor and of the murderous king in Shakespeare's play *Hamlet.*
FEMININE FORM: **Claudia.**
RELATED NAME: **Claude.**

Clayton (M) from a surname and place name meaning 'clay settlement'.
SHORT FORM: **Clay.**

Cledwyn (M) a Welsh name meaning 'rough and fair'.

Clelia (F) from the name of a Roman heroine who escaped from the Etruscans by swimming across the Tiber.

Clemence (F) a feminine form of **Clement.**
SHORT FORMS: **Clem, Clemmie.**
ALTERNATIVE FORM: **Clemency.**
RELATED NAME: **Clementine.**

Clement (M) 'merciful'. The name has been borne by several saints and popes and, more recently, by the British radio and television personality Clement Freud.
SHORT FORMS: **Clem, Clemmie.**
FEMININE FORMS: **Clemence, Clementine.**

Clementine (F) a feminine form of **Clement.** It was the name of the wife of the 20th-century British statesman Winston Churchill. Clementine is also the ill-fated heroine of a popular song with this title.
SHORT FORMS: **Clem, Clemmie.**
ALTERNATIVE FORM: **Clementina.**
RELATED NAME: **Clemence.**

Cleo (F) a short form of **Cleopatra,** sometimes given as a name in its own right. In the case of the British singer Cleo Laine, it is short for Clementina.

The name may also be regarded as an alternative form of **Clio**.

Cleopatra (F) 'father's glory'. The name of an Egyptian queen of the 1st century BC, the lover of Julius Caesar and Mark Antony, who was renowned for her beauty.
RELATED NAME: **Cleo**.

Cliff (M) a short form of **Clifford** or **Clifton**, sometimes given as a name in its own right. Since the late 1950s it has chiefly been associated with the British singer Cliff Richard (born Harry Webb).
RELATED NAME: **Clive**.

Clifford (M) from a surname and place name meaning 'ford by a cliff'.
RELATED NAME: **Cliff**.

Clifton (M) from a surname and place name meaning 'settlement on a cliff'.
RELATED NAME: **Cliff**.

Clint (M) a short form of **Clinton**, sometimes given as a name in its own right. It was popularized in the latter half of the 20th century by the US actor Clint Eastwood (whose full name is Clinton).

Clinton (M) from a surname and place name of uncertain origin.
RELATED NAME: **Clint**.

Clio (F) 'glory'. The name of the Greek muse of history. In modern times it is more familiar as the name of a car manufactured by Renault.
RELATED NAME: **Cleo**.

Cliodhna [klee-OH-na, KLEE-a-na] (F) an Irish name, possibly meaning 'shapely'. It is the name of a beautiful fairy queen in Irish legend.
ALTERNATIVE FORM: **Cliona**.

Clive (M) from a surname and place name meaning 'cliff'. Its adoption as a forename may have been influenced by the fame of the 18th-century British general Robert Clive, known as Clive of India.
RELATED NAME: **Cliff**.

Clodagh [KLOH-da] (F) from the name of a river in Ireland. An Irish name that became more widely known in the early 1970s, when the singer Clodagh Rodgers entered the Eurovision Song Contest.

Cloris (F) 'green, fresh'. From the name of a Greek goddess of vegetation. The US actress Cloris Leachman is a famous modern bearer of the name.

Clotilda (F) 'famous in battle'. St Clotilda was a 6th-century princess who married King Clovis and converted him to Christianity.
ALTERNATIVE FORMS: **Clotilde, Clothilde**.

Clover (F) from the plant name.

Clovis (M) another form of **Louis** ('famous warrior'). The name was borne by a 6th-century king who is regarded as the founder of the French monarchy.
RELATED NAMES: **Lewis, Luis,**

Ludovic, Aloysius.

Clyde (M) from the name of a river in Scotland. It was borne by the US robber and murderer Clyde Barrow, whose story is told in the film *Bonnie and Clyde* (1967).

Cody (M/F) 'helpful person'. From an Irish surname that was popularized in the late 19th century by the Wild West showman William Cody, known as Buffalo Bill.

Col (M) short for **Colin**.

Colbert (M) 'illustrious warrior'. It is more frequently found as a surname in modern times.

Cole (M) 'swarthy'. Famous bearers of the name include the nursery-rhyme character Old King Cole and the 20th-century US songwriter Cole Porter.

Coleen (F) another spelling of **Colleen**.

Coleman (M) another spelling of **Colman**.

Colette (F) a feminine form of **Nicholas** ('the people's victory'), of French origin. It was the pen-name of a famous French writer, who was born Sidonie Gabrielle Colette in 1873.
ALTERNATIVE FORM: Collette.
RELATED NAMES: Nicolette, Nicole, Nicola, Nicky.

Colin [KOL-in] (M) a short form of **Nicholas** ('the people's victory'),

given as a name in its own right. It may also be the English form of a Scottish name meaning 'puppy' or 'child' or an Irish name meaning 'little chieftain' (pronounced [KOH-lin]).
SHORT FORM: Col.
ALTERNATIVE FORM: Collin.
FEMININE FORM: Colette.
RELATED NAMES: Coll, Nicol, Nick, Nicky, Nico, Nicodemus.

Coll (M) from a Scottish name meaning 'high' or a short form of **Nicholas** ('the people's victory'), given as a name in its own right.
FEMININE FORM: Colette.
RELATED NAMES: Colin, Nicol, Nick, Nicky, Nico, Nicodemus.

Colleen (F) 'girl'. It comes from an Irish word with this meaning but is not used as a forename in Ireland. Famous bearers include the Australian novelist Colleen McCullough.
ALTERNATIVE FORM: Coleen.

Collette (F) another spelling of **Colette**.

Collin (M) another spelling of **Colin**.

Colm (M) an Irish form of **Columba**.
ALTERNATIVE FORM: Colum.
RELATED NAMES: Callum, Colman.

Colman (M) an Irish form of **Columba**. Borne by several Irish saints, it is now more frequently found as a surname, which may also mean 'charcoal burner'.

ALTERNATIVE FORM: **Coleman**.

Columba (M) 'dove'. St Columba travelled from Ireland to Scotland in the 6th century and founded a monastery on the island of Iona.
FEMININE FORM: **Columbine**.
RELATED NAMES: **Colm, Callum, Coleman**.

Columbine (F) a feminine form of Columba. It may be associated with the flower of this name or with a character in traditional Italian comedies, the sweetheart of Harlequin.

Comfort (F/M) from the word *comfort* in any of its senses. In modern times it is chiefly used as an African girls' name.

Con (M) short for various names beginning with these letters, such as **Conrad**.

Conall (M) 'mighty hound'. An Irish name borne by a number of chieftains and warriors.
ALTERNATIVE FORM: **Connell**.

Conan (M) 'little hound'. An Irish name borne by a member of the legendary band of warriors known as the Fianna. Other famous bearers include the British writer Sir Arthur Conan Doyle, who was of Irish ancestry, and the fictional character Conan the Barbarian.

Concepta (F) from a title of the Virgin Mary, referring to the Immaculate Conception. It is chiefly used by Irish Catholics.
RELATED NAMES: **Connie, Mary, Madonna, Dolores, Mercedes**.

Conn (M) an Irish name meaning 'chief'.

Connell (M) another spelling of **Conall**.

Connie (F) a short form of **Constance** or **Concepta**, sometimes given as a name in its own right. The US actress Connie Booth was born Constance Booth in 1944.

Connor (M) 'person who loves hounds'. An English form of the Irish name *Conchobar* (borne by a legendary king).
ALTERNATIVE FORM: **Conor**.

Conrad (M) 'bold counsel'. The name was borne by a number of medieval German kings.
SHORT FORM: **Con**.
RELATED NAME: **Kurt**.

Constance (F) the feminine form of Constant. The 20th-century US-born British actress Constance Cummings was a famous bearer of the name.
RELATED NAME: **Connie**.

Constant (M) 'steadfast'. Famous bearers include the 20th-century British composer Constant Lambert.
FEMININE FORM: **Constance**.
RELATED NAME: **Constantine**.

Constantine (M) another form of **Constant**. It was borne by the Roman emperor Constantine the Great, whose conversion to Christianity in the early 4th century put an end to the Roman persecution of Christians.

Cora (F) possibly from a name given to Persephone, the Greek goddess of the underworld, meaning 'maiden'. Alternatively, the name may have been coined by the US writer James Fenimore Cooper for a character in *The Last of the Mohicans* (1826).
ALTERNATIVE FORM: **Coretta**.

Coral (F) from the name of the pink substance used to make jewellery. Famous bearers include the 20th-century Australian actress Coral Browne.

Coralie (F) possibly a blend of **Cora** or **Coral** and **Rosalie**.

Corbin (M) from the surname, which means 'crow' and was originally a nickname for somebody with black hair or a raucous voice.

Cordelia (F) the name of the king's loving and virtuous daughter in Shakespeare's play *King Lear*. It may mean 'heart' or 'jewel of the sea'.
SHORT FORMS: **Cordy, Delia**.

Coretta (F) another form of **Cora**. It was borne by the wife of the 20th-century US civil-rights leader Martin Luther King.

Corey (M/F) from a surname of uncertain origin. It is more frequently given to boys than to girls.
ALTERNATIVE FORM: **Cory**.

Corin (M) 'spear'. From the Roman name *Quirinus*, borne by a number of saints. The British actor Corin Redgrave is a famous bearer.

Corinna (F) 'maiden'. The name occurs in the poetry of Ovid (in the 1st century BC) and Robert Herrick (in the 16th century).
ALTERNATIVE FORM: **Corinne**.

Corinne (F) another form of **Corinna**, of French origin. Popularized by Madame de Staël's novel *Corinne* (1807), it became the more frequent form of the name in the English-speaking world.

Cormac (M) 'charioteer's son'. A name borne by several kings of Ireland.
ALTERNATIVE FORMS: **Cormick, Cormag**.

Cornelia (F) the feminine form of **Cornelius**.
SHORT FORMS: **Corny, Nellie**.

Cornelius (M) 'horn'. The name of a minor biblical character, from a Roman family name. Famous bearers include the 19th-century US financier Cornelius Vanderbilt.
FEMININE FORM: **Cornelia**.
RELATED NAME: **Cornell**.

Cornell (M) from the surname, which

was borne by the founder of Cornell University in the USA, or another form of **Cornelius**.

ALTERNATIVE FORM: **Cornel**.

Cory (M/F) another spelling of **Corey**.

Cosima (F) the feminine form of **Cosmo**. Its best-known bearer is Cosima Wagner, wife of the 19th-century German composer Richard Wagner.

Cosmo (M) order, harmony, beauty'. Of Italian origin, the name was borne by an early Christian martyr and, in its alternative form, by two notable members of the Medici family in the 15th and 16th centuries.

ALTERNATIVE FORM: **Cosimo**.
FEMININE FORM: **Cosima**.

Courtney (F/M) from the surname, which comes either from a French place name or from a nickname meaning 'short nose'. Famous modern bearers include the British jazz musician Courtney Pine (male) and the US rock musician Courtney Love (female).

Craig (M) 'rock'. A name of Scottish origin that is now used throughout the English-speaking world.

Crawford (M) from a surname and place name meaning 'ford where crows gather'.

Creighton [KRY-t'n] (M) from a surname and place name meaning

'border settlement'. The surname was borne (in its alternative form) by a multi-talented butler in J. M. Barrie's play *The Admirable Crichton* (1902), and a phonetic spelling of the name was given to the robot manservant Kryten in the television comedy series *Red Dwarf* (1988–99).

ALTERNATIVE FORM: **Crichton**.

Cressida (F) 'gold'. The name of a legendary Trojan princess who jilted her lover Troilus.

Crispin (M) 'curly-haired'. St Crispin was a 3rd-century Christian martyr whose feast day, 25 October, was the date of the Battle of Agincourt in 1415.

ALTERNATIVE FORM: **Crispian**.

Crystal (F) from the word *crystal*, which originally meant 'ice'. Famous bearers include the US singer Crystal Gayle, who was born Brenda Gail Webb in 1951.

ALTERNATIVE FORMS: **Chrystal, Krystal, Christelle**.

Cuddy (M) a Scottish short form of **Cuthbert**.

Cullen (M) from a Scottish or Irish surname of uncertain origin.

Curt (M) another spelling of **Kurt**, which is an alternative form of **Conrad** ('bold counsel'), or a short form of **Curtis**.

Curtis (M) from the surname, meaning 'courteous'.

SHORT FORM: **Curt**.

Cuthbert (M) 'very well-known'. The name was borne in the 7th century by St Cuthbert, Bishop of Lindisfarne.
SHORT FORM: **Cuddy**.

Cy (M) short for **Cyrus**.

Cybill (F) another spelling of **Sybil** ('prophetess'), popularized in the latter half of the 20th century by the US actress Cybill Shepherd.

Cyndi (F) another spelling of **Cindy**, made famous in the late 20th century by the US singer Cyndi Lauper (whose full name is Cynthia).

Cynthia (F) one of the alternative names given to **Artemis**, the Greek goddess of hunting. Famous bearers include Cynthia Payne, who was accused of running a brothel at her London home in the 1970s.
RELATED NAMES: **Cindy, Delia**.

Cyprian (M) 'person from Cyprus'. The name was borne by the 3rd-century martyr St Cyprian, Bishop of Carthage.

Cyril (M) 'lord'. There were a number of saints with this name, including a 9th-century Greek theologian who devised the Cyrillic alphabet used for Russian and other languages.

Cyrus (M) the name of several kings of Persia in ancient times. Famous modern bearers include the US statesman Cyrus Vance.
SHORT FORM: **Cy**.

D

Daff (F) short for **Daffodil** or **Daphne**.
ALTERNATIVE FORM: **Daffy**.

Daffodil (F) from the flower name.
SHORT FORMS: **Daff, Daffy**.
RELATED NAME: **Dilly**.

Dafydd [DAV-idh] (M) a Welsh form of **David** ('beloved'). The name is borne by one of the stock characters of the television comedy series *Little Britain*, who thinks he is 'the only gay in the village'.
RELATED NAMES: **Dai, Dewi, Davy, Daud, Dawud**.

Dahlia (F) from the flower name. P. G. Wodehouse gave the name to one of Bertie Wooster's aunts in the 'Jeeves and Wooster' stories of the 1920s.
RELATED NAME: **Dalia**.

Dai [dye] (M) a Welsh name meaning 'shine' or a Welsh short form of **David** ('beloved'), sometimes given as a name in its own right.
RELATED NAMES: **Dafydd, Dewi, Davy, Daud, Dawud**.

Daire [DYE-ra, DARR-a] (M) an Irish name meaning 'fruitful, fertile'.
FEMININE FORM: **Darina**.
RELATED NAME: **Darragh**.

Daisy (F) from the name of the flower, which means 'day's eye'. It was one of the most popular flower names for girls in the early 21st century.

Dakota (F) 'friend'. From the name of an American Indian people and the territory they originally inhabited.

Dale (M/F) from the surname, meaning 'person who lives in a valley'. It has recently been popularized as a boys' name by the British television presenter Dale Winton.

Daley (M) the English form of an Irish name meaning 'frequenter of gatherings'. Its best-known bearer is the British decathlete Daley Thompson, who was born Francis Morgan Thompson in 1958.
ALTERNATIVE FORM: **Daly**.

Dalia (F) another form of **Dahlia** or a

Jewish name meaning 'flowering branch'.
ALTERNATIVE FORMS: **Daliah, Dalya.**

Dallas (M/F) from a surname and place name of Scottish origin, now chiefly associated with the US city of this name and the soap opera *Dallas* (1978–91) about an oil-rich Texan family.

Damaris [DAM-a-ris] (F) a biblical name, possibly meaning 'calf' or 'gentle person'.

Damayanti (F) 'subduing'. An Indian name borne in legend by a beautiful and intelligent princess.

Damian (M) probably another form of **Damon**. The name was borne by an early Christian martyr and, in its alternative form, by the Antichrist in the horror film *The Omen* (1976) and its sequels.
ALTERNATIVE FORM: **Damien.**

Damodar (M) 'with a rope around his belly'. An Indian name that comes from a legend about Krishna as a mischievous child who was tied to a large pot to keep him out of trouble.
FEMININE FORM: **Damodari.**

Damodari (F) the feminine form of **Damodar.**

Damon (M) 'tame'. The name was borne in the 4th century BC by the loyal friend of Pythias. More recent famous bearers include the US

writer Damon Runyon and the British racing driver Damon Hill.
RELATED NAME: **Damian.**

Dan (M) a biblical name meaning 'judge' or a short form of **Daniel**.
FEMININE FORMS: **Dana, Danuta, Danette.**
RELATED NAME: **Danny.**

Dana (F) the name of an Irish fertility goddess. It may also be regarded as a feminine form of **Dan** or **Daniel**. The name was popularized in 1970 when the Irish singer Dana (born Rosemary Brown) won the Eurovision Song Contest.
RELATED NAMES: **Danielle, Danuta, Danny, Danette.**

Dana (M) from a surname of uncertain origin. Famous modern bearers include the US actors Dana Andrews and Dana Carvey.

Dane (M) probably from the surname, which means 'person who lives in a valley', influenced by the word *Dane* meaning 'person from Denmark'.
RELATED NAME: **Dean.**

Danette (F) a feminine form of **Dan.**

Daniel (M) 'God is my judge'. A biblical name, borne by a prophet who was cast into a den of lions. More recent famous bearers include the British actors Daniel Day-Lewis, Daniel Craig, and Daniel Radcliffe.
FEMININE FORMS: **Danielle, Dana, Danuta.**
RELATED NAMES: **Dan, Danny.**

Danielle (F) a feminine form of **Daniel**, of French origin. The US writer Danielle Steel is a famous bearer of the name.

ALTERNATIVE FORMS: **Daniele, Daniella, Daniela**.

RELATED NAMES: **Danny, Dana, Danuta, Danette**.

Danika (F) 'morning star'. A name of Eastern European origin.

ALTERNATIVE FORM: **Danica**.

Danny (M/F) a short form of any name beginning with *Dan-*, sometimes given as a name in its own right. As a boys' name it may be associated with the song 'Danny Boy' (1913). The girls' name is more frequently found in one of the alternative forms.

ALTERNATIVE FORMS: **Dannie, Danni, Dani, Dannii** (F).

RELATED NAMES: **Dan** (M), **Daniel** (M), **Danielle** (F), **Dana** (F), **Danuta** (F), **Danette** (F).

Dante [DAN-ti] (M) 'steadfast, enduring'. Chiefly associated with the medieval Italian poet Dante Alighieri, it was also borne by the 19th-century poet and painter Dante Gabriel Rossetti.

Danuta (F) another form of **Dana**, of Polish origin.

RELATED NAMES: **Danny, Danielle, Danette**.

Daphne [DAFF-ni] (F) 'laurel'. The name of a nymph who was changed into a laurel in Greek mythology. The 20th-century British novelist Daphne Du Maurier was a famous bearer.

SHORT FORMS: **Daph, Daff, Daffy**.

RELATED NAMES: **Laurel, Laura**.

Dara (M/F) another form of **Darragh** or a Jewish girls' name meaning 'compassion' or 'wisdom'. The boys' name has recently been popularized by the Irish comedian Dara O'Briain.

ALTERNATIVE FORMS: **Daragh** (M).

Darby (M) from a surname and place name meaning 'deer park'. It is chiefly associated with the phrase *Darby and Joan*, referring to an elderly devoted couple.

Darcy (M/F) from a surname of French aristocratic origin, famously borne by the handsome hero of Jane Austen's novel *Pride and Prejudice* (1813). The British ballerina Darcey Bussell has popularized the girls' name in recent times.

ALTERNATIVE FORM: **Darcey** (F).

Darell (M) another spelling of **Darrell**.

Daren (M) another spelling of **Darren**.

Daria (F) the feminine form of **Darius**, borne by a 3rd-century saint.

Darien (M) possibly a blend of **Darius** and **Darren**. It is also the name of a region of Panama, made famous in a line from a poem by John Keats: 'Silent, upon a peak in Darien'.

Darin (M) another spelling of **Darren**.

Darina (F) the English form of an Irish name that is probably a feminine form of **Daire** ('fruitful, fertile').

Dario (M) another form of **Darius**, of Italian origin. Famous modern bearers include the Italian dramatist Dario Fo.

Darius (M) 'wealthy'. Borne by several ancient Persian kings, the name has recently been popularized by the British singer Darius Danesh.
FEMININE FORM: **Daria**.
RELATED NAME: **Dario**.

Darlene (F) probably a blend of the word *darling* and the name-ending *-ene*.
ALTERNATIVE FORM: **Darleen**.

Darragh [DARR-a] (M) an Irish or Scottish name meaning 'oak', or an English form of the Irish name Daire ('fruitful, fertile').
ALTERNATIVE FORMS: **Dara, Daragh**.

Darrell (M) from a surname of French aristocratic origin.
ALTERNATIVE FORMS: **Darell, Darryl**.
FEMININE FORM: **Darryl**.

Darren (M) a name of uncertain origin, possibly from a surname. It was popularized in the 1960s by

Darrin Stephens, husband of the witch Samantha, in the US television series *Bewitched*.
ALTERNATIVE FORMS: **Daren, Darrin, Darin, Darran**.

Darryl (F/M) the feminine form of **Darrell**, or another form of the boys' name. Famous modern bearers include the US film producer Darryl F. Zanuck (male) and the US actress Daryl Hannah (female).
ALTERNATIVE FORMS: **Daryl, Darryll**.

Dassah (F) a Jewish name that is another form of **Hadassah** ('myrtle').
RELATED NAMES: **Esther, Hester, Myrtle**.

Daud (M) an Arabic form of **David**.
RELATED NAMES: **Dawud, Davy, Dafydd, Dewi, Dai**.

David (M) 'beloved'. A biblical name, borne by the greatest king of Israel. The 6th-century bishop St David (or Dewi) is the patron saint of Wales. Famous modern bearers include the British artist David Hockney and the British footballer David Beckham.
SHORT FORM: **Dave**.
FEMININE FORMS: **Davida, Davina, Davinia**.
RELATED NAMES: **Davy, Dafydd, Dewi, Dai, Daud, Dawud**.

Davida (F) a feminine form of **David**.
RELATED NAMES: **Davina, Davinia**.

Davina (F) a feminine form of **David**, popularized in recent times by the British television presenter Davina McCall.
ALTERNATIVE FORM: **Davena**.
RELATED NAMES: **Davinia, Davida**.

Davinia (F) a feminine form of **David**, possibly influenced by **Lavinia**.
RELATED NAMES: **Davina, Davida**.

Davis (M) from the surname, meaning 'son of David'.
ALTERNATIVE FORM: **Davies**.

Davy (M) a short form of **David**, sometimes given as a name in its own right. Famous bearers include the US frontiersman Davy Crockett, who died defending the Alamo in 1836.
ALTERNATIVE FORMS: **Davey, Davie**.
RELATED NAMES: **Dewi, Dafydd, Dai, Daud, Dawud**.

Dawn (F) from the word *dawn*, meaning 'daybreak'. The British comic actress Dawn French is a famous bearer of the name.
RELATED NAME: **Aurora**.

Dawud (M) an Arabic form of **David**.
RELATED NAMES: **Daud, Davy, Dafydd, Dewi, Dai**.

Dayaram (M) an Arabic name meaning 'compassionate'.

Dean (M) from the surname, meaning 'person who lives in a valley' or 'senior member of the clergy'. Famous modern bearers include the US singer Dean Martin (born Dino Crocetti).
ALTERNATIVE FORMS: **Deane, Dene**.
FEMININE FORMS: **Deanna, Dena**.
RELATED NAME: **Dane**.

Deanna [dee-ANN-a] (F) another form of **Diana** or a feminine form of **Dean**. Its best-known bearer is the Canadian actress and singer Deanna Durbin, born Edna Mae Durbin in 1921, who shot to stardom at the age of 15.
ALTERNATIVE FORMS: **Deana, Deanne**.
RELATED NAME: **Dena**.

Deb (F) short for **Deborah** or **Debbie**.
ALTERNATIVE FORM: **Debs**.

Deb (M) another form of the Indian name **Dev** ('god').

Debbie (F) a short form of **Deborah**, sometimes given as a name in its own right. The US actress Debbie Reynolds was born Mary Frances Reynolds in 1932.
SHORT FORMS: **Deb, Debs**.
ALTERNATIVE FORMS: **Debby, Debi**.
RELATED NAME: **Devorah**.

Deborah (F) 'bee'. A biblical name, borne by a female judge and prophet. It was particularly popular in the mid-20th century, when the British actress Deborah Kerr was at the height of her fame.
SHORT FORMS: **Deb, Debs**.
ALTERNATIVE FORMS: **Debora, Debra**.
RELATED NAMES: **Debbie, Devorah**.

Declan (M) 'full of goodness'. Of Irish origin, it has recently been popularized by the television presenter Declan Donnelly, partner of Ant McPartlin.
SHORT FORM: Dec.

Dee (F) a short form of any name beginning with this letter, especially **Deirdre**, **Delia**, or **Dorothy**, sometimes given as a name in its own right.

Deepak (M) another form of **Dipak**.

DeForest (M) from the surname of a 19th-century US novelist. It was the middle name of the US actor known as DeForest Kelley, who played Dr Leonard 'Bones' McCoy in the television series *Star Trek*.

Deirdre [DEER-dra, DEER-dri] (F) an Irish name borne by a legendary heroine who killed herself (or died of grief) after her lover was murdered. More recent bearers include a character in the soap opera *Coronation Street*, played by Anne Kirkbride for more than 30 years.
ALTERNATIVE FORM: Deidre.
RELATED NAME: Dee.

Del (M) short for **Derek** or any name beginning with *Del-*.

Delbert (M) possibly a blend of **Delmar** or **Delroy** and the name-ending -*bert* ('illustrious'). It was popularized in the 1980s by the comic character Delbert Wilkins, a black Brixton radio DJ created by the British comedian Lenny Henry.

Delfina (F) another spelling of **Delphina**, of Italian origin.

Delia (F) one of the alternative names given to **Artemis**, the Greek goddess of hunting. Its best-known bearer in modern times is the British cookery writer Delia Smith. The name may also be used as a short form of **Cordelia**.
RELATED NAMES: Cynthia, Dee, Della.

Delicia (F) 'delight'. A name of Latin origin.
ALTERNATIVE FORMS: Delice, Delyse.

Delilah (F) a biblical name of uncertain origin, borne by Samson's deceitful and treacherous lover. It is the title of one of Tom Jones's most famous songs, which was a top ten hit in 1968.
ALTERNATIVE FORM: Delila.
RELATED NAMES: Della, Lila.

Della (F) a short form of **Adela**, given as a name in its own right, or another form of **Delia** or **Delilah**.

Delma (F) short for **Fidelma** ('beauty').

Delmar (M) 'of the sea'. Alternatively, the name may be another form of **Elmer** ('noble and famous') or of the surname *Delamare*, meaning 'of the lake'.

Delores [de-LOR-iss] (F) another form of **Dolores** ('sorrows').

Delphina (F) 'woman from Delphi'.
ALTERNATIVE FORMS: **Delphine, Delfina.**

Delphine (F) another form of **Delphina**, of French origin. Popularized by Madame de Staël's novel *Delphine* (1802), it became the more frequent form of the name in the English-speaking world.

Delroy (M) 'of the king'. Alternatively, the name may be another form of **Leroy** ('the king').

Delyse (F) another form of **Delicia**.

Delyth [DEL-ith] (F) a Welsh name meaning 'pretty'.

Demelza (F) a Cornish name that comes from a local place name. Winston Graham gave the name to the heroine of his 'Poldark' novels, which were adapted for television in the mid-1970s.

Demetria (F) the feminine form of **Demetrius**.
RELATED NAME: **Demi.**

Demetrius (M) 'follower of Demeter (the Greek goddess of agriculture and fertility)'. The name was borne by a number of Eastern European saints and became popular in Russia in the form *Dmitri*.
FEMININE FORM: **Demetria.**

Demi [de-MEE] (F) a short form of **Demetria**, popularized by the US actress Demi Moore (born Demetria Guynes in 1962) and now given as a name in its own right.

Den (M) short for **Dennis**.

Dena (F) another form of **Dina**, or a feminine form of **Dean**.
RELATED NAME: **Deanna.**

Dene (M) another form of **Dean**.

Denham (M) from a surname and place name meaning 'valley homestead'.

Denholm (M) from a surname and place name meaning 'valley island'. It is chiefly associated with the 20th-century British actor Denholm Elliott.

Denise [de-NEESS, de-NEEZ] (F) the feminine form of **Dennis**. The television personality Denise Van Outen is a famous bearer of the name. The US singer Deniece Williams popularized an alternative spelling in the late 20th century.
ALTERNATIVE FORMS: **Denese, Denice, Deniece.**
RELATED NAME: **Dionne.**

Dennis (M) 'follower of Dionysus (the Greek god of wine)'. From the Latin name *Dionysius*. St Denis (or Denys), patron saint of France, was beheaded in the 3rd century and is said to have carried his severed head to his burial-place. Famous modern bearers of the name include the comic-strip character Dennis the

Menace and the British politician Denis Healey.

SHORT FORMS: **Den, Denny**.
ALTERNATIVE FORMS: **Denis, Denys**.
FEMININE FORM: **Denise**.
RELATED NAMES: **Dion, Dwight**.

Denzil (M) from a Cornish surname and place name. Famous modern bearers include a character in the British television sitcom *Only Fools and Horses* and the US actor Denzel Washington.

ALTERNATIVE FORM: **Denzel**.

Deo (M) another form of the Indian name **Dev** ('god').

Derek (M) another form of **Theodoric** ('ruler of the people'). Famous modern bearers include Derek 'Del Boy' Trotter (the central character in the television sitcom *Only Fools and Horses*) and the British actor Derek Jacobi.

SHORT FORM: **Del**.
ALTERNATIVE FORMS: **Derrick, Deryck, Deryk**.
RELATED NAMES: **Dirk, Terry**.

Dermot (M) the English form of the Irish name **Diarmuid** ('without envy').

Dervla (F) 'poet's daughter' or 'daughter of Ireland'. Of Irish origin, it has recently been popularized by the actress Dervla Kirwan and the travel writer Dervla Murphy.

Deryn (F) a Welsh name meaning 'bird'.

Desdemona (F) 'ill-fated'. In Shakespeare's play *Othello*, Desdemona is killed by her husband (the title character) because he falsely believes that she has a lover.

Desiree [de-ZEER-ay] (F) 'desired'. A name of French origin.

ALTERNATIVE FORMS: **Desirée, Désirée**.

Desmond (M) from an Irish surname meaning 'person from South Munster'. Famous modern bearers include the South African churchman Desmond Tutu and the British singer Des O'Connor.

SHORT FORMS: **Des, Desi**.

Dev (M) an Indian name meaning 'god'.

ALTERNATIVE FORMS: **Deb, Deo**.
FEMININE FORM: **Devi**.

Devi (F) the feminine form of **Dev**, sometimes given to the wife of Shiva.

Devon (M/F) probably from the name of the English county.

Devorah (F) a Jewish form of **Deborah** ('bee').

RELATED NAME: **Debbie**.

Dewey (M) from the surname, which is associated with a system of library book classification, or another form of **Dewi**.

Dewi (M) a Welsh form of **David**. It is an alternative form of the name of the patron saint of Wales.

ALTERNATIVE FORM: **Dewey**.
RELATED NAMES: **Dafydd, Dai, Davy, Daud, Dawud**.

Dexter (M) from the surname, meaning 'dyer'. The name may also be associated with the Latin word *dexter*, which means 'right-handed' or 'auspicious'.
SHORT FORMS: **Dex, Dexy**.

Diana (F) the name of the Roman goddess of hunting, also associated with beauty and chastity. Famous modern bearers include the British actress Diana Rigg and Diana, Princess of Wales.
SHORT FORM: **Di**.
ALTERNATIVE FORMS: **Diane, Deanna**.

Diane (F) another form of **Diana**, of French origin.
SHORT FORM: **Di**.
ALTERNATIVE FORMS: **Dianne, Dyan, Dian, Deanne**.

Diarmuid [DEER-mid] (M) 'without envy'. An Irish name borne by a legendary warrior, the lover of Grainne. The name has recently been popularized by the Irish garden designer Diarmuid Gavin.
ALTERNATIVE FORM: **Diarmaid**.
RELATED NAME: **Dermot**.

Dick (M) short for **Richard**.
ALTERNATIVE FORMS: **Dickie, Dicky**.

Dickon (M) a short form of **Richard** ('powerful ruler'), sometimes given as a name in its own right. It is

borne by a character in *The Secret Garden* (1911), a children's novel by Frances Hodgson Burnett.
RELATED NAMES: **Rick, Ricky, Richie**.

Digby (M) from a surname and place name meaning 'farm by a ditch'.

Diggory (M) 'lost, astray'. The name is chiefly found in literature.
ALTERNATIVE FORM: **Digory**.

Dil (F) short for **Dilys**.
ALTERNATIVE FORM: **Dill**.

Dilip (M) 'protector of Delhi'. An Indian name borne by several legendary kings.

Dillon (M) from an Irish surname of uncertain origin, or another spelling of **Dylan** 'sea'.

Dilly (F) a short form of **Dilys** or **Daffodil**, sometimes given as a name in its own right.

Dilys (F) a Welsh name meaning 'steadfast, sincere'.
SHORT FORMS: **Dil, Dill**.
ALTERNATIVE FORM: **Dylis**.
RELATED NAME: **Dilly**.

Dima (F) an Arabic name meaning 'downpour'.

Dimity (F) from the word *dimity*, referring to a light cotton fabric.

Dina (F) a short form of any Italian name ending with these letters (pronounced [DEE-na]), given as a name in its own right, or another

spelling of **Dinah** (pronounced [DYE-na]).
ALTERNATIVE FORM: **Dena.**

Dinah [DYE-na] (F) 'judgement'. A biblical name, borne by a daughter of Jacob. Famous modern bearers include the British actress Dinah Sheridan.
ALTERNATIVE FORM: **Dina.**

Dinesh (M) an Indian name meaning 'lord of the day'.

Dion (M) 'follower of Dionysus (the Greek god of wine)'. A short form of the Latin name *Dionysius*, sometimes given as a name in its own right. The 19th-century Irish dramatist Dion Boucicault (whose real name was Dionysius Boursiquot) was a famous bearer.
FEMININE FORM: **Dionne.**
RELATED NAMES: **Dennis, Dwight.**

Dionne (F) the feminine form of **Dion**. It was made famous in the 1960s by the US singer Dionne Warwick.
RELATED NAME: **Denise.**

Dipak (M) 'lamp'. An Indian name sometimes used with reference to Kama, the god of love.
ALTERNATIVE FORM: **Deepak.**

Dirk (M) another form of **Theodoric** ('ruler of the people'), of Dutch origin. Its best-known bearer is the 20th-century British actor Dirk Bogarde (whose real name was Derek van den Bogaerde). The name

may also be associated with the Scottish word *dirk*, meaning 'dagger'.
RELATED NAMES: **Derek, Terry.**

Dixie (F) from the nickname of the southern states of the USA.

Diya (M) an Arabic name meaning 'brightness'.

Dodie (F) a short form of **Dorothy**, sometimes given as a name in its own right. As a short form it was used by the 20th-century British novelist and dramatist Dodie Smith, author of *The Hundred and One Dalmatians* (1956).
RELATED NAMES: **Dorothea, Dee, Dolly, Thea, Theodora, Theda, Dora.**

Dolly (F) a short form of **Dorothy**, **Dora**, or **Dolores**, sometimes given as a name in its own right (in which case it may be associated with a child's word for a doll). Famous modern bearers include the US singer Dolly Parton and the title character of the musical *Hello, Dolly!* (1964).

Dolly (M) short for **Adolph**, or a Scottish pet form of **Donald**.

Dolores [de-LOR-iss] (F) 'sorrows'. From a Spanish title of the Virgin Mary.
ALTERNATIVE FORM: **Delores.**
RELATED NAMES: **Dolly, Lola, Lolita, Mary, Madonna, Mercedes, Concepta.**

Dolph (M) short for **Adolph.**

Dominic (M) 'lord'. The name was borne by St Dominic, who founded the Dominican order of monks in 1216.
SHORT FORM: **Dom.**
ALTERNATIVE FORM: **Dominick.**
FEMININE FORMS: **Dominica, Dominique.**

Dominica (F) a feminine form of **Dominic.**
RELATED NAME: **Dominique.**

Dominique (F) another form of **Dominica,** of French origin. It is also used as a boys' name in France.

Don (M) a short form of **Donald** or **Donovan,** sometimes given as a name in its own right. The US singer Don McLean is a famous bearer of the name.
ALTERNATIVE FORM: **Donn.**
RELATED NAME: **Donny.**

Donal (M) the Irish form of **Donald.**
RELATED NAMES: **Don, Donny, Dolly.**

Donald (M) 'world ruler'. The English and Scottish form of a Gaelic name that sounds like **Donal,** which is the Irish form of the name. The name was borne by a number of kings of Scotland. More recent bearers include the British actor Donald Sinden and the cartoon character Donald Duck.
FEMININE FORM: **Donella.**

RELATED NAMES: **Don, Donny, Dolly.**

Donella (F) a feminine form of **Donald.**

Donn (M) an Irish name meaning 'brown' or 'chieftain', or another spelling of **Don.**

Donna (F) 'lady'. A name of recent origin, not found before the 1920s.

Donny (M) a short form of **Donald** or **Donovan,** sometimes given as a name in its own right. As a short form it is used by the US singer Donny Osmond (whose full name is Donald).
ALTERNATIVE FORM: **Donnie.**
RELATED NAME: **Don.**

Donovan (M) an Irish name meaning 'dark brown' or 'dark chieftain'. It was popularized in the 1960s by the British singer whose full name was Donovan Leitch.
RELATED NAMES: **Don, Donny.**

Dora (F) 'gift'. A short form of **Theodora, Isidora, Eudora,** or **Dorothy,** often given as a name in its own right. Famous modern bearers include the British actress Dora Bryan.
RELATED NAMES: **Dolly, Dory.**

Doran (M) an Irish name meaning 'pilgrim, wanderer, stranger, exile'. It is more often found as a surname.

Dorcas (F) 'doe, gazelle'. A biblical name, borne by a charitable and industrious woman (also called **Tabitha**) who was raised from the dead by St Peter.

Dorean (F) the English form of an Irish name meaning 'daughter of Finn'.

Doreen (F) probably a blend of **Dora** and the name-ending *-een*.
SHORT FORM: **Reenie**.
ALTERNATIVE FORMS: **Dorene, Dorine**.

Dorian (M) possibly from the name of a people of ancient Greece. Alternatively, it may have been coined by Oscar Wilde for the dissolute title character of his novel *The Picture of Dorian Gray* (1891).
ALTERNATIVE FORM: **Dorien**.

Dorien (M/F) another form of **Dorian**. It is usually given to boys, a notable exception being the sex-obsessed character played by Lesley Joseph in the television sitcom *Birds of a Feather*.

Dorinda (F) a blend of **Dora** and the name-ending *-inda*.

Doris (F) from the name of a region of ancient Greece, applied to the women who lived there. It is also the name of a Greek sea goddess. It was popular in the first part of the 20th century, when the actress Doris Day and the novelist Doris Lessing were born.

Dorothea [dorr-a-THEE-a] (F) 'gift of God'. George Eliot gave the name in this form to the heroine of her novel

Middlemarch (1872), but it is more frequently found in the alternative form **Dorothy**.
RELATED NAMES: **Thea, Theodora, Theda, Dee, Dolly, Dodie, Dora**.

Dorothy (F) the usual form of the name **Dorothea**. It was popularized in the first half of the 20th century by the US actress Dorothy Lamour and by the young heroine of the film *Wizard of Oz* (1939), played by Judy Garland.
SHORT FORMS: **Dot, Dottie**.
RELATED NAMES: **Dee, Dolly, Dodie, Thea, Theodora, Theda, Dora**.

Dory (F) a pet form of **Dora**, sometimes given as a name in its own right, in which case it may be associated with the French word *doré*, meaning 'gilded'. It is also the name of a type of fish and of a fish character in the cartoon film *Finding Nemo* (2003).

Dot (F) short for **Dorothy**.
ALTERNATIVE FORMS: **Dottie, Dotty**.

Dougal (M) 'dark stranger'. The English form of a Scottish name, spelt as it sounds. Famous fictional bearers include a long-haired dog in the children's television series *The Magic Roundabout* (1965–77) and the childlike character played by Ardal O'Hanlon in the television sitcom *Father Ted* (1995–8).
SHORT FORM: **Dougie**.
ALTERNATIVE FORM: **Dugald**.
RELATED NAME: **Doyle**.

Douglas (M) from the Scottish surname, which comes from a place name meaning 'black stream'. Famous bearers include the US actors Douglas Fairbanks and Douglas Fairbanks Jnr.
SHORT FORMS: **Doug, Dougie, Duggie**.

Dov (M) a Jewish name meaning 'bear'.

Doyle (M) another form of **Dougal** that comes from an Irish surname.

Dreda (F) a short form of **Etheldreda**, sometimes given as a name in its own right.
RELATED NAME: **Audrey**.

Drew (M/F) a short form of the boys' name **Andrew** ('man, warrior'), often given as a name in its own right. The name is now sometimes borne by girls, popularized by the US actress Drew Barrymore, in whose case it is a family surname.

Drogo (M) 'dear' or 'ghost'. The name was borne by a 12th-century saint and by various members of the aristocratic Montagu family.

Drusilla (F) 'dew'. The name of a minor biblical character, from a Roman family name.

Duane (M) the English form of an Irish name meaning 'black, dark'. It was popularized in the 1950s by the US guitarist Duane Eddy.

ALTERNATIVE FORMS: **Dwayne, Dwane, Dwain**.

Dudley (M) from an aristocratic surname that comes from an English place name. Famous bearers of the forename include the British actor, comedian, and musician Dudley Moore and the fictional character Dudley Dursley in J. K. Rowling's *Harry Potter* books.
SHORT FORM: **Dud**.

Dugald (M) another form of **Dougal**.

Duggie (M) short for **Douglas**.
ALTERNATIVE FORM: **Dougie**.

Duke (M) from the noble title *duke*, or a short form of **Marmaduke**. It was popularized in the 20th century by the US jazz musician Duke Ellington (whose real name was Edward).

Dulcie (F) 'sweet'. Famous modern bearers include the British actress Dulcie Gray.

Duncan (M) the English form of a Scottish name meaning 'dark warrior'. It was borne by a number of Scottish kings, including Duncan I, who was killed by Macbeth in 1040. More recent famous bearers include the British swimmer Duncan Goodhew.

Dunstan (M) 'dark stone'. St Dunstan was a 10th-century Archbishop of Canterbury whose name is now chiefly associated with a charity for blind ex-servicemen and ex-servicewomen.

Durga (F) 'inaccessible'. An Indian name given to the wife of Shiva in her fearsome form.

Dustin (M) from a surname, possibly meaning 'Thor's stone'. The best-known bearer of the forename is the US actor Dustin Hoffman.
SHORT FORM: **Dusty**.
FEMININE FORM: **Dusty**.

Dusty (M/F) a short form or feminine form of **Dustin**. As a girls' name it is chiefly associated with the 20th-century British singer Dusty Springfield (born Mary O'Brien).

Dwayne (M) another spelling of **Duane** ('black, dark').
ALTERNATIVE FORMS: **Dwane, Dwain**.

Dwight (M) from a surname that may ultimately come from the Latin name *Dionysius*, meaning 'follower of Dionysus (the Greek god of wine)'. It was borne in the 20th century by the US president Dwight D. Eisenhower.
RELATED NAMES: **Dennis, Dion**.

Dyan (F) another spelling of **Diane**, made famous by the US actress Dyan Cannon.

Dylan (M) 'sea'. A Welsh name, its best-known bearer is the 20th-century poet Dylan Thomas. It may also be associated with the surname of the US singer and songwriter Bob Dylan, born Robert Allen Zimmerman in 1941.
ALTERNATIVE FORM: **Dillon**.

Dylis (F) another spelling of the Welsh name **Dilys** ('steadfast, sincere').

Dymphna (F) 'fawn'. An Irish name borne by the patron saint of people with mental disorders.
ALTERNATIVE FORM: **Dympna**.

E

Eamon [AY-mun] (M) the Irish form of **Edmund** ('protector of wealth'). Famous modern bearers include the Irish president Eamon de Valera and the Irish television presenter Eamonn Andrews.
ALTERNATIVE FORM: **Eamonn.**

Earl (M) from the noble title *earl*.
ALTERNATIVE FORMS: **Earle, Erle.**

Earnest (M) another spelling of **Ernest** ('serious').

Ebba (F) 'fortress of wealth'. The name was borne by a 7th-century Northumbrian princess who became a saint.

Ebenezer (M) 'stone of help'. A name taken from the Bible, where it refers to a commemorative stone (rather than a person). The best-known bearer is the miser Ebenezer Scrooge in Charles Dickens' book *A Christmas Carol* (1843).
SHORT FORM: **Eb.**

Ebony (F) from the name of the black wood. It became a popular name among African-Americans in the latter half of the 20th century.

Echo (F) the name of a nymph in Greek mythology who was punished for talking too much by being deprived of the ability to say anything but the last part of what others said.

Ed (M) short for any name beginning with these letters, especially **Edward**.

Eddie (M) a short form of any name beginning with **Ed-**, especially **Edward**, sometimes given as a name in its own right. As a short form it is used by the US actor Eddie Murphy.
ALTERNATIVE FORM: **Eddy.**

Eden (M/F) from the name of the Garden of Eden in the Bible, meaning 'place of pleasure'. The boys' name has the alternative meaning 'wealthy bear cub'.

Edgar (M) 'wealthy spearman'. Famous bearers of the name include a 10th-century English king and the 19th-century US writer Edgar Allan Poe.

Edina (F) a feminine form of **Eddie** coined for the character played by Jennifer Saunders in the British television sitcom *Absolutely Fabulous*. It is also a Hungarian name, of uncertain origin.

Edith (F) 'prosperous in battle'. The name was popular in the first half of the 20th century, when it was borne by the British poet Dame Edith Sitwell and the British actress Dame Edith Evans.
SHORT FORM: **Edie**.

Edmund (M) 'protector of wealth'. The New Zealand mountaineer Sir Edmund Hillary is a well-known bearer of the name.
ALTERNATIVE FORM: **Edmond**.
RELATED NAME: **Eamon**.

Edna (F) 'delight'. A biblical name that occurs in one of the books of the Apocrypha. It is also used as an English form of the Irish name Eithne ('kernel'). Famous modern bearers include Dame Edna Everage, a larger-than-life female persona adopted by the Australian comedian Barry Humphries.

Edom (M) 'red'. An alternative name for the biblical character Esau, possibly from the colour of the soup for which he sold his birthright to his brother Jacob.

Edric (M) 'rich and powerful'.

Edsel (M) 'noble' or 'father'. The name was borne by Edsel Ford, son of the car manufacturer Henry Ford.

Edward (M) 'guardian of wealth'.

There have been many royal bearers of the name, including the 11th-century English king Edward the Confessor and Prince Edward, the youngest son of Elizabeth II.
SHORT FORM: **Ed**.
FEMININE FORM: **Edwina**.
RELATED NAMES: **Eddie, Ned, Ted, Teddy**.

Edwin (M) 'wealthy friend'. The 19th-century British artist Sir Edwin Landseer was a famous bearer of the name.
ALTERNATIVE FORM: **Edwyn**.
FEMININE FORM: **Edwina**.

Edwina (F) a feminine form of Edwin or Edward. The best-known bearer in modern times is the British politician Edwina Currie.

Effie (F) a short form of **Euphemia** ('well-regarded') or **Hephzibah** ('my delight'), sometimes given as a name in its own right.
RELATED NAME: **Eppie**.

Egan (M) the English form of an Irish name meaning 'fire'. It is more frequently found as a surname.

Egbert (M) 'illustrious swordsman'. The name was borne by a 9th-century English king.
RELATED NAMES: **Bert, Bertie**.

Eglantine (F) from the name of a type of rose.

Eileen (F) the English form of an Irish name that is probably another form of **Aveline**. It was particularly popular in the first half of the 20th century.

RELATED NAMES: **Aileen, Evelyn.**

Eilidh [AY-lee] (F) a Scottish form of **Ellie.**
ALTERNATIVE FORM: **Ailie.**

Eilis [AY-lish, EYE-lish] (F) the Irish form of **Elizabeth** ('oath of God').
ALTERNATIVE FORM: **Eilish.**
RELATED NAMES: **Eliza, Elsa, Elsie, Elspeth, Elise, Liza, Lisa, Lizzie, Libby, Lizbeth, Lili, Lisette, Beth, Bethan, Betty, Betsy, Bess, Babette, Buffy, Isabel.**

Eiluned (F) another form of the Welsh name **Eluned** ('idol, image').

Eilwen (F) a Welsh name meaning 'fair brow'.

Eimear [EE-mer] (F) an Irish name borne by a legendary heroine who was beautiful, wise, and chaste.
ALTERNATIVE FORM: **Emer.**

Eira [EYE-ra] (F) a Welsh name meaning 'snow'.

Eirlys [IRE-lis] (F) a Welsh name meaning 'snowdrop'.

Eithne [ETH-nee, EN-ya] (F) 'kernel'. An Irish name borne by several saints, one of whom was the mother of St Columba in the 6th century.
ALTERNATIVE FORMS: **Aithne, Ethne, Enya.**
RELATED NAMES: **Ena, Edna.**

Elaine (F) another form of **Helen** ('light'). The name is borne by various characters in Arthurian legend, including the heroine of Tennyson's poem 'The Lady of Shalott' (1832).
ALTERNATIVE FORMS: **Elain, Elayne, Alaine.**
RELATED NAMES: **Helena, Ellen, Elen, Elena, Ilona.**

Eldon (M) from a surname and place name.
ALTERNATIVE FORM: **Elden.**

Eleanor [EL-in-er] (F) a name of French origin brought to England in the 12th century by Eleanor of Aquitaine, wife of Henry II. Famous modern bearers include the British actress Eleanor Bron.
ALTERNATIVE FORMS: **Elinor, Eleanora.**
RELATED NAMES: **Ellie, Ella, Nell, Eleonora, Leonora, Lenora.**

Eleazar [el-i-AY-za] (M) 'God is my help'. A biblical name, borne by one of Aaron's sons.
ALTERNATIVE FORM: **Eliezer.**
RELATED NAME: **Lazarus.**

Elen (F) a Welsh form of **Helen** ('light'). It may also be associated with the Welsh word *elen*, meaning 'nymph'.
ALTERNATIVE FORM: **Elin.**
RELATED NAMES: **Ellen, Helena, Nell, Elaine, Elena, Ilona.**

Elena (F) another form of **Helen** ('light'), of Italian or Spanish origin.

RELATED NAMES: **Helena, Ilona, Ellen, Elen, Nell, Elaine.**

Eleonora [el-i-a-NOR-a] (F) another form of **Eleanor**, of Italian origin.
RELATED NAMES: **Leonora, Lenora, Nora, Ellie, Ella, Nell.**

Eleri (F) a Welsh name of uncertain origin, possibly related to a river name.

Elfleda (F) 'noble beauty'. The name was borne in its original Old English form by one of the daughters of Alfred the Great.

Elfreda (F) 'elf strength'. The name was borne in its original Old English form by the mother of Ethelred the Unready.
ALTERNATIVE FORMS: **Elfrida, Alfreda.**
RELATED NAME: **Freda.**

Eli (M) 'exalted'. A biblical name, borne by the priest who raised the prophet Samuel.

Elias [i-LYE-us] (M) the Greek form of the Hebrew name **Elijah**.
RELATED NAMES: **Ellis, Elliot.**

Eliezer (M) another form of **Eleazar**.

Elijah (M) 'Jehovah is God'. A biblical name, borne by one of the best-known prophets of the Israelites. More recent famous bearers include the US actor Elijah Wood.
RELATED NAMES: **Elias, Ellis, Elliot, Joel.**

Elin (F) another form of **Elen**, which is a Welsh form of **Helen** ('light').

Elinor (F) another spelling of **Eleanor**. The name is borne in this form by one of the heroines of Jane Austen's novel *Sense and Sensibility* (1811).

Eliot (M) another spelling of **Elliot**.

Elisabeth (F) another spelling of **Elizabeth**.

Elise [el-EEZ] (F) another form of **Elizabeth**, of French origin.
ALTERNATIVE FORM: **Élise.**
RELATED NAMES: *see list at* **Elizabeth.**

Elisha [i-LYE-sha] (M) 'God is my salvation'. A biblical name, borne by a disciple of Elijah.

Elita [el-EE-ta] (F) from the word *elite*, meaning 'chosen'.

Eliza [i-LYE-za] (F) a short form of **Elizabeth**, sometimes given as a name in its own right. A famous fictional bearer is Eliza Doolittle, the heroine of George Bernard Shaw's play *Pygmalion* (1913) and its musical version *My Fair Lady* (1957).
RELATED NAMES: *see list at* **Elizabeth.**

Elizabeth (F) 'oath of God'. A biblical name, borne by the mother of John the Baptist. The name was popularized in the 16th century by Elizabeth I and in the 20th century by the wife of George VI and her daughter Elizabeth II.

SHORT FORM: Liz.

ALTERNATIVE FORM: Elisabeth.

RELATED NAMES: Eliza, Elsa, Elsie, Elspeth, Elise, Eilis, Liza, Lisa, Lizzie, Libby, Lizbeth, Lili, Lisette, Beth, Bethan, Betty, Betsy, Bess, Babette, Buffy, Isabel.

Elkanah (M) 'created by God' or 'possessed by God'. A biblical name, borne by the father of the prophet Samuel.

ALTERNATIVE FORM: Elkan.

FEMININE FORM: Elke.

Elke (F) a Jewish name that is probably a feminine form of **Elkanah**. The British singer Elkie Brooks (whose real name is Elaine Bookbinder) has popularized the alternative form.

ALTERNATIVE FORM: Elkie.

Ella (F) a short form of various names beginning with *El*-, such as **Eleanor** or **Ellen**, given as a name in its own right. Famous bearers include the 20th-century US jazz singer Ella Fitzgerald.

RELATED NAMES: Ellie, Nell.

Elle (F) a short form of various names beginning with *El*- or the letter 'L', now often given as a name in its own right. It may also be associated with the French word *elle*, meaning 'she'. The name has recently been popularized by the Australian model Elle MacPherson (whose full name is Eleanor).

Ellen (F) another form of **Helen** ('light'). Famous modern bearers include the British sailor Ellen MacArthur.

RELATED NAMES: Ella, Elen, Nell, Helena, Elaine, Elena, Ilona.

Ellie (F) a short form of various names beginning with *El*-, especially **Eleanor**, now often given as a name in its own right.

ALTERNATIVE FORM: Elly.

RELATED NAMES: Ella, Eilidh, Nell.

Elliot (M) from the surname, which originated as another form of **Elias**. The US actor Elliott Gould is a famous bearer of the name.

ALTERNATIVE FORMS: Elliott, Eliot.

RELATED NAMES: Ellis, Elijah.

Ellis (M/F) from the surname, which originated as another form of the boys' name **Elias**. The girls' name may also be the English form of a Welsh name meaning 'kind'. The 20th-century British writer Ellis Peters was born Edith Pargeter.

RELATED NAMES: Elliot (M), Elijah (M).

Elma (F) possibly a combination of two names containing these letters, such as **Elizabeth** and **Mary**, or a feminine form of **Elmer**.

Elmer (M) 'noble and famous'. The US writer Sinclair Lewis gave the name to the title character of his novel *Elmer Gantry* (1927).

ALTERNATIVE FORMS: Aylmer, Delmar.

FEMININE FORM: Elma.

Elmore (M) from the surname, meaning 'river bank with elms'.

Elodia (F) 'foreign riches'. The Spanish form of a name that is also sometimes found in the French form Élodie (or Elodie) in English-speaking countries.

Eloise (F) a name of uncertain origin, borne in the 12th century by the wife of the French philosopher Peter Abelard. The tragic story of their love and separation has been told by various authors.

ALTERNATIVE FORMS: Éloise, Heloise, Héloïse.

Elroy (M) another form of Leroy ('the king').

Elsa (F) another form of Elizabeth. In the latter half of the 20th century the best-known bearer of the name was a lioness, whose story was told by Joy Adamson in a series of books beginning with *Born Free* (1960).

RELATED NAMES: *see list at* Elsie.

Elsie (F) another form of Elizabeth, which originated in Scotland as a short form of Elspeth. It was particularly popular in the early 20th century.

RELATED NAMES: Eliza, Elsa, Elise, Eilis, Liza, Lisa, Lizzie, Libby, Lizbeth, Lili, Lisette, Beth, Bethan, Betty, Betsy, Bess, Babette, Buffy, Isabel.

Elspeth (F) another form of Elizabeth, of Scottish origin.

SHORT FORM: Elspie.

RELATED NAMES: *see list at* Elsie.

Elton (M) from a surname and place name. In modern times it is chiefly associated with the British singer and songwriter Elton John (born Reginald Dwight).

Eluned [el-IN-ed] (F) a Welsh name meaning 'idol, image'.

ALTERNATIVE FORM: Eiluned.

RELATED NAME: Lynette.

Elvina (F) a feminine form of Alvin ('elf friend').

Elvira (F) a name of Spanish origin, possibly meaning 'true to all'. It is the name of the title characters of Noël Coward's play *Blithe Spirit* (1941) and the Swedish film *Elvira Madigan* (1967).

Elvis (M) a name of uncertain origin. Since the 1950s it has been almost exclusively associated with the US singer Elvis Presley.

Elwyn (M) a Welsh name of uncertain origin, possibly meaning 'fair brow' or 'elf friend'.

ALTERNATIVE FORM: Elwin.

Elysia (F) 'heavenly, blissful'. From *Elysium*, the name of the place where dead heroes enjoyed eternal rest in classical mythology.

Em (F) short for various names beginning with these letters, such as **Emma** or **Emily**.

Emanuel (M) another spelling of **Emmanuel**.

Emelia (F) another form of **Amelia** ('hard-working').

Emer [EE-mer] (F) another spelling of the Irish name **Eimear**.

Emerald (F) from the name of the gemstone.
RELATED NAME: **Esmeralda**.

Emerson (M) from the surname, meaning 'son of Emery'. Famous bearers include the Brazilian racing driver Emerson Fittipaldi, who was named after the 19th-century US writer Ralph Waldo Emerson.

Emery (M) another form of **Amory** ('brave ruler').

Emile [e-MEEL] (M) 'striving, competing'. A French name (which comes from a Roman family name) that is sometimes found in English-speaking countries.
ALTERNATIVE FORMS: **Émile, Emil**.
RELATED NAME: **Emlyn**.

Emilia (F) another form of **Amelia** ('hard-working') or **Emily**. Famous modern bearers include the British actress Emilia Fox.

Emily (F) 'striving, competing'. From a Roman family name, which may also have influenced the coining of **Amelia**. Borne in the 19th century

by the British novelist Emily Brontë and the US poet Emily Dickinson, the name came back into fashion in the late 20th century.
SHORT FORM: **Em**.
ALTERNATIVE FORM: **Emilie**.
RELATED NAMES: **Emilia, Emmie, Emmeline**.

Emlyn (M) a Welsh name, either of Celtic origin or from a Roman family name meaning 'striving, competing'. Famous 20th-century bearers include the dramatist Emlyn Williams and the footballer Emlyn Hughes.
RELATED NAME: **Emile**.

Emma (F) 'whole, universal'. The name is borne by the heroine of Jane Austen's novel *Emma* (1816). It came back into fashion in the latter half of the 20th century, popularized by the fictional character Emma Peel (played by Diana Rigg) in the British television series *The Avengers* (1965–7).
SHORT FORM: **Em**.
RELATED NAMES: **Emmie, Emmeline, Irma**.

Emmanuel (M) 'God with us'. A biblical name used with reference to the Messiah.
SHORT FORM: **Manny**.
ALTERNATIVE FORM: **Emanuel**.
FEMININE FORM: **Emmanuelle**.
RELATED NAMES: **Immanuel, Manuel**.

Emmanuelle (F) a feminine form of

Emmanuel. The name is chiefly associated with the title character of a series of pornographic films.

Emmeline (F) another form of **Emma** or **Emily**, of Old French origin. Famous bearers include the British suffragette Emmeline Pankhurst.
ALTERNATIVE FORM: **Emmaline**.

Emmet (M) from a surname that originated as another form of the girls' name **Emma**. It is sometimes given in honour of the 18th-century Irish patriot Robert Emmet.
ALTERNATIVE FORM: **Emmett**.

Emmie (F) a short form of various names beginning with *Em-*, such as **Emma** or **Emily**, sometimes given as a name in its own right. The alternative form is the name of a US television award.
ALTERNATIVE FORM: **Emmy**.

Emrys (M) the Welsh form of **Ambrose** ('immortal').

Ena (F) an English form of the Irish name **Eithne** ('kernel'). It fell from popularity in the latter half of the 20th century, when it was chiefly associated with Ena Sharples, an unattractive character in the soap opera *Coronation Street*.

Enid (F) a name of Celtic origin, possibly meaning 'soul'. It is borne by the virtuous wife of Geraint in Arthurian legend. Since the 1930s the name has largely been associated with the British children's writer Enid Blyton.

Enoch (M) a biblical name, possibly meaning 'experienced'. In the Bible, Enoch is the son of Cain. Famous modern bearers include the British politician Enoch Powell.

Enola (F) a name of uncertain origin. The aircraft that dropped the first atomic bomb on Hiroshima in 1945 was named the 'Enola Gay' after the mother of its pilot.

Enos (M) 'mankind'. A biblical name, borne by the son of Seth.

Enya (F) another form of the Irish name **Eithne** ('kernel'), spelt as it sometimes sounds. It is chiefly associated with the Irish singer known as Enya (whose real name is Eithne).

Eoghan (M) 'born of the yew tree'. A Gaelic name that is usually pronounced [owE-in] in Ireland and [YOO-un] in Scotland.
RELATED NAMES: **Ewan, Owen, Eugene**.

Eoin [owE-in] (M) an Irish form of **John** ('God is gracious'). The Irish writer Eoin Colfer is a famous bearer of the name.
RELATED NAMES: **Sean, Shaun, Shane, Evan, Sion, Ian, Ivan, Juan, Johnny, Jack, Jackie, Jake, Jock, Hank**.

Ephraim [EE-frame] (M) 'fruitful'. A biblical name, borne by one of

Joseph's sons and one of the tribes of Israel.

Eppie (F) a short form of **Euphemia** ('well-regarded') or **Hephzibah** ('my delight'), sometimes given as a name in its own right.
RELATED NAME: **Effie**.

Erasmus (M) 'beloved'. The name is chiefly associated with the 16th-century Dutch scholar Desiderius Erasmus.

Erastus (M) 'beloved'. The name of a minor biblical character, converted to Christianity by St Paul.
RELATED NAME: **Rastus**.

Eric (M) 'one ruler'. The name is of Scandinavian origin, borne by the 10th-century explorer Eric the Red. It was popular in the UK in the first part of the 20th century, when the comedians Eric Morecambe and Eric Sykes were born.
ALTERNATIVE FORM: **Erik**.
FEMININE FORM: **Erica**.

Erica (F) the feminine form of **Eric**. It is also the name of various plants, including some heathers. Famous modern bearers include the US novelist Erica Jong.
ALTERNATIVE FORM: **Erika**.

Erin (F) from a poetic name for Ireland. The name is borne by the British writer and campaigner Erin Pizzey, famous for helping the victims of domestic violence.
ALTERNATIVE FORM: **Eryn**.

Erle (M) another spelling of **Earl**, borne by the US writer Erle Stanley Gardner, creator of the fictional lawyer and detective Perry Mason.

Erma (F) another spelling of **Irma**.

Ermintrude (F) 'wholly beloved'. The name was borne by a singing cow in the children's television series *The Magic Roundabout* (1965–77).
RELATED NAME: **Trudy**.

Ernest (M) 'serious'. The name forms the central part of the plot of Oscar Wilde's comedy *The Importance of Being Earnest* (1895). Famous bearers include the 20th-century US novelist Ernest Hemingway.
SHORT FORMS: **Ern, Ernie**.
ALTERNATIVE FORM: **Earnest**.
FEMININE FORMS: **Ernestine, Ernestina, Ernesta**.

Ernestine (F) a feminine form of **Ernest**.
ALTERNATIVE FORMS: **Ernestina, Ernesta**.

Errol (M) from a surname and place name of Scottish origin. It was made famous in the 1930s by the Australian-born actor Errol Flynn.
ALTERNATIVE FORMS: **Erroll, Erol**.

Erskine (M) from a Scottish surname and place name. It was the middle name of the writer and Irish nationalist known as Erskine Childers.

Eryn (F) another spelling of **Erin**.

Esau (M) 'hairy'. A biblical name borne by the elder twin brother of Jacob, to whom Esau sold his birthright for a bowl of soup.

Esme (F/M) 'esteemed, loved'. Originally a boys' name, of French origin, it is now more frequently given to girls.
ALTERNATIVE FORMS: **Esmé, Esmee** (F).

Esmeralda (F) 'emerald'. The name is borne by the beautiful gypsy girl loved by Quasimodo in Victor Hugo's novel *The Hunchback of Notre Dame* (1831).
ALTERNATIVE FORMS: **Esmaralda, Esmerelda**.
RELATED NAME: **Emerald**.

Esmond (M) 'gracious protector'.
ALTERNATIVE FORM: **Esmund**.

Estelle (F) 'star'. In its alternative form it is borne by a beautiful but aloof young woman in Charles Dickens' novel *Great Expectations* (1861).
ALTERNATIVE FORM: **Estella**.
RELATED NAMES: **Stella, Astra, Esther**.

Esther (F) 'myrtle' or 'star'. A biblical name borne by the Jewish wife of a Persian king, who persuaded him to save her people. Other famous bearers include the heroine of Charles Dickens' novel *Bleak House* (1853) and the British television presenter Esther Rantzen.
SHORT FORMS: **Essie, Ettie**.
ALTERNATIVE FORM: **Esta**.
RELATED NAMES: **Hester, Etta, Hadassah, Dassah, Myrtle, Stella, Estelle, Astra**.

Ethan (M) 'firm' or 'long-lived'. The name of a minor biblical character, it was popularized in the USA by the 18th-century patriot Ethan Allen. More recent famous bearers include the US actor Ethan Hawke.

Ethel (F) 'noble'. It may have originated as a short form of a name beginning with these letters, such as **Etheldreda**. The name was popular in the first part of the 20th century, when it was borne by the US actresses Ethel Barrymore and Ethel Merman.
SHORT FORM: **Eth**.

Etheldreda (F) from an Old English name meaning 'noble strength'. It was borne by a 6th-century saint who is better known as St Audrey.
SHORT FORM: **Dreda**.
RELATED NAME: **Audrey**.

Ethne [ETH-nee] (F) another spelling of **Eithne** ('kernel').

Etta (F) a short form of **Esther** or of any name ending with these letters, such as **Henrietta**, sometimes given as a name in its own right. Famous bearers include Etta Place, a companion of the US outlaws Butch Cassidy and the Sundance Kid.

Ettie (F) short for **Esther** or **Henrietta**.
ALTERNATIVE FORM: **Etty**.

Euan (M) another spelling of **Ewan**.

Eudora (F) 'good gift'. The 20th-century US writer Eudora Welty was a famous bearer of the name.
RELATED NAME: **Dora**.

Eugene [YOO-jeen] (M) 'well-born'. In Ireland the name is sometimes regarded as an English form of **Eoghan**. Famous bearers include the 20th-century US dramatist Eugene O'Neill.
FEMININE FORMS: **Eugenie, Eugenia**.
RELATED NAMES: **Gene, Owen**.

Eugenie [yoo-ZHAY-nee] (F) a feminine form of **Eugene**. Of French origin, the name was borne by Empress Eugénie, the wife of Napoleon III, who came to England in the early 1870s. It was given by the Duke and Duchess of York to their second daughter, Princess Eugénie, in 1990.
ALTERNATIVE FORMS: **Eugénie, Eugenia**.

Eulalia (F) 'well-spoken'. Saint Eulalia was a Spanish girl who was martyred in the early 4th century.
SHORT FORMS: **Eula, Lalia, Lallie**.
ALTERNATIVE FORM: **Eulalie**.

Eunice [YOO-niss] (F) 'good victory'.

The name occurs in the Bible, borne by the mother of Timothy.

Euphemia (F) 'well-regarded'. The name of an early Christian martyr.
SHORT FORM: **Phemie**.
RELATED NAMES: **Effie, Eppie**.

Eurydice [yoor-RID-i-see] (F) 'wide justice'. In Greek mythology the name was borne by the wife of Orpheus, who tried to bring her back to the land of the living after her death.

Eustace [YOOST-us] (M) 'good harvest'. The novelist L. P. Hartley gave the name to the hero of his *Eustace and Hilda* trilogy, published in the mid-1940s.
FEMININE FORM: **Eustacia**.
RELATED NAME: **Stacy**.

Eustacia [yoo-STAY-si-a] (F) the feminine form of **Eustace**. The name is borne by the capricious heroine of Thomas Hardy's novel *The Return of the Native* (1878).
RELATED NAME: **Stacey**.

Eva (F) another form of **Eve**, or the English form of the Irish name **Aoife** ('beautiful'). It is pronounced [EE-va] in English and [AY-va] in some European languages. Famous bearers include Eva Perón, wife of the President of Argentina in the mid-20th century, whose story is told in the musical *Evita*.
RELATED NAMES: **Ava, Evie**.

Evadne (F) a name of uncertain

meaning, borne in Greek mythology by a woman who committed suicide by throwing herself on to her husband's funeral pyre. In the 1970s it was made famous by the musician Dr Evadne Hinge, a female persona adopted by George Logan in the comedy partnership Hinge and Bracket.

Evan (M) a Welsh form of **John** ('God is gracious').
SHORT FORM: **Van**.
RELATED NAMES: **Sion, Sean, Shaun, Shane, Eoin, Ian, Ivan, Juan, Johnny, Jack, Jackie, Jake, Jock, Hank**.

Evander (M) 'good man'. The name of hero in Roman legend. More recent famous bearers include the US boxer Evander Holyfield.

Evangeline (F) 'good news'. The name was popularized in the mid-19th century as the title of a poem by Henry Wadsworth Longfellow.
ALTERNATIVE FORM: **Evangelina**.

Eve (F) 'alive'. A biblical name borne by the first woman, the wife of Adam.
RELATED NAMES: **Eva, Evie, Chaya**.

Evelina (F) another form of Evelyn, or a compound of **Eve** and the name-ending –*lina*. The name was popularized in the 18th century by the title character of Fanny Burney's novel *Evelina* (1778).
ALTERNATIVE FORM: **Eveline**.

Evelyn [EEV-lin, EV-lin] (F/M) another form of **Aveline** that became a surname and was later readopted as a forename for boys or girls. The British writer Evelyn Waugh was briefly married to a woman who bore the same name. As a girls' name it is sometimes regarded as a compound of **Eve** and **Lynn**.
ALTERNATIVE FORM: **Evelyne** (F).
RELATED NAMES: **Evelina** (F), **Evie** (F), **Aileen** (F), **Eileen** (F).

Everard (M) 'brave boar'. In the 1970s it became familiar as the name of a fictitious friend of the British comedian Larry Grayson.
RELATED NAME: **Everett**.

Everett (M) from a surname that originated as another form of **Everard**.

Everton (M) from a surname and place name meaning 'wild boar settlement'. It is sometimes given as a forename in honour of Everton Football Club.

Evette (F) another spelling of **Yvette** ('yew'), or a compound of **Eve** and the name-ending -*ette*.

Evie (F) a pet form of **Eve, Eva**, or various other names beginning with *Ev*-, now sometimes given as a name in its own right.

Evonne (F) another spelling of **Yvonne** ('yew'). Famous bearers of the name in this form include the

Australian tennis player Evonne
Goolagong Cawley.

Ewan (M) a Scottish form of the
Gaelic name **Eoghan** ('born of the
yew tree'), spelt as it sounds. The
Scottish actor Ewan McGregor is a
famous bearer of the name.
ALTERNATIVE FORM: **Euan**.

Ewart (M) from a Scottish surname
of uncertain origin. Famous bearers
include the 19th-century British
statesman William Ewart Gladstone.

Ezekiel (M) 'God strengthens'. A
biblical name, borne by a prophet
whose sayings are to be found in the
book of the Bible that bears his
name.
RELATED NAME: **Zeke**.

Ezra (M) 'help'. The name of a
biblical prophet and the book of the
Bible containing his story. Other
famous bearers include the 20th-
century US poet Ezra Pound.

F

Fabia (F) a feminine form of **Fabian**.
RELATED NAME: **Fabienne**.

Fabian (M) from a Roman family name that comes from the Latin word *faba*, meaning 'bean'. Famous bearers include a 3rd-century pope and a US singer who rose to stardom in the late 1950s.
FEMININE FORMS: **Fabia, Fabienne**.

Fabienne (F) a feminine form of **Fabian**, of French origin.
RELATED NAME: **Fabia**.

Fadi (M) an Arabic name meaning 'saviour'.
FEMININE FORM: **Fadia**.

Fadia (F) the feminine form of **Fadi**.

Fae (F) another spelling of **Fay**.

Fahim (M) an Arabic name meaning 'scholar'.
FEMININE FORM: **Fahmida**.

Fahmida (F) the feminine form of **Fahim**.

Faisal [FYE-s'l] (M) 'judge'. An Arabic name borne by the last king of Iraq, assassinated in 1958.
ALTERNATIVE FORMS: **Faysal, Feisal**.

Faith (F) from the word *faith*, especially in the sense 'religious belief'. Like many other names representing virtues, it was popular with the Puritans in the 17th century. The name has come back into fashion in recent years.

Falk (M) a Jewish name meaning 'falcon'.

Fancy (F) from the word *fancy*, especially in the sense 'imagination' or 'whim'. Thomas Hardy gave the name to the capricious heroine of his novel *Under the Greenwood Tree* (1872).

Fanny (F) a short form of **Frances** ('French person'), sometimes given as a name in its own right. Famous bearers include Fanny Hill, the heroine of John Cleland's notorious novel *Memoirs of a Woman of Pleasure* (1749), and Fanny Cradock, a formidable television cook of the 1950s and 1960s.
ALTERNATIVE FORM: **Fannie**.

Farah (F) an Arabic name meaning 'joy'.
ALTERNATIVE FORM: **Farrah**.

Faraj (M) an Arabic name meaning 'remedy'.

Farid (M) an Arabic name meaning 'unique'.
FEMININE FORM: **Farida**.

Farida (F) a feminine form of **Farid**.
ALTERNATIVE FORM: **Faridah**.

Farouk (M) 'person who knows right from wrong'. An Arabic name borne by the last king of Egypt, who abdicated in 1952.
ALTERNATIVE FORMS: **Faruk, Faruq**.

Farrah (F) another spelling of **Farah** or an English name of uncertain origin, made famous in the 1970s by the US actress Farrah Fawcett-Majors.

Fatima [FAT-im-a] (F) 'chaste' or 'motherly'. An Arabic name borne in the 7th century by the favourite daughter of Muhammad. The best-known modern bearer of the name is the British athlete Fatima Whitbread.

Fay (F) 'fairy'. Famous modern bearers of the name include the British writer Fay Weldon and the US actress Faye Dunaway.
ALTERNATIVE FORMS: **Faye, Fae**.

Faysal (M) another spelling of **Faisal**.

Fedelma (F) another form of **Fidelma** ('beauty').

Feisal (M) another spelling of **Faisal**.

Felicia (F) the feminine form of **Felix**.

Felicity (F) from the word *felicity*, meaning 'good fortune' or 'happiness'. The British actress Felicity Kendal is a famous bearer of the name.
SHORT FORMS: **Flick, Fliss**.

Felix (M) 'happy, fortunate'. The name was borne by several saints and popes. More recent famous bearers include the British actor Felix Aylmer and the cartoon character Felix the Cat.
FEMININE FORM: **Felicia**.

Fenella (F) an English form of the Gaelic name **Fionnuala** ('fair-shouldered'). The British actress Fenella Fielding is a famous bearer.
SHORT FORM: **Nella**.
RELATED NAMES: **Finola, Nola, Nuala**.

Fenton (M) from a surname and place name meaning 'marsh settlement'.

Ferdinand (M) 'ready to travel'. Of Spanish origin, the name was borne by a number of European monarchs.
SHORT FORMS: **Ferdie, Ferdy**.
FEMININE FORM: **Nanda**.

Fergal (M) 'man of valour'. Of Gaelic origin, the name was borne in the 8th century by a High King of

Ireland. The Irish journalist Fergal Keane is a famous modern bearer.

Fergus (M) 'man of vigour'. Of Gaelic origin, the name was borne by a legendary Irish hero but is now chiefly associated with Scotland.
SHORT FORM: **Fergie**.

Fern (F) from the plant name. Famous modern bearers include the British television presenter Fern Britton.

Feroz (M) another form of the Arabic name **Firoz** ('victorious, successful').

Festus (M) 'steadfast'. The name of a minor biblical character, a Roman who refused to condemn St Paul to death.

Ffion (F) a Welsh name meaning 'foxglove', or a Welsh form of **Fiona** ('white, fair').

Fi (F) short for **Fiona**.

Fidelia (F) the feminine form of **Fidelis**.

Fidelis (M) 'faithful'. The name of a 6th-century saint. It is most familiar in the Spanish form *Fidel*, borne by the Cuban president Fidel Castro.
FEMININE FORM: **Fidelia**.

Fidelma (F) 'beauty'. An Irish name borne by several saints and a legendary warrior renowned for her beauty.
SHORT FORM: **Delma**.
ALTERNATIVE FORM: **Fedelma**.

Fife (M) from the Scottish surname and place name, which comes from the name of a legendary hero.
ALTERNATIVE FORM: **Fyfe**.

Fifi (F) a short form of **Josephine**, of French origin, sometimes given as a name in its own right. It is generally regarded as a frivolous name, used for poodles and similar dogs.

Fikri (M) an Arabic name meaning 'intellectual'.
FEMININE FORM: **Fikriyya**.

Fikriyya (F) the feminine form of **Fikri**.

Filbert (M) another spelling of **Philbert** ('very illustrious'). The word *filbert* also refers to a type of nut, so called because it ripens around the time of St Philbert's feast day.

Fina (F) short for **Seraphina**.

Finbar (M) 'fair-haired'. Of Irish origin, the name was borne in the 6th century by St Finbar, patron saint of Cork.
ALTERNATIVE FORM: **Finnbar**.
RELATED NAME: **Barry**.

Fingal (M) 'fair stranger'. Of Gaelic origin, the name is chiefly associated with Fingal's Cave, on the Scottish island of Staffa. Fingal was the second forename of the Irish dramatist Oscar Wilde.
ALTERNATIVE FORM: **Fingall**.

Finlay (M/F) 'fair hero'. The English

form of a Scottish boys' name, spelt as it sounds. The name is now sometimes given to girls, especially in the alternative form Finley.

ALTERNATIVE FORMS: **Finley, Findlay.**

Finn (M) from a surname meaning 'person from Finland', or another form of the Gaelic name **Fionn**, spelt as it sounds.

Finnbar (M) another spelling of **Finbar.**

Finola (F) an English form of **Fionnuala.**

RELATED NAMES: **Nola, Nuala, Fenella.**

Fintan (M) 'white fire'. An Irish name borne by a number of saints.

Fiona (F) 'fair'. Possibly coined by the 18th-century Scottish poet James Macpherson as a feminine form of **Fionn**, it was further popularized by the 19th-century Scottish writer William Sharp, who used the pen-name Fiona Mcleod for his romantic works.

SHORT FORM: **Fi.**

RELATED NAME: **Ffion.**

Fionn [fin] (M) 'fair'. A Gaelic name borne by the legendary Irish hero Fionn MacCool, renowned for his strength, courage, and wisdom.

ALTERNATIVE FORM: **Finn.**

FEMININE FORM: **Fiona.**

Fionnuala [fi-NOO-la] (F) a Gaelic name meaning 'fair-shouldered'.

According to Irish legend, a princess of this name was turned into a swan by her stepmother and only regained human form when Christianity came to Ireland.

RELATED NAMES: **Fenella, Finola, Nuala, Nola.**

Firoz (M) an Arabic name meaning 'successful'.

ALTERNATIVE FORM: **Feroz.**

Fitzgerald (M) from the surname, meaning 'son of Gerald'.

SHORT FORM: **Fitz.**

Fitzroy (M) from the surname, which means 'son of Roy' and was originally given to the illegitimate son of a king.

SHORT FORM: **Fitz.**

Flann (M) an Irish name meaning 'red, ruddy'. Famous bearers include the 20th-century Irish writer Flann O'Brien, whose real name was Brian O'Nolan.

ALTERNATIVE FORM: **Flannan.**

RELATED NAME: **Flynn.**

Flavia (F) 'yellow-haired'. From a Roman family name. Princess Flavia is one of the central characters in Anthony Hope's novel *The Prisoner of Zenda* (1894).

Fletcher (M) from the surname, meaning 'maker of arrows'. The forename was famously borne in the 18th century by Fletcher Christian, who led the mutiny on the *Bounty*. The surname is associated with the habitual criminal played by Ronnie Barker in the television sitcom *Porridge*.

Fleur (F) 'flower'. Of French origin, the name was popularized in the English-speaking world by a character in John Galsworthy's series of novels *The Forsyte Saga* (1922), adapted for television in 1967.
RELATED NAME: **Flora**.

Flick (F) short for **Felicity**.

Fliss (F) short for **Felicity**.

Flo (F) short for **Flora** or **Florence**.

Floella (F) a compound of **Flo** and **Ella**. The best-known bearer of the name is the children's television presenter Floella Benjamin, born in Trinidad.

Flora (F) 'flower'. The name of the Roman goddess of the spring. Famous bearers include Flora Macdonald, who helped Bonnie Prince Charlie to escape from the Scottish mainland in 1746.
SHORT FORMS: **Flo, Florrie**.
RELATED NAME: **Fleur**.

Florence (F) 'blossoming'. The 19th-century British nurse Florence Nightingale was named after the city of Florence in Italy, where she was born.
SHORT FORMS: **Flo, Florrie, Floss, Flossie**.
ALTERNATIVE FORM: **Florentina**.

Florinda (F) a blend of **Flora** and the name-ending -*inda*.

Floyd (M) from the surname, which is another form of **Lloyd** ('grey-haired'), respelt to avoid the hard-to-pronounce Welsh *Ll*- sound. The US boxer Floyd Patterson is a famous bearer.

Flynn (M) another form of **Flann** ('red, ruddy') that comes from an Irish surname.

Fonsie (M) short for **Alphonse**.
ALTERNATIVE FORM: **Fonzie**.

Ford (M) from the surname, which comes from the word *ford* meaning 'shallow crossing-place'. Famous bearers of the name include the 19th-century British painter Ford Madox Brown and his grandson, the writer Ford Madox Ford.

Forrest (M) from the surname, meaning 'person who lives in or by a forest'. The forename is now chiefly associated with the simple-minded title character of the film *Forrest Gump* (1994), played by Tom Hanks.
ALTERNATIVE FORM: **Forest**.

Frances (F) a feminine form of **Francis**. Famous modern bearers include the actress Frances de la Tour.
SHORT FORMS: **Fran, Franny, Francie**.
RELATED NAMES: **Francesca, Francine, Frankie, Fanny**.

Francesca [fran-CHESK-a] (F) a feminine form of **Francis**, of Italian origin. The name was borne by the legendary Italian beauty Francesca di Rimini.

RELATED NAMES: **Frances, Francine, Frankie.**

Francine (F) a feminine form of **Francis**, of French origin.

ALTERNATIVE FORM: **Francene.**
RELATED NAMES: **Frances, Francesca.**

Francis (M) 'French person'. Its first bearer (in the Italian form *Francesco*) was St Francis of Assisi, so called because his family had connections with France.

FEMININE FORMS: **Frances, Francesca, Francine.**
RELATED NAMES: **Frank, Frankie.**

Frank (M) from the name of a people who settled in what is now called France in the 4th century. It is also a short form of **Francis** (as in the case of the US singer Frank Sinatra) or **Franklin**.

RELATED NAME: **Frankie.**

Frankie (M/F) a pet form of **Frank, Francis, Frances**, or **Francesca**, sometimes given as a name in its own right. Famous male bearers include the British comedian Frankie Howerd (whose full name was Francis).

Franklin (M) from the surname, meaning 'freeborn landholder'. It was popularized as a forename in the first half of the 20th century by the US president Franklin D. Roosevelt.

ALTERNATIVE FORM: **Franklyn.**
RELATED NAME: **Frank.**

Franny (F) short for **Frances**.

ALTERNATIVE FORM: **Frannie.**

Fraser (M) from a Scottish surname of uncertain origin. In its alternative forms it is borne by the British actor Frazer Hines and the title character of the US television sitcom *Frasier*.

ALTERNATIVE FORMS: **Frazer, Frasier.**

Fred (M) a short form of **Frederick** or **Alfred** ('elf counsel'), sometimes given as a name in its own right.

Freda (F) 'peace', 'strength', or 'counsel'. A short form of various names containing the letters -*fred*-, such as **Frederica, Winifred, Elfreda**, or **Alfreda**, given as a name in its own right.

Freddie (M/F) a short form of **Frederick** or **Frederica**, sometimes given as a name in its own right. Famous bearers include the singer Freddie Mercury, who was born Farrokh Bulsara in Zanzibar in 1946.

ALTERNATIVE FORM: **Freddy.**

Frederica (F) the feminine form of **Frederick**. The British writer A. S. Byatt gave the name to the central character of a quartet of novels, beginning with *The Virgin in the Garden* (1978).

RELATED NAMES: **Freda, Freddie, Ricki.**

Frederick (M) 'peaceful ruler'. The name was borne in the 18th century by Frederick the Great, King of Prussia, and Frederick Louis, Prince of Wales (the father of George III).
ALTERNATIVE FORMS: **Frederic, Fredrick, Fredric.**
FEMININE FORM: **Frederica.**

Freya [FRAY-a] (F) 'lady'. The name of the goddess of love in Scandinavian mythology. Famous bearers include the 20th-century travel-writer Freya Stark.

Fuad (M) an Arabic name meaning 'heart'.

Fulton (M) from a Scottish surname and place name. The 20th-century Scottish actor Fulton Mackay was a famous bearer of the forename.

Fulvia (F) from a Roman family name meaning 'dusky'. The name was borne in the 1st century BC by a wife of Mark Antony.

Fyfe (M) another spelling of **Fife**, borne by the 20th-century Scottish broadcaster Fyfe Robertson.

G

Gabriel [GAY-bri-ul] (M) 'man of God'. A biblical name, borne by the archangel who told Mary that she would give birth to Jesus. Other famous bearers include the farmer Gabriel Oak in Thomas Hardy's novel *Far from the Madding Crowd* (1874).
FEMININE FORM: **Gabrielle**.
RELATED NAME: **Gaby**.

Gabrielle [gab-ri-EL] (F) the feminine form of **Gabriel**.
ALTERNATIVE FORM: **Gabriella**.
RELATED NAME: **Gaby**.

Gaby (F/M) a short form of **Gabrielle** or **Gabriel**, sometimes given as a name in its own right. The British television presenter Gaby Roslin is a famous female bearer.
ALTERNATIVE FORM: **Gabby**.

Gae (F) another spelling of **Gay**.

Gaenor (F) a Welsh spelling of **Gaynor**. It is also sometimes regarded as another form of a Welsh saint's name meaning 'beautiful maiden'.

Gaia [GUY-a] (F) the name of the goddess of the earth in classical mythology.

Gail (F) a short form of **Abigail** ('father's joy'), usually given as a name in its own right.
ALTERNATIVE FORMS: **Gayle, Gale**.
RELATED NAME: **Abbie**.

Gaius [GUY-us] (M) another form of **Caius** (possibly meaning 'rejoice').

Galahad (M) a name of uncertain origin. In Arthurian legend, Sir Galahad is a virtuous knight who finds the Holy Grail.

Galen [GAY-lun] (M) 'calm'. The name may be given in honour of the 2nd-century Greek physician Claudius Galenus, who is generally known as Galen.

Galia (F) a Jewish name meaning 'Wave'.

Gamaliel (M) 'benefit of God'. A biblical name, borne by a teacher of St Paul.

Ganesh (M) 'lord of hosts'. An Indian name borne by Shiva's elder son, the god of wisdom, who is usually depicted with the head of an elephant.

Gareth (M) a Welsh name of uncertain origin, borne by a character in Arthurian legend. More recent famous bearers include the Welsh rugby player Gareth Edwards and the English singer Gareth Gates.
RELATED NAME: **Gary**.

Garfield (M) from the surname, meaning 'triangular field'. It is the full name of the West Indian cricketer known as Gary Sobers, but is probably more familiar as the name of a cartoon cat.
RELATED NAME: **Gary**.

Garnet (M/F) from a surname of uncertain origin, or from the name of the gemstone.
ALTERNATIVE FORM: **Garnett**.

Garret (M) from a surname that is another form of **Gerald** or **Gerard**, or from the Irish equivalent of these names (as in the case of the Irish politician Garret Fitzgerald).
ALTERNATIVE FORM: **Garrett**.
RELATED NAMES: **Jarrett, Jarrod, Ged, Gerry**.

Garrick (M) from a surname that either means 'spear ruler' or (as in the case of the 18th-century actor David Garrick) comes from the French word *garrigue*, referring to open scrubland.

Garrison (M) from the surname. It was popularized as a forename in the late 20th century by the US writer Garrison Keillor (whose real name is Gary).

Garth (M) from the surname, meaning 'enclosure'. It is borne by a fictional superhero, who first appeared in a *Daily Mirror* cartoon strip in the 1940s.

Gary (M) 'spear'. From the surname of a US industrialist whose steel company founded the town of Gary, Indiana in 1906. This place name was adopted as a stage name by the US actor Gary Cooper (whose real name was Frank). It is also regarded as a short form of **Gareth** or **Garfield**.
SHORT FORM: **Gaz**.
ALTERNATIVE FORM: **Garry**.

Gauri (F) 'white'. An Indian name sometimes given to the wife of Shiva.
ALTERNATIVE FORM: **Gowri**.

Gautam (M) 'descendant of Gotam'. An Indian name associated with the Buddha (whose original name was Gautama Siddhartha).

Gavin (M) another form of **Gawain**. It is the usual form of the name in modern times. Famous bearers include the Scottish naturalist and writer Gavin Maxwell.

Gawain (M) the name of one of the knights of King Arthur's Round Table, possibly meaning 'white hawk'.
ALTERNATIVE FORM: **Gavin**.

Gay (F) 'cheerful'. From the word *gay* in its original meaning. The new sense 'homosexual' caused the name to fall from favour in the second half of the 20th century.
ALTERNATIVE FORMS: **Gae, Gaye**.

Gayle (F) another spelling of **Gail**, borne by the US actress Gayle Hunnicutt.

Gaynor (F) another form of **Guinevere** ('fair and soft').
ALTERNATIVE FORM: **Gaenor**.
RELATED NAMES: **Jennifer, Ginevra**.

Gaz (M) short for **Gary**.

Ged (M) a short form of **Gerald** or **Gerard**, sometimes given as a name in its own right.
ALTERNATIVE FORM: **Jed**.

Geena (F) another spelling of **Gina**, used by the US actress Geena Davis (whose full name is Virginia).

Geeta (F) another spelling of the Indian name **Gita** ('song').

Gemma (F) 'gem'. Of Italian origin, the name was borne in the late 19th century by St Gemma Galgani.
ALTERNATIVE FORM: **Jemma**.

Gene (M) a short form of **Eugene** ('well-born'), sometimes given as a name in its own right. Famous bearers include the US singer Gene Pitney and the US actors Gene Hackman and Gene Kelly (whose full names were Eugene).

Geneva (F) from the name of the Swiss city, or another form of **Genevieve** or **Jennifer**.
RELATED NAME: **Ginevra**.

Genevieve [jen-a-VEEV] (F) a name of French origin, possibly meaning 'tribeswoman'. The name was borne in the 5th century by St Genevieve, patron saint of Paris. In the mid-20th century it was given to a veteran car in the film *Genevieve* (1953).
ALTERNATIVE FORMS: **Geneviève, Geneva, Ginevra**.

Geoffrey [JEF-ri] (M) a name of uncertain origin. The *-frey* ending means 'peace', but the meaning of the first part is unknown. Famous bearers include the 14th-century poet Geoffrey Chaucer.
SHORT FORM: **Geoff**.
ALTERNATIVE FORM: **Jeffrey**.

Geordie (M) a pet form of **George**. Chiefly used in northern England and Scotland, it gave rise to the word *Geordie* meaning 'person from Tyneside'.
RELATED NAME: **Georgie**.

George (M) 'farmer'. The name of the patron saint of England, as well as six British monarchs and various US presidents. Although it is not a girls' name, it has had some notable female bearers, including the 19th-century writer George Eliot (born Mary Ann Evans) and a fictional tomboy (whose full name was

Georgina) in Enid Blyton's 'Famous Five' books.

FEMININE FORMS: **Georgina, Georgette, Georgia, Georgiana**.

RELATED NAMES: **Georgie, Geordie**.

Georgette (F) a feminine form of George, of French origin.

RELATED NAMES: **Georgie, Georgina, Georgia, Georgiana, Gina**.

Georgia (F) a feminine form of George, of French origin. It is also the name of an American state and a European country.

RELATED NAMES: **Georgie, Georgiana, Georgina, Georgette, Gina**.

Georgiana (F) a feminine form of George, of French origin.

RELATED NAMES: **Georgie, Georgina, Georgia, Georgette, Gina**.

Georgie (M/F) a short form of George, Georgina, Georgette, Georgia, or Georgiana, sometimes given as a name in its own right. The girls' name was popularized in the 1960s by the film *Georgy Girl* and its title song.

ALTERNATIVE FORM: **Georgy**.

RELATED NAMES: **Geordie** (M), **Gina** (F).

Georgina (F) a feminine form of George.

RELATED NAMES: **Georgie, Gina, Georgiana, Georgia, Georgette**.

Geraint (M) a Welsh name, possibly meaning 'old man'. (The name rhymes with *pint* and the G is hard, as in *guy*.) Famous modern bearers include the Welsh opera singer Geraint Evans.

Gerald (M) 'rule of the spear'. The British naturalist and writer Gerald Durrell was a famous 20th-century bearer of the name.

FEMININE FORM: **Geraldine**.

RELATED NAMES: **Gerry, Ged, Garret, Jarrett, Jarrod**.

Geraldine (F) the feminine form of Gerald. Famous modern bearers include the British actress Geraldine James.

RELATED NAME: **Gerry**.

Gerard (M) 'brave with a spear'. The name was borne by the 19th-century British poet Gerard Manley Hopkins.

ALTERNATIVE FORM: **Gerrard**.

RELATED NAMES: **Gerry, Ged, Garret, Jarrett, Jarrod**.

Gerda [GIR-da] (F) a name of Scandinavian origin, possibly meaning 'enclosure', borne by the young heroine of Hans Christian Andersen's story 'The Snow Queen'.

Germaine [jer-MANE] (F/M) the feminine form of the French name *Germain*, meaning 'brother'. Germaine is now used for either sex in English-speaking countries, but the boys' name is more frequently found in the alternative form Jermaine. Famous bearers include

the Australian feminist writer Germaine Greer (female) and the US singer Jermaine Jackson (male).
ALTERNATIVE FORM: **Jermaine**.

Gerry (M/F) a short form of **Gerald**, **Gerard**, or **Geraldine**, sometimes given as a name in its own right. The British singer Geri Halliwell was born Geraldine Halliwell in 1972.
ALTERNATIVE FORMS: **Jerry**, **Geri** (F), **Gerri** (F), **Gerrie** (F).

Gershom (M) 'exile' or 'stranger'. A biblical name, borne by a son of Moses.

Gertrude [GIR-trood] (F) 'strong with a spear'. The name was popular in the late 19th and early 20th centuries.
SHORT FORMS: **Gert**, **Gertie**.
RELATED NAME: **Trudy**.

Gervase [JER-vaze, jer-VAZE] (M) a name of uncertain origin, possibly meaning 'spear servant'. St Gervase was an early Christian martyr about whom little is known.
ALTERNATIVE FORM: **Gervaise**.
RELATED NAME: **Jarvis**.

Gerwyn [GIR-win] (M) a Welsh name meaning 'fair love'.

Gethin [GETH-in] (M) a Welsh name meaning 'dusky, swarthy'.

Ghada (F) an Arabic name meaning 'graceful young lady'.

Ghassan (M) an Arabic name meaning 'youth'.

Ghislain (M) 'pledge'. The name was borne by a 7th-century Belgian saint.
FEMININE FORM: **Ghislaine**.

Ghislaine (F) the feminine form of **Ghislain**.
RELATED NAME: **Giselle**.

Gideon (M) 'hewer' or 'destroyer'. A biblical name, borne by a leader of the Israelites. It is also the name of an organization that distributes free copies of the Bible.

Gigi [ZHEE-zhee] (F) a short form of **Giselle** (or another name beginning with the same sound), sometimes given as a name in its own right. It is chiefly associated with the novel *Gigi* (1945), by the French writer Colette, and the musical based on it, about a Parisian girl (whose full name is Gilberte) being groomed for a career as a courtesan.

Gilbert (M) 'bright pledge'. The name was borne in the 12th century by St Gilbert of Sempringham, who founded an English order of monks and nuns.
SHORT FORMS: **Gil**, **Gib**.

Gilda (F) 'sacrifice' or 'golden'. Famous fictional bearers include the tragic heroine of Verdi's opera *Rigoletto* (1851) and a *femme fatale* (played by Rita Hayworth) in the film *Gilda* (1946).

Giles (M) 'young goat' or 'shield'. St Giles is the patron saint of beggars and cripples. The name became associated with farmers after Robert Bloomfield used it for the title character of his poem *The Farmer's Boy* (1800).

ALTERNATIVE FORM: **Gyles**.

Gill (F) another spelling of **Jill**, chiefly used as a short form of **Gillian** rather than a name in its own right.

ALTERNATIVE FORM: **Gilly**.

Gillian (F) a feminine form of **Julian**. It was particularly popular in the mid-20th century.

ALTERNATIVE FORM: **Jillian**.

RELATED NAMES: **Jill, Jilly, Juliana, Julia, Julie, Juliet**.

Gina [JEE-na] (F) a short form of **Georgina** (or various other names containing the letters *-gin-*, such as **Virginia**), sometimes given as a name in its own right. The Italian actress Gina Lollobrigida was born Luigina Lollobrigida in 1927.

ALTERNATIVE FORM: **Geena**.

Ginette (F) another spelling of **Jeanette** ('God is gracious').

Ginevra (F) another form of **Guinevere** ('fair and soft'), **Genevieve** (possibly meaning 'tribeswoman'), or **Geneva**, of Italian origin. The name is borne by a character in J. K. Rowling's *Harry Potter* books.

SHORT FORM: **Ginny**.

RELATED NAMES: **Jennifer, Gaynor**.

Ginger (M/F) from a nickname for a

red-haired person. In the case of the US film star Ginger Rogers, it was a pet form of her real name, Virginia.

Ginny (F) short for **Virginia** or **Ginevra**.

ALTERNATIVE FORMS: **Ginnie, Jinny**.

Giselle [zhi-ZEL] (F) 'pledge'. Of French origin, the name is chiefly associated with the tragic heroine of the ballet *Giselle*, first performed in the mid-19th century.

ALTERNATIVE FORMS: **Gisele, Gisela**.

RELATED NAMES: **Gigi, Ghislaine**.

Gita [GHEE-ta] (F) an Indian name meaning 'song'.

ALTERNATIVE FORM: **Geeta**.

Gladwin (M) from the surname, meaning 'bright friend'.

Gladys (F) from a Welsh name of uncertain origin, possibly meaning 'princess'. It was popularized in the early 20th century by the British actress Dame Gladys Cooper.

SHORT FORM: **Glad**.

Glenda (F) 'holy and good'. Of Welsh origin, the name is borne by the British actress and politician Glenda Jackson.

SHORT FORM: **Glen**.

Glenn (M/F) from a Scottish word meaning 'valley'. The girls' name may also be short for **Glenda** or **Glenys**, especially in the alternative form Glen. Famous modern bearers include the US bandleader Glenn

Miller (male) and the US actress Glenn Close (female).

ALTERNATIVE FORMS: **Glen, Glenna** (F).

RELATED NAME: **Glyn** (M).

Glenys (F) a Welsh name meaning 'pure, holy'. The Welsh politician Glenys Kinnock is a famous bearer of the name.

ALTERNATIVE FORMS: **Glenis, Glynis**.

Gloria (F) 'glory'. The name was popularized by the actress Gloria Swanson in the early 20th century.

ALTERNATIVE FORM: **Glory**.

Glyn (M) from a Welsh word meaning 'valley'.

ALTERNATIVE FORM: **Glynn**.

FEMININE FORM: **Glynis**.

RELATED NAME: **Glenn**.

Glynis (F) another form of **Glenys**, or a feminine form of **Glyn**. The Welsh actress Glynis Johns is a famous bearer of the name.

Gobind (M) another form of **Govind**, borne in the 17th century by the tenth guru of Sikhism.

Godfrey (M) 'God's peace'. The name is most familiar in modern times as the surname of one of the elderly soldiers in the British sitcom *Dad's Army*.

Godwin (M) 'friend of God'. The name was borne in the 11th century by an Anglo-Saxon nobleman, the father of Harold II.

Golda (F) 'gold'. A Jewish name, borne by the 20th-century Israeli stateswoman Golda Meir.

ALTERNATIVE FORM: **Golde**.

Goldie (F) from a nickname for a fair-haired person. The best-known bearer of the name is the US actress Goldie Hawn.

Gomer (M) 'complete'. A biblical name, borne by a grandson of Noah.

Gopal (M) 'cowherd'. An Indian name sometimes used with reference to the god Krishna.

Gordon (M) from a Scottish surname and place name, possibly meaning 'great hill'. Famous Scottish-born bearers include the actor Gordon Jackson and the politician Gordon Brown.

Gotam (M) 'the best ox'. An Indian name borne by a Hindu sage.

Govind (M) 'cattle finder'. An Indian name sometimes used with reference to the god Krishna.

ALTERNATIVE FORM: **Gobind**.

Gowri (F) another spelling of the Indian name **Gauri** ('white').

Grace (F) from the word *grace* in any of its senses. Grace Darling was a British lighthouse-keeper's daughter who heroically helped her father rescue nine shipwrecked people on a stormy day in 1838.

RELATED NAME: **Gracie**.

Gracie (F) a pet form of **Grace**, now

often given as a name in its own right. Famous bearers include the 20th-century British singer Gracie Fields (born Grace Stansfield).

Graham (M) from a Scottish surname that comes from the English place name Grantham. The British novelist Graham Greene was a famous bearer.
SHORT FORM: **Gray**.
ALTERNATIVE FORMS: **Graeme, Grahame**.

Grainne [GRAHN-ya] (F) 'grain'. An Irish name borne by the goddess of the harvest and by a legendary princess who eloped with Diarmuid.
ALTERNATIVE FORMS: **Gráinne, Grania**.

Grant (M) from the Scottish surname, meaning 'tall'. Grant Mitchell, a character in the soap opera *EastEnders*, is a famous fictional bearer of the name.

Granville (M) from the surname, which comes from a French place name. The forename is chiefly associated with the downtrodden grocer's assistant played by David Jason in the British television sitcom *Open All Hours*.

Gray (M) from the surname, meaning 'grey-haired', or a short form of **Graham**.

Greer (F) from a surname that originated as another form of **Gregory**. It was the maiden name of

the mother of the British actress Greer Garson (born Eileen Evelyn Greer Garson), who popularized it as a girls' name in the 20th century.
ALTERNATIVE FORM: **Grier**.

Greg (M) a short form of **Gregory**, sometimes given as a name in its own right.
ALTERNATIVE FORM: **Gregg, Greig**.

Gregor (M) a Scottish form of **Gregory**.

Gregory (M) 'watchful, vigilant'. The name was borne by a number of saints and popes. More recent famous bearers include the US actor Gregory Peck and the teenage hero of the film *Gregory's Girl* (1980).
RELATED NAMES: **Gregor, Grigor**.

Grenville (M) from the surname, which comes from a French place name.

Greta [GRET-a, GREE-ta] (F) another form of **Margaret** ('pearl'), of German or Scandinavian origin. The name was popularized in the 20th century by the Swedish-born actress Greta Garbo.
ALTERNATIVE FORM: **Gretta**.
RELATED NAMES: **Gretel, Gretchen, Margarita, Rita, Marguerite, Margot, Margaux, Margery, Marjorie, Madge, Maggie, Meg, Megan, Peggy, Mairead, Maisie, May, Molly, Pearl**.

Gretchen (F) another form of

Margaret ('pearl'), of German origin.
RELATED NAMES: *see list at* **Greta**.

Gretel (F) another form of **Margaret** ('pearl'), of German origin. The name is borne by one of the central characters in the fairy tale 'Hansel and Gretel' by the Brothers Grimm.
RELATED NAMES: *see list at* **Greta**.

Grier (F) another spelling of **Greer**.

Griffith (M) 'lord, prince'. Another form of a Welsh name, spelt as it sounds. The Welsh-born comedian Griff Rhys Jones uses the short form of the name.
SHORT FORM: **Griff**.

Grigor (M) a Welsh form of **Gregory**.

Griselda (F) 'grey warrior'. In the tale of 'Patient Griselda', told by Chaucer (among others), the name is borne by an obedient and long-suffering wife.
ALTERNATIVE FORM: **Grizel**.
RELATED NAME: **Zelda**.

Grover (M) from the surname, meaning 'person who lives near a grove of trees'. It was the middle name of the 19th-century US president known as Grover Cleveland. It is also the name of a likeable character in the US children's television series *Sesame Street*.

Gudrun (F) 'secret of the gods'. Of Scandinavian origin, the name is borne by a heroine of Norse mythology and by one of the title

characters of D. H. Lawrence's novel *Women in Love* (1920).

Guinevere (F) 'fair and soft'. The name of King Arthur's wife, who fell in love with Sir Lancelot.
RELATED NAMES: **Gaynor, Jennifer, Ginevra**.

Gulzar (F) a Muslim name meaning 'rose garden'.

Gus (M) short for **Angus, Augustus, Augustine**, or **Gustav**.

Gussie (M/F) short for **Augustus, Augustine, Augusta**, or **Augustina**.

Gustav (M) a name of Scandinavian origin, possibly meaning 'staff of the Goths' or 'staff of the gods'. The British composer Gustav Holst, of Swedish ancestry, was a famous bearer of the name.
SHORT FORM: **Gus**.
ALTERNATIVE FORMS: **Gustave, Gustavus**.

Guy (M) 'wide' or 'wood'. Famous bearers include the 16th-century conspirator Guy Fawkes and the title character of Sir Walter Scott's novel *Guy Mannering* (1815).

Gwen (F) a Welsh name meaning 'fair', or a short form of various names beginning with these letters, such as **Gwendolen**. The Welsh-born artist Gwen John was a famous bearer.

Gwenda (F) a Welsh name meaning 'fair and good'.
SHORT FORM: **Gwen**.

Gwendolen (F) 'white ring'. Of Welsh origin, it is borne by one of the central characters in Oscar Wilde's comedy *The Importance of Being Earnest* (1895).
SHORT FORMS: **Gwen, Wendy**.
ALTERNATIVE FORMS: **Gwendolyn, Gwendoline**.

Gwilym (M) the Welsh form of William ('resolute protector').
ALTERNATIVE FORM: **Gwillym**.
RELATED NAMES: **Will, Billy, Liam, Wilkie**.

Gwyn (M/F) a Welsh boys' name meaning 'fair', or a short form of the girls' name **Gwyneth**.
ALTERNATIVE FORMS: **Gwynn, Wyn** (M).

Gwyneth (F) from a Welsh word meaning 'luck, happiness', or from the name of the Welsh region Gwynedd. The US actress Gwyneth Paltrow has popularized the name in recent times.
SHORT FORM: **Gwyn**.
ALTERNATIVE FORM: **Gwynneth**.

Gwynfor (M) a Welsh name meaning 'fair and great'. The 20th-century Welsh politician Gwynfor Evans was a famous bearer.

Gyles (M) another spelling of **Giles**, borne by the British writer and broadcaster Gyles Brandreth.

Gypsy (F) from the word *gypsy*, referring to a member of a travelling people. Famous bearers include the 20th-century US dancer and actress Gypsy Rose Lee (born Rose Louise Hovick).

H

Habib (M) an Arabic name meaning 'beloved'.
FEMININE FORM: **Habiba**.

Habiba (F) the feminine form of Habib.

Hadassah (F) a Jewish name meaning 'myrtle'. It is the Hebrew name of the biblical character better known as Esther.
RELATED NAMES: **Dassah, Esther, Hester, Myrtle**.

Hadley (M) from a surname and place name meaning 'heathery field'.
ALTERNATIVE FORM: **Hadleigh**.

Hadrian (M) 'person from Hadria in Italy'. Hadrian's Wall in northern England was built in the 2nd century by the Roman emperor of that name. Its more common English form is **Adrian**.

Hafiz (M) 'guardian'. An Arabic name, originally used with reference to somebody who had learnt the Koran by heart.
ALTERNATIVE FORM: **Hafeez**.

Hafsa (F) 'gathering' or

'motherliness. An Arabic name borne by one of Muhammad's wives.
ALTERNATIVE FORM: **Hafza**.

Hagar [HAY-gar] (F) 'flight'. A biblical name, borne by the handmaid of Abraham's wife Sarah and the mother of his son Ishmael.

Haidar [HYE-da] (M) 'lion'. An Arabic name that formed part of a title given to Muhammad's son-in-law Ali.
ALTERNATIVE FORMS: **Haider, Hyder**.

Hailey (F) another spelling of Hayley.

Hakim (M) an Arabic name meaning 'wise'.

Hal (M) short for **Harry, Harold**, or **Henry**.

Hala (F) an Arabic name meaning 'halo (round the moon)'.

Hale (M) from a surname and place name meaning 'nook, recess'.

Haley (F) another spelling of **Hayley**.

Halle [HAL-i] (F) from the surname

(as in the case of the US model and actress Halle Berry), or another form of **Hallie**.

Hallie (F) a short form of **Harriet**, sometimes given as a name in its own right, or another form of **Halle**.
RELATED NAME: **Hattie**.

Ham (M) short for **Abraham**.

Hamid (M) an Arabic name meaning 'thankful, praising'.

Hamilton (M) from a surname and place name meaning 'flat-topped hill'.

Hamish (M) a Scottish form of **James** ('supplanter').
RELATED NAMES: **Seamus, Jamie, Jim, Jimmy, Jem, Jacob, Jake, Jago**.

Hamza (M) an Arabic name meaning 'steadfast'.

Hana (F) an Arabic name meaning 'happiness'.

Hanan (F) an Arabic name meaning 'tenderness'.

Hanif (M) an Arabic name meaning 'true, upright'. The Pakistani-British writer Hanif Kureishi is a famous bearer.

Hank (M) a pet form of **John** ('God is gracious'), sometimes given as a name in its own right. The British guitarist Hank Marvin was born Brian Rankin in 1941.
RELATED NAMES: **Johnny, Jack,**

Jackie, Jake, Jock, Ian, Sean, Shaun, Shane, Eoin, Evan, Sion, Ivan, Juan.

Hannah (F) 'favour' or 'grace'. A biblical name (literally meaning 'God has favoured me') borne by the mother of Samuel, who had begun to despair of having children of her own. The name came back into fashion in the late 20th century, replacing Anne, which had previously been more popular.
ALTERNATIVE FORM: **Hanna**.
RELATED NAMES: **Anne, Anna, Anya, Anita, Annette, Annie, Anneka, Anouska, Anais, Nancy, Nanette**.

Hannibal (M) 'grace of Baal'. The name was borne by a famous Carthaginian general in the 3rd century BC. A notorious fictional bearer is Hannibal Lecter, a cannibalistic serial killer created by the US writer Thomas Harris in a series of novels that includes *The Silence of the Lambs* (1988), filmed in 1991.

Hardy (M) from the surname, meaning 'brave, tough'. It was the middle name of the 20th-century British fashion designer known as Hardy Amies.

Hari (M) 'brown, yellow' or 'monkey, lion'. An Indian name sometimes given to the gods Vishnu and Krishna.

Harish (M) 'lord of the monkeys'. An

Indian name sometimes given to the god Vishnu.

Harlan (M) from a surname and place name meaning 'hare land'.
ALTERNATIVE FORM: **Harland**.

Harley (M/F) from a surname and place name meaning 'hare meadow'. The name is also associated with the motorcycles manufactured by Harley-Davidson.

Harmony (F) from the word *harmony*, meaning 'concord'.

Harold (M) 'army commander'. The name fell from favour after the death of Harold II at the Battle of Hastings in 1066. It became fashionable again in the late 19th century and was borne by the 20th-century British statesmen Harold Macmillan and Harold Wilson.
SHORT FORM: **Hal**.
RELATED NAME: **Harry**.

Haroun (M) another spelling of **Harun**.

Harper (M/F) from the surname, meaning 'harp player'. It is the middle name of the female US novelist known as Harper Lee.

Harriet (F) a feminine form of **Henry** ('lord of the manor') or **Harry**. Famous bearers include the 19th-century US writer Harriet Beecher Stowe.
ALTERNATIVE FORM: **Harriette**.
RELATED NAMES: **Henrietta, Hallie, Hattie**.

Harris (M) from the surname, meaning 'of Harry'. It is also a Scottish place name and is particularly popular in Scotland.

Harrison (M) from the surname, meaning 'son of Harry'. The US actor Harrison Ford is a famous bearer of the name.

Harry (M) a short form of **Harold** ('army commander') or **Henry** ('lord of the manor'), now often given as a name in its own right. It has recently been popularized by Harry Potter, the young hero of a series of children's books by J. K. Rowling.
SHORT FORM: **Hal**.
FEMININE FORM: **Harriet**.

Hartley (M) from a surname and place name meaning 'deer wood'.

Harun [ha-ROON] (M) the Arabic form of **Aaron** (possibly meaning 'high mountain'). Harun al-Rashid was an 8th-century caliph of Islam.
ALTERNATIVE FORM: **Haroun**.

Harvey (M) from the surname, meaning 'battle worthy'. Famous modern bearers include the US actor Harvey Keitel.
SHORT FORMS: **Harv, Harve**.

Hashim (M) 'breaker'. An Arabic name given to an ancestor of Muhammad because he broke bread to feed pilgrims.

Hassan (M) 'good, beautiful'. An Arabic name borne by a grandson of

Muhammad, the brother of Hussein.
ALTERNATIVE FORM: **Hasan**.
RELATED NAME: **Hussein**.

Hattie (F) a short form of **Harriet**, sometimes given as a name in its own right. It is chiefly associated with the 20th-century British comedy actress Hattie Jacques (whose real name was Josephine).
RELATED NAME: **Hallie**.

Haya [HY-a] (F) another spelling of the Jewish name **Chaya** ('alive').

Hayden (M) from a surname and place name meaning 'hay valley' or 'heather hill', or another form of **Haydn**. It has recently been popularized by the Canadian actor Hayden Christensen, who played Anakin Skywalker in two of the *Star Wars* films.
ALTERNATIVE FORM: **Haydon**.

Haydn (M/F) 'heathen'. From the surname of the 18th-century Austrian composer Joseph Haydn. Famous female bearers include the British actress Haydn Gwynne.
ALTERNATIVE FORMS: **Hayden**, **Haydon**.

Hayfa (F) an Arabic name meaning 'slender'.

Hayley (F) from a surname and place name meaning 'hay field'. It was popularized in the mid-20th century by the British child actress

Hayley Mills, who was named after her mother, Mary Hayley Bell.
ALTERNATIVE FORM: **Haley, Hailey**.

Haytham (M) an Arabic name meaning 'young eagle'.

Hazel (F) from the name of the tree or the colour of its nuts, used to describe a person's eyes.

Heath (M) from the surname, meaning 'person who lives on heathland'. It was the middle name of the British cartoonist known as Heath Robinson, famous for his drawings of absurd machines.

Heather (F) from the plant name. It is particularly popular in Scotland. Famous bearers include Heather Mills, former wife of Paul McCartney.

Hebe [HEE-bee] (F) 'young'. The name of the Greek goddess of youth, and also of a type of flowering shrub.

Hector (M) 'holding fast'. The name of a Trojan hero in Greek mythology. In the late 1960s the name was borne by an affable puppet dog in the children's television series *Hector's House*.

Hedda (F) another form of **Hedwig**, of Scandinavian origin. The name is borne by the heroine of Henrik Ibsen's play *Hedda Gabler* (1890).
RELATED NAME: **Hedy**.

Hedley (M) from a surname and

place name meaning 'heather meadow'.

Hedwig (F) 'warfare'. A name of German origin, borne by a white owl in J. K. Rowling's *Harry Potter* books.
RELATED NAMES: **Hedda, Hedy.**

Hedy [HED-i] (F) a short form of **Hedwig**, sometimes given as a name in its own right. As a short form it was used by the Austrian-born film star Hedy Lamarr.
RELATED NAME: **Hedda.**

Heidi (F) 'of noble kind'. A short form of the German name *Adelheid*, it was popularized in the English-speaking world by the children's novel *Heidi* (1880) by Johanna Spyri.
RELATED NAMES: **Adelaide, Alice, Ailish, Ally, Alison.**

Helen (F) 'light'. Helen of Troy was a legendary Greek heroine renowned for her beauty. The name was popular in the mid-20th century, when the British singer Helen Shapiro and the British actress Helen Mirren were born.
RELATED NAMES: **Helena, Ellen, Elen, Nell, Elaine, Elena, Ilona.**

Helena [HEL-in-a] (F) another form of **Helen**. Famous bearers include a 3rd-century saint and, more recently, the British actress Helena Bonham Carter.

RELATED NAMES: **Lena, Elena, Ilona, Ellen, Elen, Nell, Elaine.**

Helga (F) 'prosperous, successful'. A name of Scandinavian or German origin, made famous in the UK by a character in the television sitcom *'Allo 'Allo*.
RELATED NAME: **Olga.**

Heloise (F) another form of **Eloise**.
ALTERNATIVE FORM: **Héloïse.**

Henrietta (F) a feminine form of **Henry**. The name was borne in the 17th century by the wife of Charles I.
SHORT FORMS: **Hen, Hennie, Hettie, Ettie.**
ALTERNATIVE FORM: **Henriette.**
RELATED NAMES: **Harriet, Etta.**

Henry (M) 'lord of the manor'. The name has had many royal bearers, including eight kings of England and the younger son of Prince Charles, who is known as Prince Harry.
SHORT FORM: **Hal.**
FEMININE FORMS: **Henrietta, Harriet.**
RELATED NAMES: **Harry.**

Hephzibah [HEF-zi-bah, HEP-si-bah] (F) 'my delight'. A biblical name, borne by the wife of Hezekiah, King of Judah.
SHORT FORM: **Hepsie.**
RELATED NAMES: **Effie, Eppie.**

Herbert (M) 'illustrious army'. The British actor Sir Herbert Beerbohm Tree was a famous bearer of the name in the late 19th and early 20th centuries.

SHORT FORMS: **Herb, Herbie.**

RELATED NAMES: **Bert, Bertie.**

Hercules (M) 'glory of Hera (the wife of Zeus)'. The name of the son of Zeus in Greek mythology, a man of great strength who became a god.

Hereward [HERR-i-wud] (M) 'army guardian'. The name was borne in the 11th century by the Anglo-Saxon leader Hereward the Wake.

Herman (M) 'soldier, warrior'. Famous bearers include the US writer Herman Melville and the German Nazi politician Hermann Goering.

ALTERNATIVE FORM: **Hermann.**

RELATED NAME: **Armand.**

Hermia (F) a feminine form of *Hermes*, the name of the Greek messenger god. Hermia is one of the central characters in Shakespeare's play *A Midsummer Night's Dream*.

RELATED NAME: **Hermione.**

Hermione [her-MY-a-ni] (F) another form of **Hermia**. Famous fictional bearers include the virtuous wife of the king of Sicily in Shakespeare's play *The Winter's Tale* and a friend of Harry Potter in the books by J. K. Rowling.

Hershel (M) another form of the Jewish name **Hirsh** ('deer').

ALTERNATIVE FORM: **Herschel.**

Hester (F) another form of **Esther** ('myrtle' or 'star').

SHORT FORM: **Hettie.**

RELATED NAMES: **Hadassah, Dassah, Myrtle.**

Hettie (F) short for **Henrietta** or **Hester**.

ALTERNATIVE FORM: **Hetty.**

Hezekiah (M) 'God is strength'. A biblical name, borne by a king of Judah.

Hiba (F) an Arabic name meaning 'gift'.

Hilary (F/M) 'cheerful'. Originally a boys' name, borne by the 4th-century theologian St Hilary of Poitiers, it is now usually given to girls. The US lawyer and politician Hillary Clinton uses the alternative spelling of the name.

SHORT FORM: **Hil.**

ALTERNATIVE FORM: **Hillary.**

Hilda (F) 'battle'. The name was borne in the 7th century by St Hilda, who founded an abbey at Whitby.

ALTERNATIVE FORM: **Hylda.**

Hildegard (F) 'battle enclosure'. The name was borne in the 12th century by the German abbess and mystic Hildegard of Bingen.

ALTERNATIVE FORM: **Hildegarde.**

Hillel (M) a Jewish name meaning 'praise'. The name occurs in the Bible and was borne in the 1st century by a highly respected and influential rabbi.

Hiram (M) a biblical name, possibly meaning 'my brother is exalted'. In the Bible, the name is borne by a king of Tyre who played an important role in the building of King Solomon's temple.

Hirsh (M) a Jewish name meaning 'deer'.
ALTERNATIVE FORMS: **Hirsch, Hershel, Herschel**.

Hisham (M) 'generous'. An Arabic name borne by an 8th-century caliph.

Hobart (M) another form of **Hubert** ('bright spirit'), possibly influenced by the name of the capital of Tasmania.

Holden (M) from a surname and place name meaning 'hollow valley'. The best-known bearer of the forename is the fictional teenager Holden Caulfield in J. D. Salinger's novel *The Catcher in the Rye* (1951).

Holly (F) from the plant name, associated with Christmas. Famous modern bearers include the US actress Holly Hunter.
ALTERNATIVE FORM: **Hollie**.

Homer (M) the name of an ancient Greek poet, possibly meaning 'hostage'. It is now chiefly associated with Homer Simpson, the lazy and gluttonous father of the cartoon family featured in the television series *The Simpsons*.

Honor (F) 'honour'. The US actress Honor Blackman is a famous bearer of the name.
ALTERNATIVE FORMS: **Honoria, Honora, Honour**.

Honora (F) another form of **Honor**.
RELATED NAME: **Nora**.

Honoria (F) another form of **Honor** that originated as the feminine form of the Latin boys' name *Honorius*.

Hope (F) from the word *hope*, originally adopted as a forename with reference to the Christian expectation of eternal life.

Horace [HORR-iss] (M) from the Roman family name *Horatius*, possibly meaning 'hour, time'. The Roman poet Horace was born Quintus Horatius Flaccus in 65 BC. Other famous bearers include the 18th-century British writer Horace Walpole.
SHORT FORM: **Horry**.
ALTERNATIVE FORM: **Horatio**.
FEMININE FORM: **Horatia**.

Horatia (F) the feminine form of **Horace** or **Horatio**.

Horatio (M) another form of **Horace**, borne by the 18th-century British admiral Horatio Nelson.
FEMININE FORM: **Horatia**.

Hortense (F) from a Roman family name, possibly meaning 'garden'.
ALTERNATIVE FORM: **Hortensia**.

Hosanna (F) from the word *hosanna*,

a biblical exclamation of praise that means 'save, we pray'.

Howard (M) from an aristocratic surname, possibly meaning 'high guardian'. The US businessman and millionaire Howard Hughes was a famous bearer of the name.
SHORT FORM: **Howie**.

Howell (M) an English form of the Welsh name **Hywel** ('eminent'), spelt as it sounds.

Hubert (M) 'bright spirit'. Famous bearers include the 8th-century bishop St Hubert and the 20th-century US statesman Hubert Humphrey.
ALTERNATIVE FORM: **Hobart**.
RELATED NAMES: **Bert, Bertie**.

Huda (F) an Arabic name meaning 'right guidance'.

Hugh (M) 'heart, mind'. Famous bearers include the 12th century bishop St Hugh of Lincoln and, more recently, the British actor Hugh Grant.
ALTERNATIVE FORM: **Huw**.
RELATED NAMES: **Hughie, Hugo**.

Hughie (M) a pet form of Hugh, sometimes given as a name in its own right. The television presenter Hughie Green was a well-known bearer.
ALTERNATIVE FORM: **Huey**.
RELATED NAME: **Hugo**.

Hugo (M) another form of **Hugh**.
RELATED NAME: **Hughie**.

Hulda (F) 'weasel'. A biblical name, borne by a prophetess. It is also a Scandinavian name meaning 'lovable'.
ALTERNATIVE FORM: **Huldah**.

Humbert (M) 'illustrious warrior'. It is chiefly associated with the fictional character Humbert Humbert, the narrator of Vladimir Nabokov's novel *Lolita* (1955).

Humphrey (M) 'peaceful warrior'. The fame of the US actor Humphrey Bogart in the mid-20th century did little to popularize the name.
SHORT FORM: **Humph**.
ALTERNATIVE FORM: **Humphry**.

Hunter (M) from the surname, meaning 'person who hunts'. It is the middle name of the British writer known as Hunter Davies.

Husam (M) an Arabic name meaning 'sword'.

Hussein (M) another form of **Hassan** ('good, beautiful'). An Arabic name borne by a grandson of Muhammad, the brother of Hassan.
ALTERNATIVE FORMS: **Husayn, Hussain**.

Huw (M) a Welsh spelling of **Hugh**, borne by the broadcaster Sir Huw Weldon.

Hyacinth (F) from the flower name. It was originally a boys' name, borne by a beautiful youth in classical mythology. In modern times it is

chiefly associated with the snobbish Hyacinth Bucket (played by Patricia Routledge) in the television sitcom *Keeping Up Appearances*.
SHORT FORM: **Hy**.
RELATED NAME: **Jacinta**.

Hyam (M) a Jewish name meaning 'life'.
SHORT FORMS: **Hy, Hymie**.
ALTERNATIVE FORMS: **Chaim, Hyman**.

Hyder (M) another spelling of the Arabic name **Haidar** ('lion').

Hylda (F) another spelling of **Hilda** ('battle').

Hywel [HOW-ul, HUH-wul] (M) a Welsh name meaning 'eminent'. Famous bearers include the Welsh actor Hywel Bennett.
RELATED NAME: **Howell**.

I

Ian (M) the Scottish form of **John** ('God is gracious'). Famous modern bearers include the British novelist Ian Fleming, creator of James Bond, and the British actor Sir Ian McKellen.

ALTERNATIVE FORM: **Iain**.

RELATED NAMES: **Johnny, Jack, Jackie, Jake, Jock, Hank, Sean, Shaun, Shane, Eoin, Evan, Sion, Ivan, Juan.**

Ianthe [eye-ANTH-ee] (F) 'violet flower'. The name of a sea nymph in Greek mythology, it is also found in 19th-century poetry.

RELATED NAME: **Iolanthe**.

Ibby (F) short for **Isabel**.

Ibrahim (M) the Arabic form of **Abraham** ('father of a multitude').

Ida (F) 'work'. Famous bearers of the name include the title character of the Gilbert and Sullivan opera *Princess Ida* (1884) and the 20th-century actress Ida Lupino.

Idris (M) a Welsh name meaning 'ardent lord', borne by a legendary sorcerer, or an Arabic name borne by the founder of the first Shiite dynasty.

Iestyn [YES-tin] (M) the Welsh form of **Justin** ('just, fair').

Ifor [EYE-vor, EYE-va] (M) a Welsh name of uncertain origin, possibly meaning 'lord'.

ALTERNATIVE FORM: **Ivor**.

Ignatius (M) from a Roman family name that became associated with the Latin word *ignis*, meaning 'fire'. St Ignatius Loyola, the 16th-century Spanish founder of the Jesuits, was a famous bearer of the name.

RELATED NAME: **Inigo**.

Igor (M) another form of **Ivor** ('archer') or of the Scandinavian name *Ingvar* (meaning 'Ing's warrior'), of Russian origin. Famous bearers include the hunchbacked assistant of Dr Frankenstein in some film versions of the story.

Ike (M) short for **Isaac**. It was also a nickname for the 20th-century US president Dwight D. Eisenhower, based on his surname.

Ilan (M) a Jewish name meaning 'tree'. FEMININE FORM: **Ilana**.

Ilana (F) the feminine form of **Ilan**.

Ilona (F) another form of **Helen** ('light'), of Hungarian origin.
RELATED NAMES: **Helena, Elena, Ellen, Elen, Nell, Elaine**.

Iman (F) an Arabic name meaning 'faith, belief'.

Imelda (F) 'all-conquering'. Famous modern bearers of the name include the Filipino politician Imelda Marcos and the British actress Imelda Staunton.
SHORT FORM: **Mel**.

Immanuel (M) the Hebrew form of **Emmanuel** ('God with us'). The 18th-century German philosopher Immanuel Kant was a famous bearer of the name in this form.
RELATED NAME: **Manuel**.

Imogen (F) from the Celtic name *Innogen*, meaning 'girl, maiden', which was accidentally changed to Imogen in Shakespeare's play *Cymbeline*. Famous modern bearers include the British actress Imogen Stubbs.
SHORT FORM: **Immy**.

Imran (M) the Arabic name for the father of Moses. Famous modern bearers include the Pakistani former cricketer Imran Khan.

Ina (F) a short form of various names ending with these letters, such as **Edwina** or **Georgina**, sometimes given as a name in its own right.

Inderjit (M/F) an Indian name meaning 'conqueror of Indra'.

India (F) from the name of the country. It was popularized in the late 20th century by the model India Hicks, a goddaughter and second cousin of Prince Charles.

Indiana (M/F) from the name of the American state. It was originally given to girls, but a series of films featuring Harrison Ford as the intrepid archaeologist Indiana Jones have popularized it as a boys' name.
SHORT FORM: **Indy**.

Indira (F) 'beauty'. An Indian name sometimes given to the goddess Lakshmi, wife of Vishnu. It was borne in the 20th century by the Indian stateswoman Indira Gandhi.

Indra (M) 'possessing drops of rain'. An Indian name borne by the god of the sky.

Ines (F) another form of **Agnes** ('pure, holy'), of Spanish origin.
ALTERNATIVE FORMS: **Inés, Inez**.
RELATED NAMES: **Annis, Nesta**.

Inga (F) an English form of *Inge* (short for various Scandinavian or German names beginning with *Ing-*, such as **Ingrid**), spelt as it sounds.

Ingram (M) from the surname,

possibly meaning 'Engel's raven' or 'Ing's raven'. (Engel means 'Angle', referring to the tribe of that name, and Ing was a Norse fertility god.)

Ingrid (F) 'fair Ing (a Norse fertility god)'. Of Scandinavian origin, the name was popularized in the 20th century by the Swedish-born actress Ingrid Bergman.
RELATED NAME: **Inga**.

Inigo [IN-ig-oh] (M) another form of **Ignatius**, of Spanish origin. The 17th-century English architect Inigo Jones was a famous bearer of the name.

Innes [INN-iss] (M) from the surname, which is another form of **Angus** based on the pronunciation of the Gaelic name from which it comes.

Iola [eye-OH-la] (F) 'violet'. The name was borne (in its original form *Iole*) by a beautiful princess in Greek mythology.

Iolanthe [eye-a-LANTH-ee] (F) 'violet flower'. The name is chiefly associated with the Gilbert and Sullivan opera *Iolanthe* (1882), in which it is borne by a fairy who has married a mortal.
RELATED NAME: **Ianthe**.

Iolo [YOL-oh, YOH-loh] (M) a short form of **Iorwerth**, sometimes given as a name in its own right.
RELATED NAME: **Yorath**.

Iona [eye-OH-na] (F) from the name

of the Scottish island where St Columba founded a monastery in the 6th century.

Ione [eye-OH-ni] (F) a name of uncertain origin, which possibly comes from the Greek place name **Ionia**.

Iorwerth [YOR-werth] (M) a Welsh name meaning 'handsome lord'.
RELATED NAMES: **Iolo, Yorath**.

Ira (M) 'watchful'. The name of a minor biblical character. Famous modern bearers include the 20th-century US lyricist Ira Gershwin (whose real name was Israel).

Irene [EYE-reen, eye-REEN] (F) 'peace'. Originally pronounced [eye-REE-nee], it was the name of a Greek goddess and an 8th-century Byzantine empress. In the 20th century it was popularized by a character in John Galsworthy's series of novels *The Forsyte Saga* (1922).
RELATED NAME: **Rene**.

Iris (F) 'rainbow' or 'iris (the flower)'. Famous modern bearers of the name include the British novelist Iris Murdoch.

Irma (F) 'whole, universal'. In the film *Irma la Douce* (1963), which is based on a French musical, the title character is a prostitute.
ALTERNATIVE FORM: **Erma**.
RELATED NAME: **Emma**.

Irving (M) from a Scottish surname and place name. Famous bearers

include the 20th-century US songwriter Irving Berlin (born Israel Baline).
ALTERNATIVE FORM: **Irvine**.

Irwin (M) 'boar friend'. It is more frequently found as a surname in modern times.
ALTERNATIVE FORM: **Irvine**.

Isaac (M) a biblical name, possibly meaning 'laughter'. In the Bible, Isaac is the younger son of Abraham and the father of Esau and Jacob. Other famous bearers include the 17th-century English scientist Sir Isaac Newton.
SHORT FORMS: **Ike, Izzy**.
ALTERNATIVE FORM: **Izaak**.
RELATED NAMES: **Zak, Yitzhak**.

Isabel (F) another form of **Elizabeth** ('oath of God'), of Spanish origin. It has had various royal bearers in the alternative form Isabella, including two medieval queens of England.
SHORT FORMS: **Izzy, Ibby, Isa, Bel**.
ALTERNATIVE FORMS: **Isabelle, Isobel, Ysabel, Isabella, Ishbel**.
RELATED NAMES: **Eliza, Elsa, Elsie, Elspeth, Elise, Eilis, Liza, Lisa, Lizzie, Libby, Lizbeth, Lili, Lisette, Beth, Bethan, Betty, Betsy, Bess, Babette, Buffy**.

Isadora (F) another form of **Isidora**.

Isaiah (M) 'God is salvation'. The name of a major biblical prophet and the book of the Bible that contains his sayings. Famous

modern bearers include the British philosopher Isaiah Berlin.

Isam (M) an Arabic name meaning 'pledge, security, protection'.

Ishbel (F) another form of **Isabel**, of Scottish origin.

Ishmael [ISH-mail] (M) 'God will listen'. A biblical name borne by the elder son of Abraham. Herman Melville gave the name to the narrator of his novel *Moby-Dick* (1851), who introduces himself in the famous opening line 'Call me Ishmael'.
RELATED NAME: **Ismail**.

Isidora (F) the feminine form of **Isidore**. It is more familiar in its alternative form, made famous in the early 20th century by the US dancer Isadora Duncan.
ALTERNATIVE FORM: **Isadora**.
RELATED NAME: **Dora**.

Isidore (M) 'gift of Isis (an Egyptian goddess)'. The name was borne in the 7th century by St Isidore of Seville.
FEMININE FORM: **Isidora**.

Isla [EYE-la] (F) from the place name Islay, a Scottish island that is famous for its whisky.

Ismail [iz-ma-EEL] (M) the Arabic form of **Ishmael**.

Ismat (M) an Arabic name meaning 'infallible'.

Isobel (F) another spelling of **Isabel**.

Isolde (F) 'beautiful'. In Celtic legend, Isolde is a beautiful princess who is engaged to the elderly King Mark of Cornwall but falls in love with the young knight Tristan.
ALTERNATIVE FORM: **Isolda**.

Isra (F) an Arabic name meaning 'night journey', referring to Muhammad's journey to Jerusalem to meet Jesus and Moses.

Israel (M) 'he struggles with God'. A biblical name, given to Jacob and subsequently applied to his descendants and the modern Jewish state.

Issachar [ISS-a-kar] (M) 'hireling'. A biblical name, borne by one of Jacob's sons.

Itamar (M) 'palm island'. A biblical name, borne by one of Aaron's sons.

Ivan (M) another form of **John** ('God is gracious'), of Russian origin. Famous bearers include the 16th-century Russian emperor Ivan the Terrible.
SHORT FORM: **Van**.

RELATED NAMES: **Ian, Sean, Shaun, Shane, Eoin, Evan, Sion, Juan, Johnny, Jack, Jackie, Jake, Jock, Hank**.

Ivo [EE-vo] (M) another form of **Yves** ('yew'), of German origin.
ALTERNATIVE FORM: **Ivon**.

Ivor (M) from a Scandinavian name meaning 'archer', or another form of the Welsh name **Ifor** (possibly meaning 'lord'). The Welsh songwriter, singer, and actor Ivor Novello was born David Ivor Davies.
RELATED NAME: **Igor**.

Ivy (F) from the plant name. Famous bearers include the 20th-century British novelist Dame Ivy Compton-Burnett.

Izaak (M) another spelling of **Isaac**, borne by the 17th-century English writer and angler Izaak Walton.

Izzy (F/M) short for various names beginning with *Is-*, especially **Isabel** and **Isaac**.
ALTERNATIVE FORM: **Izzie**.

J

Jabez (M) a biblical name meaning 'sorrowful'.

Jabir (M) an Arabic name meaning 'comforter'.

Jacinta (F) another form of Hyacinth, of Spanish origin.
ALTERNATIVE FORM: **Jacintha**.

Jack (M) a pet form of **John** ('God is gracious'), now usually given as a name in its own right. It has been one of the most popular names for baby boys born in the UK since the 1990s.
RELATED NAMES: **Jackie, Jake, Jock, Hank, Johnny, Ian, Sean, Shaun, Shane, Eoin, Evan, Sion, Ivan, Juan**.

Jackie (F) a short form of Jacqueline, sometimes given as a name in its own right. It was the title of a magazine for teenage girls that was particularly popular in the 1970s.
ALTERNATIVE FORMS: **Jacky, Jacqui**.
RELATED NAMES: **Jacquetta, Jacoba, Jamesina, Jamie, Jaime**.

Jackie (M) a pet form of **John** or Jack, sometimes given as a name in its own right. The British racing driver Jackie Stewart (whose real name is John) is a famous bearer of the name.
ALTERNATIVE FORM: **Jacky**.
RELATED NAMES: *see list at* **Jack**.

Jacklyn (F) another form of Jacqueline.
ALTERNATIVE FORM: **Jaclyn**.

Jackson (M) from the surname, meaning 'son of Jack'. Famous modern bearers include the US artist Jackson Pollock.

Jacob (M) 'supplanter'. A biblical name borne by Esau's younger twin brother, who cunningly gained Esau's birthright. More recent famous bearers include the US-born sculptor Sir Jacob Epstein.
ALTERNATIVE FORM: **Jakob**.
FEMININE FORMS: **Jacoba, Jacobina, Jacqueline, Jackie, Jacquetta**.
RELATED NAMES: **Jake, Jago, James, Jamie, Jim, Jimmy, Jem, Hamish, Seamus**.

Jacoba (F) a feminine form of **Jacob**.
ALTERNATIVE FORM: **Jacobina**.
RELATED NAMES: **Jacqueline, Jackie, Jacquetta, Jamesina, Jamie, Jaime**.

Jacqueline (F) a feminine form of **Jacob** or **James**, of French origin. The 20th-century British cellist Jacqueline du Pré was a famous bearer of the name.
ALTERNATIVE FORMS: **Jacquelyn, Jacklyn, Jaclyn**.
RELATED NAMES: **Jackie, Jacquetta, Jacoba, Jamesina, Jamie, Jaime**.

Jacquetta (F) a feminine form of **Jacob** or **James** that is a blend of the French name **Jacqueline** and its Italian equivalent *Giachetta*.
RELATED NAMES: **Jackie, Jacoba, Jamesina, Jamie, Jaime**.

Jade (F) from the name of the gemstone. The name became popular in the 1970s, after the British rock singer Mick Jagger and his wife Bianca gave it to their daughter. In the early years of the 21st century it was chiefly associated with the reality TV celebrity Jade Goody.
ALTERNATIVE FORM: **Jada**.

Jaden (M) another spelling of **Jayden**.

Jael [JAY-ul] (F) another form of the Jewish name **Yael** ('wild goat').

Jafar (M) an Arabic name meaning 'stream'.

Jagdish (M) an Indian name meaning 'ruler of the world'.

Jago (M) a Cornish form of **James** or **Jacob**.
RELATED NAMES: **Jake, Jamie, Jim, Jimmy, Jem, Hamish, Seamus**.

Jahangir (M) 'holder of the world'. An Indian name borne by a 17th-century Mogul emperor.

Jai (M) another spelling of the Indian name **Jay** ('victory').

Jaime [JAY-mi] (F) a feminine form of **James**, influenced by a boys' name with the same spelling that is the Spanish form of James.
ALTERNATIVE FORMS: **Jaimie, Jamie**.
RELATED NAMES: **Jamesina, Jacqueline, Jackie, Jacquetta, Jacoba**.

Jake (M) a pet form of **John** ('God is gracious') or a short form of **Jacob** ('supplanter'), now usually given as a name in its own right. Famous modern bearers include the British singer Jake Thackray (whose real name was John) and the hero of Kingsley Amis's novel *Jake's Thing* (1978).
RELATED NAMES: **Jack, Jackie, Jock, Hank, Johnny, Ian, Sean, Shaun, Shane, Eoin, Evan, Sion, Ivan, Juan, Jago, James, Jamie, Jim, Jimmy, Jem, Hamish, Seamus**.

Jakob (M) another spelling of **Jacob**.

Jalal (M) an Arabic name meaning 'greatness, glory'.

Jamal (M/F) an Arabic name meaning 'good looks'.

Jameel (M) another spelling of Jamil.

Jameela (F) another spelling of Jamila.

James (M) another form of Jacob ('supplanter'). The name was borne by two of Jesus Christ's apostles and seven kings of Scotland. More recent famous bearers include the Irish novelist James Joyce and the fictional secret agent James Bond, created by Ian Fleming.
FEMININE FORMS: Jamesina, Jaime, Jamie, Jacqueline, Jackie, Jacquetta.
RELATED NAMES: Jamie, Jim, Jimmy, Jem, Hamish, Seamus, Jake, Jago.

Jamesina (F) a feminine form of James.
RELATED NAMES: Jaime, Jamie, Jacqueline, Jackie, Jacquetta, Jacoba.

Jamie (M/F) a short form of James, sometimes given as a name in its own right, or a feminine form of James. Famous bearers include the British chef Jamie Oliver (male) and the US actress Jamie Lee Curtis (female).
ALTERNATIVE FORMS: Jamey, Jaimie.
RELATED NAMES: see lists at James and Jamesina.

Jamil (M) an Arabic name meaning 'good-looking'.
ALTERNATIVE FORM: Jameel.

FEMININE FORM: Jamila.

Jamila (F) the feminine form of Jamil.
ALTERNATIVE FORM: Jameela.

Jamshed (M) a name of uncertain origin, possibly meaning 'shining river', borne by a legendary king of Persia.

Jan (F) short for various names beginning with these letters, such as Janet or Janice.

Jancis (F) probably a blend of Jan and Frances, coined by the British writer Mary Webb for a character in her novel *Precious Bane* (1924) and further popularized by the British wine expert Jancis Robinson.

Jane (F) a feminine form of John ('God is gracious'). Famous bearers include the heroine of Charlotte Brontë's novel *Jane Eyre* (1847) and the 19th-century US frontierswoman known as Calamity Jane.
ALTERNATIVE FORM: Jayne.
RELATED NAMES: Janie; see also list at Janet.

Janeen (F) another spelling of Janine ('God is gracious').
ALTERNATIVE FORMS: Jeanine, Jeannine.

Janelle (F) a compound of Jan and the name-ending -elle.

Janet (F) a feminine form of John ('God is gracious'). It was particularly popular in the mid-20th century, when it was given to one of the title characters of the 'Janet and John' books used to teach children to read.

SHORT FORM: **Jan**.

ALTERNATIVE FORM: **Janette**.

RELATED NAMES: **Jane, Jean, Joan, Joanna, Joni, Jeanette, Janine, Juanita, Sian, Shana, Shauna, Siobhan, Shevaun, Sinead, Sheena, Shona**.

Janice (F) probably a compound of Jan and the name-ending -*ice*, coined by the US writer Paul Leicester Ford for his novel *Janice Meredith* (1899). The US singer Janis Joplin was a famous bearer of the name in its alternative form.

SHORT FORM: **Jan**.

ALTERNATIVE FORM: **Janis**.

Janie (F) a pet form of **Jane**, sometimes given as a name in its own right.

ALTERNATIVE FORM: **Janey**.

Janine (F) a feminine form of **John** ('God is gracious'), of French origin.

ALTERNATIVE FORMS: **Janeen, Jeanine, Jeannine**.

RELATED NAMES: *see list at* **Janet**.

Japheth (M) 'expansion'. A biblical name, borne by Noah's eldest son.

Jared [JARR-ud] (M) 'descent'. A biblical name, borne by the father of Enoch.

ALTERNATIVE FORMS: **Jarred, Jarrod, Jarod**.

Jarrett (M) from a surname that is another form of **Gerald** ('rule of the spear') or **Gerard** ('brave with a spear').

ALTERNATIVE FORM: **Jarrod**.

RELATED NAMES: **Garret, Ged, Gerry**.

Jarvis (M) from a surname that originated as another form of **Gervase** (possibly meaning 'spear servant'). Famous modern bearers include the British rock musician Jarvis Cocker.

Jasmine (F) from the flower name.

ALTERNATIVE FORM: **Jasmin**.

RELATED NAMES: **Yasmin, Jessamine**.

Jason (M) 'healer'. The name of the leader of the Argonauts in Greek mythology. Famous modern bearers include the Australian actor and singer Jason Donovan.

ALTERNATIVE FORM: **Jayson**.

Jasper (M) 'treasurer'. The name was borne by one of the three Magi (now known by the alternative form Caspar). Famous modern bearers include the British comedian Jasper Carrott (born Robert Davies) and the British fashion designer Jasper Conran.

RELATED NAME: **Caspar**.

Jaswinder (M) an Indian name meaning 'Indra of the thunderbolt'. (Indra is the god of the sky.)

Javan (M) 'wine'. A biblical name, borne by a grandson of Noah.

Javed (M) a Muslim name meaning 'eternal'.

Jay (M) an Indian name meaning 'victory'.
ALTERNATIVE FORM: **Jai**.
FEMININE FORM: **Jaya**.

Jay (M/F) a short form of any name beginning with this letter, sometimes given as a name in its own right. Famous male bearers include the wealthy title character of F. Scott Fitzgerald's novel *The Great Gatsby* (1925).
ALTERNATIVE FORM: **Jaye**.

Jaya (F) the feminine form of the Indian name **Jay**.

Jayant (M) 'victorious'. An Indian name borne by a son of Indra.
FEMININE FORM: **Jayanti**.

Jayanti (F) the feminine form of **Jayant**.

Jayden (M) a name of uncertain origin. It may be a blend of **Jay** and **Hayden**, or another spelling of a biblical name.
ALTERNATIVE FORM: **Jaden**.

Jaye (M/F) another spelling of **Jay**.

Jayne (F) another spelling of **Jane**, popularized in the 20th century by the US actress Jayne Mansfield and the British ice dancer Jayne Torvill.

Jayson (M) another spelling of **Jason**.

Jean (F) a feminine form of **John** ('God is gracious'). It was chiefly used in Scotland until the 20th century, when it was popularized by the English actress Jean Simmons.
RELATED NAMES: **Jeannie, Jeanette, Jane, Joan, Joanna, Joni, Janet, Janine, Juanita, Sian, Shana, Shauna, Siobhan, Shevaun, Sinead, Sheena, Shona**.

Jeanette (F) a feminine form of **John** ('God is gracious'), of French origin. Famous modern bearers include the British writer Jeanette Winterson.
SHORT FORMS: **Netta, Nettie**.
ALTERNATIVE FORMS: **Jeannette, Ginette**.
RELATED NAMES: *see list at* **Jean**.

Jeanine (F) another spelling of **Janine** ('God is gracious').
ALTERNATIVE FORMS: **Jeannine, Janeen**.

Jeannie (F) a pet form of **Jean**, sometimes given as a name in its own right.
ALTERNATIVE FORM: **Jeanie**.

Jed (M) a short form of **Jedidiah**, sometimes given as a name in its own right, or another spelling of **Ged**.

Jedidiah (M) 'beloved of God'. In the Bible, it is an alternative name given to Solomon at his birth.
RELATED NAME: **Jed**.

Jefferson (M) from the surname, meaning 'son of Jeffrey'. Famous bearers of the forename include the 19th-century US statesman Jefferson Davis, who was born during Thomas Jefferson's presidency.

Jeffrey (M) another spelling of Geoffrey.
SHORT FORM: Jeff.
ALTERNATIVE FORM: Jeffery.

Jem (M/F) a short form of James, Jeremy, Jeremiah, or Jemima, sometimes given to boys as a name in its own right.
ALTERNATIVE FORM: Jemmy.

Jemima (F) 'dove' or 'bright as day'. A biblical name, borne by Job's eldest daughter. Other famous bearers include Jemima Puddle-Duck, one of the animal characters created by Beatrix Potter for her children's stories.
SHORT FORMS: Jem, Jemmy, Jemma.

Jemma (F) another spelling of Gemma ('gem') or a short form of Jemima. The British actress Jemma Redgrave is a famous bearer of the name.

Jenna (F) a short form of Jennifer, usually given as a name in its own right. It was popularized by a character in the US soap opera *Dallas* (1978–91).
SHORT FORM: Jen.
RELATED NAME: Jenny.

Jennifer (F) another form of Guinevere ('fair and soft'). Famous

modern bearers include the British comedian Jennifer Saunders and the US actress Jennifer Aniston.
ALTERNATIVE FORMS: Jenifer, Geneva.
RELATED NAMES: Jenny, Jenna, Gaynor, Ginevra.

Jenny (F) a short form of Jennifer, sometimes given as a name in its own right.
SHORT FORM: Jen.
ALTERNATIVE FORMS: Jennie, Jenni, Jeni.
RELATED NAME: Jenna.

Jenson (M) from the surname, meaning 'son of John'. The British racing driver Jenson Button has popularized the name in recent times.

Jeremiah (M) 'appointed by God'. The name of a biblical prophet and the book of the Bible that contains his sayings.
RELATED NAMES: Jeremy, Jem, Jerry.

Jeremy (M) another form of Jeremiah. The usual form of the name in modern times, it is borne by the British broadcasters Jeremy Paxman and Jeremy Clarkson.
RELATED NAMES: Jerry, Jem.

Jermaine (M) another form of Germaine.

Jerome (M) 'holy name'. St Jerome translated the Bible into Latin in the late 4th century. The British writer

Jerome K. Jerome wrote the comic novel *Three Men in a Boat* (1889).
RELATED NAME: **Jerry**.

Jerry (M/F) a short form of **Jeremy**, **Jeremiah**, or **Jerome**, sometimes given as a name in its own right, or another spelling of **Gerry**. Famous bearers include the mouse in the 'Tom and Jerry' cartoons (male) and the US model and actress Jerry Hall (female).

Jess (F/M) a short form of **Jessica**, **Jessamine**, **Jessie**, or **Jesse**, sometimes given as a name in its own right.

Jessamine (F) another form of **Jasmine**, from an alternative name for the flower.
ALTERNATIVE FORMS: **Jessamyn**, **Jessamy**.
RELATED NAMES: **Yasmin, Jess, Jessie**.

Jesse [JESS-i] (M/F) 'gift'. A biblical name for boys, borne by King David's father. As a girls' name it is an alternative spelling of **Jessie**. Other famous male bearers include the 19th-century US outlaw Jesse James.
RELATED NAME: **Jess**.

Jessica (F) a name coined by Shakespeare for a Jewish character in *The Merchant of Venice*, possibly based on a biblical name meaning 'God beholds'. Famous modern bearers include the US actress Jessica Lange.

RELATED NAMES: **Jess, Jessie**.

Jessie (F/M) a short form of **Jessica** or **Jessamine**, sometimes given as a name in its own right, or an alternative spelling of **Jesse**.
RELATED NAME: **Jess**.

Jethro (M) 'excellence'. A biblical name, borne by the father-in-law of Moses. It was popularized in the 1970s by the rock group Jethro Tull, named after an English agricultural reformer of the 18th century.

Jevon (M) from the surname, meaning 'young'.

Jewel (F) from the word *jewel*, meaning 'gemstone'.

Jill (F) a short form of **Gillian** (which is a feminine form of **Julian**), sometimes given as a name in its own right. It features in the nursery rhyme 'Jack and Jill'.
ALTERNATIVE FORM: **Gill**.
RELATED NAMES: **Jilly, Juliana, Julia, Julie, Juliet**.

Jillian (F) another spelling of **Gillian**.

Jilly (F) a short form of **Gillian**, sometimes given as a name in its own right. The writer Jilly Cooper is a famous bearer.
ALTERNATIVE FORMS: **Jillie, Gilly**.
RELATED NAMES: **Jill, Juliana, Julia, Julie, Juliet**.

Jim (M) a short form of **James**, sometimes given as a name in its own right.

RELATED NAMES: **Jimmy, Jem, Jamie, Hamish, Seamus, Jacob, Jake, Jago.**

Jimmy (M) a short form of **James**, sometimes given as a name in its own right. The US rock guitarist Jimi Hendrix (whose full name was James) used an alternative spelling of the name.
ALTERNATIVE FORMS: **Jimmie, Jimi.**
RELATED NAMES: *see list at* **Jim.**

Jinan (M/F) an Arabic name meaning 'garden' or 'paradise'.

Jinny (F) another spelling of **Ginny**, which is short for **Virginia** or **Ginevra**.

Jitendra (M) an Indian name meaning 'conqueror of Indra (the god of the sky)'.
ALTERNATIVE FORM: **Jitender.**

Jo (F) a short form of various names beginning with these letters, especially **Joanna** or **Josephine**, sometimes given as a name in its own right. Famous bearers include Jo March, one of the heroines of Louisa M. Alcott's novel *Little Women* (1868), and the British comedian Jo Brand.

Jo (M) another spelling of **Joe**, or a short form of any name beginning with these letters.

Joachim [jo-a-kim] (M) 'established by God'. A biblical name, borne by a king of Judah. It is also said to have

been the name of the Virgin Mary's father.

Joan (F) a feminine form of **John**. Joan of Arc is the English name for the 15th-century French heroine Jeanne d'Arc. More recent famous bearers include the British actress Joan Collins.
RELATED NAMES: **Joanie, Joni, Joanna, Jane, Jean, Janet, Jeanette, Janine, Juanita, Sian, Shana, Shauna, Siobhan, Shevaun, Sinead, Sheena, Shona.**

Joanie (F) a pet form of **Joan**, sometimes given as a name in its own right, especially in its alternative form.
ALTERNATIVE FORM: **Joni.**

Joanna (F) a feminine form of **John**. Famous modern bearers include the British writer Joanna Trollope and the British actress Joanna Lumley.
SHORT FORM: **Jo.**
ALTERNATIVE FORMS: **Joanne, Johanna.**
RELATED NAMES: **Jo;** *see also list at* **Joan.**

Job [jobe] (M) 'persecuted'. In the Bible, Job is a man whose patience and faith is tested by a series of misfortunes sent by God.
RELATED NAME: **Joby.**

Joby (M) a pet form of **Job**, given as a name in its own right, or a blend of **Joe** and **Toby**.
ALTERNATIVE FORM: **Jobie.**

Jocasta (F) a name of uncertain origin, possibly meaning 'shining moon'. Jocasta was the mother and wife of Oedipus in Greek mythology.

Jocelyn [JOSS-a-lin, JOSS-lin] (F/M) from an Old French name of uncertain origin. It was originally a boys' name but is now more frequently given to girls.
ALTERNATIVE FORMS: **Joscelyn, Joslyn** (F), **Jocelyne** (F).
RELATED NAME: **Joss**.

Jock (M) a pet form of **John** ('God is gracious'), sometimes given as a name in its own right. It is chiefly associated with Scotland.
RELATED NAMES: **Jack, Jackie, Jake, Hank, Johnny, Ian, Sean, Shaun, Shane, Eoin, Evan, Sion, Ivan, Juan**.

Jody (F/M) possibly a pet form of **Jude, Judith,** or a name beginning with *Jo-*. The US actress Jodie Foster (whose real name is Alicia) is a famous female bearer.
ALTERNATIVE FORMS: **Jodie, Jodi**.

Joe (M) a short form of **Joseph**, sometimes given as a name in its own right. Joe Bloggs is a name used in the UK to refer to any member of the public.
ALTERNATIVE FORM: **Jo**.
FEMININE FORMS: **Jo, Joely**.
RELATED NAMES: **Joey, Jose, Yusuf**.

Joel (M) 'Jehovah is God'. The name is borne by a number of biblical characters, including a prophet whose sayings are to be found in the book that bears his name.
FEMININE FORMS: **Joelle, Joely**.
RELATED NAME: **Elijah**.

Joelle (F) a feminine form of **Joel**.
RELATED NAME: **Joely**.

Joely (F) a feminine form of **Joe** or **Joel**, another spelling of **Jolie**, or another form of **Jolene**. The British actress Joely Richardson is a well-known bearer of the name.
RELATED NAMES: **Jo, Joelle**.

Joey (M) a short form of **Joseph** or a pet form of **Joe**, sometimes given as a name in its own right. The name is borne by the title character of the musical *Pal Joey* and by one of the central characters of the US television series *Friends*.
RELATED NAMES: **Jose, Yusuf**.

Johanna (F) another form of **Joanna**, which is a feminine form of **John**. The 19th-century Swiss writer Johanna Spyri, author of *Heidi* (1880), was a famous bearer of the name in this form.

John (M) 'God is gracious'. A biblical name, borne by John the Baptist and one of Jesus Christ's apostles. Other famous bearers include a 12th-century king of England, numerous saints and popes, John Bull (the typical Englishman), and the 20th-century singer and songwriter John Lennon.

ALTERNATIVE FORM: **Jon.**

FEMININE FORMS: **Jane, Jean, Joan, Joanna, Joni, Janet, Jeanette, Janine, Juanita, Sian, Shana, Shauna, Siobhan, Shevaun, Sinead, Sheena, Shona.**

RELATED NAMES: **Johnny, Jack, Jackie, Jake, Jock, Hank, Ian, Sean, Shaun, Shane, Eoin, Evan, Sion, Ivan, Juan.**

Johnathan (M) a blend of **John** and **Jonathan**.

ALTERNATIVE FORM: **Johnathon.**

Johnny (M) a pet form of **John**, sometimes given as a name in its own right. The US actor Johnny Depp was born John Christopher Depp II in 1963.

ALTERNATIVE FORMS: **Johnnie, Jonny.**

RELATED NAMES: *see list at* **John.**

Jolene (F) a compound of **Jo** and the name-ending *-lene*. In Dolly Parton's song 'Jolene' it is borne by a woman who seems likely to take the singer's man.

ALTERNATIVE FORMS: **Joleen, Joely.**

Jolie [JO-lee, zho-LEE] (F) 'pretty'. It is the middle name of the US actress known as Angelina Jolie.

ALTERNATIVE FORM: **Joely.**

Jolyon [JOE-li-un] (M) another form of **Julian**. It is chiefly associated with a character in John Galsworthy's series of novels *The Forsyte Saga* (1922).

RELATED NAMES: **Jules, Julius.**

Jon (M) another spelling of **John** or a short form of **Jonathan**. Famous bearers include the British actor Jon Pertwee (whose real name was John) and the US actor Jon Voight (whose full name is Jonathan).

RELATED NAMES: **Jonny, Jonty.**

Jonah (M) 'dove'. The name of a biblical character who was swallowed by a large fish (or a whale) and survived.

ALTERNATIVE FORM: **Jonas.**

Jonathan (M) 'gift of God'. A biblical name borne by one of King Saul's sons, who was David's closest friend. Other famous bearers include the Irish writer Jonathan Swift, author of *Gulliver's Travels* (1726), and the British television presenter Jonathan Ross.

ALTERNATIVE FORM: **Jonathon.**

RELATED NAMES: **Jon, Jonny, Jonty.**

Joni (F) a pet form of **Joan**, sometimes given as a name in its own right. The Canadian singer Joni Mitchell was born Roberta Joan Anderson in 1943.

ALTERNATIVE FORM: **Joanie.**

RELATED NAMES: **Jane, Jean, Joanna, Janet, Jeanette, Janine, Juanita, Sian, Shana, Shauna, Siobhan, Shevaun, Sinead, Sheena, Shona.**

Jonny (M) another spelling of Johnny, a pet form of **Jon**, or a short form of **Jonathan**.

RELATED NAME: **Jonty.**

Jonquil (F) from the flower name.

Jonty (M) a short form of **Jonathan**, sometimes given as a name in its own right.
RELATED NAMES: **Jon, Jonny.**

Jools (M/F) another spelling of **Jules**, borne by the British musician and television presenter Jools Holland (whose full name is Julian).

Jordan (M/F) from the name of the river, which means 'flowing down'. It was originally given to children baptized in water that was said to come from there. Famous female bearers include the British topless model and celebrity whose real name is Katie Price.
SHORT FORM: **Jordy.**
ALTERNATIVE FORM: **Jordyn.**
RELATED NAME: **Judd.**

Jos (M/F) another form of **Joss**.

Joscelyn (M/F) another spelling of **Jocelyn**.

Jose [ho-ZAY, ho-SAY] (M) another form of **Joseph**, of Spanish origin. It occurs in the popular phrase 'No way, Jose!'
ALTERNATIVE FORM: **José.**
RELATED NAMES: **Joe, Joey, Yusuf.**

Joseph (M) 'God will add'. A name borne by three biblical characters: one of Jacob's sons (whose story is told in the musical *Joseph and the Amazing Technicolor Dreamcoat*), the husband of the Virgin Mary, and Joseph of Arimathea, who buried Jesus.
FEMININE FORMS: **Josephine, Josephina, Josie, Josette.**
RELATED NAMES: **Joe, Joey, Jose, Yusuf.**

Josephine (F) a feminine form of **Joseph**. The name was borne by the French empress Joséphine (whose real name was Marie Josèphe Rose), wife of Napoleon Bonaparte.
ALTERNATIVE FORM: **Josephina.**
RELATED NAMES: **Jo, Josie, Josette, Fifi.**

Josette (F) another form of **Josephine**, of French origin.
RELATED NAMES: **Jo, Josie, Fifi.**

Josh (M) a short form of **Joshua**, sometimes given as a name in its own right.

Joshua (M) 'God is salvation'. The name of a biblical character who led the Israelites into the Promised Land after the death of Moses. In the 18th century it was borne by the British artist Sir Joshua Reynolds.
RELATED NAME: **Josh.**

Josiah [jo-SYE-a, jo-ZYE-a] (M) 'God heals'. A biblical name, borne by a king of Judah. Other famous bearers include the 18th-century British potter Josiah Wedgwood.
ALTERNATIVE FORM: **Josias.**

Josie (F) a short form of **Josephine**,

sometimes given as a name in its own right.

RELATED NAMES: **Jo, Josette, Fifi.**

Joslyn (F) another spelling of the girls' name **Jocelyn**.

Joss (F/M) a short form of **Jocelyn** or of various names beginning with *Jos-*, sometimes given as a name in its own right. Famous bearers include the male British actor Joss Ackland (whose full name is Jocelyn) and the female British singer Joss Stone (whose full name is Joscelyn).

ALTERNATIVE FORM: **Jos.**

Joy (F) from the word *joy*, meaning 'happiness'. It is sometimes regarded as a short form of **Joyce.** The naturalist and writer Joy Adamson was a famous bearer of the name.

RELATED NAME: **Letitia.**

Joyce (F) a name meaning 'lord' that was given to boys in the Middle Ages but became a girls' name, associated with the word *joy*, in the 16th century. The comic entertainer Joyce Grenfell popularized the name in the mid-20th century.

RELATED NAME: **Joy.**

Juan [hwahn] (M) another form of **John** ('God is gracious'), of Spanish origin. The most famous bearer of the name is Don Juan, a legendary nobleman and seducer of women.

FEMININE FORM: **Juanita.**

RELATED NAMES: **Johnny, Jack,**

Jackie, Jake, Jock, Hank, Ian, Sean, Shaun, Shane, Eoin, Evan, Sion, Ivan.

Juanita [hwa-NEE-ta] (F) a feminine form of **John** ('God is gracious'), of Spanish origin.

RELATED NAMES: **Jane, Jean, Joan, Joanna, Joni, Janet, Jeanette, Janine, Sian, Shana, Shauna, Siobhan, Shevaun, Sinead, Sheena, Shona.**

Judah (M) 'praised'. A biblical name, borne by one of the sons of Jacob.

RELATED NAMES: **Judas, Jude.**

Judas (M) another form of **Judah.** Borne by Judas Iscariot, who betrayed Jesus, the name has become another word for a traitor.

RELATED NAME: **Jude.**

Judd (M) from the surname, which originated as a short form of **Jordan.**

Jude (F) a short form of **Judith** or **Judy**, sometimes given as a name in its own right.

Jude (M) a short form of **Judas**, given as a name in its own right. It is borne in the Bible by the author of one of the epistles. Other famous bearers include the title character of Thomas Hardy's novel *Jude the Obscure* (1895) and, more recently, the British actor Jude Law.

RELATED NAME: **Judah.**

Judith (F) 'Jewish woman'. A biblical name, borne by a Jewish heroine who saves the people of her town by

beheading the commander of an invading army. The name was popular with Jews and Christians alike in the 20th century.
RELATED NAMES: **Judy, Jude.**

Judy (F) a short form of **Judith**, sometimes given as a name in its own right. Famous bearers include the long-suffering wife in the traditional 'Punch and Judy' puppet show. The British actress Judi Dench (whose full name is Judith) uses an alternative spelling.
ALTERNATIVE FORMS: **Judi, Judie.**
RELATED NAMES: **Jude.**

Jules [joolz] (M/F) another form of **Julius**, of French origin, or a short form of various names beginning with *Jul-* (such as **Julian** or **Julie**), sometimes given as a name in its own right.
ALTERNATIVE FORM: **Jools.**

Julia (F) a feminine form of **Julius**. The name of a minor biblical character and a number of saints. Famous modern bearers include the US actress Julia Roberts (whose real name is Julie).
RELATED NAMES: **Julie, Juliet, Jules, Juliana, Gillian, Jill, Jilly.**

Julian (M) from the Roman name *Julianus*, which was another form of **Julius**. It is borne by two famous British musicians, the classical guitarist Julian Bream and the cellist Julian Lloyd Webber, as well as the comedian and television presenter

Julian Clary. In former times the name was also occasionally given to girls.
FEMININE FORMS: **Juliana, Gillian.**
RELATED NAMES: **Jules, Jolyon.**

Juliana (F) a feminine form of **Julian**.
RELATED NAMES: **Gillian, Jill, Jilly, Julia, Julie, Juliet.**

Julianna (F) a compound of **Julie** and **Anna**.
RELATED NAME: **Julianne.**

Julianne (F) a compound of **Julie** and **Anne**. The name is borne by the US actress Julianne Moore.
ALTERNATIVE FORMS: **Julieann, Julieanne.**
RELATED NAME: **Julianna.**

Julie (F) a feminine form of **Julius**, of French origin. It was popularized in the 1960s by the British actresses Julie Andrews (whose real name is Julia) and Julie Christie.
RELATED NAMES: **Julia, Juliet, Jules, Juliana, Gillian, Jill, Jilly.**

Juliet (F) a feminine form of **Julius**, of French or Italian origin. It is chiefly associated with the tragic heroine of Shakespeare's play *Romeo and Juliet*.
ALTERNATIVE FORM: **Juliette.**
RELATED NAMES: **Julia, Julie, Jules, Juliana, Gillian, Jill, Jilly.**

Julius (M) from a Roman family name, possibly meaning 'youthful'. It was borne by the Roman emperor Caius Julius Caesar in the 1st century BC.

FEMININE FORMS: **Julia, Julie, Juliet.**
RELATED NAMES: **Jules, Julian.**

June (F) from the name of the month. The British actress June Whitfield is a famous bearer.

Juniper (F) from the plant name.

Juno (F) the name of a Roman goddess, or another form of the Gaelic name **Una** ('lamb' or 'one'). The hard-working Irishwoman Juno Boyle in Sean O'Casey's play *Juno and the Paycock* (1924) is apparently so nicknamed because she was born and married in June.
RELATED NAME: **Unity.**

Justin (M) 'just, fair'. The name was borne by a number of early saints. More recent famous bearers include the US singer Justin Timberlake.
ALTERNATIVE FORM: **Justyn.**
FEMININE FORMS: **Justine, Justina.**
RELATED NAME: **Iestyn.**

Justine (F) a feminine form of **Justin**, borne by the title characters of novels by the Marquis de Sade (1791) and Lawrence Durrell (1957).
ALTERNATIVE FORM: **Justina.**

Jyoti (F) an Indian name meaning 'light'.

K

Kacey (M/F) another spelling of Casey.

Kaddy (F) short for **Katherine**.

Kade (M) another form of **Cade**.

Kaden (M) another form of **Caden**.

Kai [kye] (M) a name of uncertain origin. It may be another spelling of Cai (possibly meaning 'rejoice') or from a Hawaiian word meaning 'the sea'. In the alternative form Kay (sometimes pronounced as it is spelt) it was borne by one of the knights of King Arthur and by a character in Hans Christian Andersen's story 'The Snow Queen'. ALTERNATIVE FORMS: **Cai, Kay**.

Kailey (F) another spelling of **Kayleigh**.

Kaitlyn (F) another spelling of **Caitlin**, the Irish form of **Catherine** ('pure').

Kalie (F) another spelling of **Kayleigh**.

Kalpana (F) an Indian name meaning 'fantasy' or 'ornament'.

Kalyan (M) an Indian name meaning 'beautiful' or 'auspicious'. FEMININE FORM: **Kalyani**.

Kalyani (F) the feminine form of Kalyan.

Kamal (M) an Arabic name meaning 'perfection' or an Indian name meaning 'pink'. FEMININE FORM: **Kamala**.

Kamala (F) the feminine form of the Indian name **Kamal**. It is sometimes given to the goddess Lakshmi, wife of Vishnu.

Kamil (M) an Arabic name meaning 'perfect'.

Kane (M) 'little warrior'. Of Irish origin, it is generally preferred to the biblical name **Cain** with its murderous associations.

Kanta (F) an Indian name meaning 'beautiful'.

Kapil (M) an Indian name meaning 'reddish-brown'. Famous bearers include an ancient Hindu sage and, more recently, the Indian cricketer Kapil Dev.

Kara (F) another spelling of **Cara** ('beloved' or 'friend').

Karan (M) an Indian name meaning 'ear'.

Karen (F) another form of **Catherine** ('pure'), of Scandinavian origin. It became popular in the English-speaking world in the latter half of the 20th century.
ALTERNATIVE FORMS: **Karin, Karyn, Caryn**.
RELATED NAMES: **Kate, Katie, Kathy, Kathleen, Caitlin, Catriona, Katrina, Kitty, Kay, Katha, Katya, Karina**.

Karenza (F) a Cornish name meaning 'loving'.
ALTERNATIVE FORM: **Carenza**.

Karim (M) an Arabic name meaning 'noble, generous'. The name is borne by one of the central characters of Hanif Kureishi's novel *The Buddha of Suburbia* (1990).
FEMININE FORM: **Karima**.

Karima (F) the feminine form of **Karim**.

Karin (F) another spelling of **Karen**.

Karina (F) another spelling of **Carina** ('beloved') or another form of **Karen**.
RELATED NAMES: **Cara, Carita**: *see also list at* **Karen**.

Karis (F) another form of **Charis** ('grace'), borne by the daughter of the British rock singer Mick Jagger and Marsha Hunt.

Karl (M) another form of **Charles** ('free man'), of German origin. The best-known bearer of the name in this form is the 19th-century German political theorist Karl Marx.
ALTERNATIVE FORM: **Carl**.
RELATED NAMES: **Carlo, Carlos, Charlie, Chay, Chuck, Carol**.

Karyn (F) another spelling of **Karen**.

Kasey (M/F) another spelling of **Casey**.

Kat (F) short for **Katherine**.

Kate (F) a short form of **Catherine** ('pure'), often given as a name in its own right. Famous modern bearers include the British actress Kate Winslet.
ALTERNATIVE FORM: **Cate**.
RELATED NAMES: *see list at* **Karen**.

Katelyn (F) another spelling of **Caitlin** (the Irish form of **Catherine**), or a compound of **Kate** and **Lynn**.
RELATED NAMES: *see list at* **Karen**.

Katha (F) a short form of **Katherine**, sometimes given as a name in its own right.
RELATED NAMES: *see list at* **Karen**.

Katherine (F) another spelling of **Catherine** ('pure'). The alternative form borne by the US actress

Katharine Hepburn is less common.

SHORT FORMS: **Kath, Kat, Kaddy.**

ALTERNATIVE FORMS: **Katharine, Kathryn.**

RELATED NAMES: **Kathy, Kate, Katie, Kathleen, Caitlin, Catriona, Katrina, Karen, Kitty, Kay, Katha, Katya.**

Kathleen (F) another form of **Katherine**, of Irish origin. Famous modern bearers include the US actress Kathleen Turner.

SHORT FORM: **Kath.**

ALTERNATIVE FORM: **Cathleen.**

RELATED NAMES: *see list at* **Katie.**

Kathy (F) a short form of **Katherine**, sometimes given as a name in its own right.

ALTERNATIVE FORM: **Cathy.**

RELATED NAMES: *see list at* **Katie.**

Katie (F) a short form of **Catherine** ('pure'), often given as a name in its own right. It was popularized by the heroine of a series of children's books by Susan Coolidge, beginning with *What Katy Did* (1872).

ALTERNATIVE FORM: **Katy.**

RELATED NAMES: **Kate, Caitlin, Kitty, Kathy, Kathleen, Catriona, Katrina, Karen, Kay, Katha, Katya.**

Katrina (F) another form of **Catherine** ('pure'). It may be an alternative spelling of **Catriona**, which is of Scottish or Irish origin,

or a shortening of *Katerina* or *Katarina* (used in various European countries).

SHORT FORM: **Trina.**

ALTERNATIVE FORMS: **Catrina, Katrine.**

RELATED NAMES: *see list at* **Katie.**

Katya (F) another form of **Catherine** ('pure'), of Russian origin.

ALTERNATIVE FORM: **Katia.**

RELATED NAMES: *see list at* **Katie.**

Kay [kay] (F) a short form of any name beginning with this letter, especially **Katherine**, often given as a name in its own right. It was popularized in the mid-20th century by the British actress Kay Kendall.

ALTERNATIVE FORM: **Kaye.**

RELATED NAMES: *see list at* **Katie.**

Kay [kay, kye] (M) another form of **Kai.**

Kayla (F) another form of **Kayleigh** or a short form of **Michaela.**

Kayleigh (F) a compound of **Kay** and **Leigh.** Alternatively, it may come from an Irish name meaning 'slender'. The song 'Kayleigh' by the band Marillion, which was a top ten hit single in 1985, popularized the name in the UK.

ALTERNATIVE FORMS: **Kayley, Kaylee, Kaylie, Kailey, Kalie, Kayla.**

Kaylin (F) another form of **Keelin** ('slender and fair').

Keane [keen] (M) an English form of the Irish name **Cian** ('ancient').
ALTERNATIVE FORM: **Kean**.
RELATED NAMES: **Kian, Keenan**.

Keanu [kee-AH-noo] (M) 'cool breeze'. A Hawaiian name, recently popularized by the actor Keanu Reeves.

Keelan (M) another form of the Irish name **Caolan** ('slender'), spelt as it sounds.
ALTERNATIVE FORM: **Kelan**.

Keeley (F) 'slender'. A name of Irish origin, borne by the British actress Keeley Hawes.
ALTERNATIVE FORM: **Keely**.

Keelin (F) another form of an Irish name meaning 'slender and fair'.
ALTERNATIVE FORM: **Kaylin**.

Keenan (M) from the Irish surname, which comes from a pet form of the Irish name **Cian** ('ancient').
RELATED NAMES: **Keane, Kian**.

Keeva (F) another spelling of **Keva**.

Keir [keer] (M) from the Scottish surname. It was the middle name of the Scottish politician known as Keir Hardie.
FEMININE FORM: **Keira**.

Keira [KEER-a] (F) another spelling of **Kiera** ('little dark-haired one') or a feminine form of **Keir**. It has

recently been popularized by the British actress Keira Knightley.

Keiran [KEER-un] (M) another spelling of **Kieran** ('little dark-haired one'), probably influenced by **Keir**.
FEMININE FORM: **Keira**.

Keisha [KAY-sha, KEE-sha] (F) a name of uncertain origin, possibly from an African word meaning 'favourite daughter'.

Keith (M) from a Scottish surname and place name meaning 'wood'. It was a popular forename in the mid-20th century, when the British rock musician Keith Richards was born.

Kelan (M) another form of the Irish name **Caolan** ('slender'), spelt as it sounds.
ALTERNATIVE FORM: **Keelan**.

Kelly (F/M) 'bright-headed' or 'strife'. Another form of an Irish boys' name, which gave rise to the surname Kelly. As a forename it is now more frequently given to girls.
ALTERNATIVE FORMS: **Kelley, Kellie** (F).

Kelsey (F/M) from the surname, which may come from a boys' name meaning 'ship victory'. It is the middle name of the US actor known as Kelsey Grammer. In the UK it is more frequently given to girls.
ALTERNATIVE FORM: **Kelsie** (F).

Kelvin (M) from the name of a river in Scotland, made famous as the

title of the 19th-century Scottish scientist Lord Kelvin.
ALTERNATIVE FORM: **Kelvyn**.

Ken (M) a short form of various names beginning with these letters, especially **Kenneth**.

Kendall (M/F) from the surname, which comes from the place name Kendal or from a Welsh name meaning 'high image'.
ALTERNATIVE FORM: **Kendal**.

Kendra (F) the feminine form of Kendrick.

Kendrick (M) from the surname, which may mean 'high hill', 'son of Henry', or 'bold power'.
ALTERNATIVE FORM: **Kenrick**.
FEMININE FORM: **Kendra**.

Kenelm (M) 'bold protector'. The name was borne in the 9th century by St Kenelm of Mercia.

Kennard (M) from the surname, which may mean 'bold and strong' or 'royal guardian'.

Kennedy (M/F) 'ugly head'. Originally an English form of an Irish boys' name, it became a surname and was later readopted as a forename for either sex, probably in honour of the US president John Kennedy, assassinated in 1963.

Kenneth (M) 'handsome' or 'born of fire'. Of Scottish origin, the name is now used throughout the English-speaking world. Famous modern

bearers include the actor Kenneth Branagh, who was born in Northern Ireland.
SHORT FORM: **Ken**.
ALTERNATIVE FORMS: **Kennith, Kenith, Keneth**.
RELATED NAME: **Kenny**.

Kenny (M) a short form of **Kenneth**, sometimes given as a name in its own right. Famous bearers include the British disc jockey and comedian Kenny Everett (whose real name was Maurice Cole).

Kenrick (M) another form of Kendrick.

Kent (M) from the surname, which comes from the name of the English county, meaning 'border'.

Kenton (M) from a surname and place name. It is borne by the fictional character Kenton Archer, twin brother of Shula, in the BBC radio soap opera *The Archers*.

Kenzie (M/F) a short form of **Mackenzie** ('son of Kenneth'), sometimes given as a name in its own right.

Keren (F) a short form of the biblical name *Keren-Happuch*, meaning 'horn of kohl', borne by a daughter of Job.
ALTERNATIVE FORM: **Kerena**.

Kermit (M) from a Gaelic surname meaning 'son of Diarmuid'. It is now chiefly associated with the *Muppet Show* character Kermit the Frog.

Kerry (F/M) from the name of the Irish county. Famous modern bearers include the Australian media tycoon Kerry Packer (male) and the New Zealand writer Keri Hulme (female).
ALTERNATIVE FORMS: **Kerrie** (F), **Kerri** (F), **Keri** (F), **Ceri** (F).

Kester (M) another form of **Christopher** ('carrier of Christ'), of medieval Scottish origin.

Keturah (F) 'incense'. A biblical name, borne by Abraham's second wife.

Keva (F) another form of the Irish name **Caoimhe** (gentle, beautiful'), spelt as it sounds. It may be given as a feminine form of **Kevin**.
ALTERNATIVE FORM: **Keeva**.

Kevin (M) 'handsome' or 'gentle'. A name of Irish origin, borne by one of the patron saints of Dublin. More recent famous bearers include the US actors Kevin Kline and Kevin Costner, as well as the troublesome teenager created and played by the British comedian Harry Enfield.
SHORT FORM: **Kev**.
ALTERNATIVE FORM: **Kevan**.

Kezia [kez-EYE-a] (F) from the Hebrew name of a cinnamon-like spice (or the tree from which it is obtained), known in English as *cassia*. A biblical name, it was borne by a daughter of Job.
ALTERNATIVE FORM: **Keziah**.

RELATED NAMES: **Cassia, Kizzy**.

Khadija (F) 'premature child'. An Arabic name borne by Muhammad's first wife.
ALTERNATIVE FORM: **Khadiga**.

Khalid (M) 'eternal'. An Arabic name borne by a famous military commander of the 7th century.
FEMININE FORM: **Khalida**.

Khalida (F) the feminine form of **Khalid**.

Khalil (M) an Arabic name meaning 'close friend'.

Kian [KEE-un] (M) another spelling of the Irish name **Cian** ('ancient').
RELATED NAMES: **Keane, Keenan**.

Kiara [ki-AR-a] (F) another spelling of **Chiara**, which is a form of **Clara** ('bright, clear') of Italian origin.

Kiera [KEER-a] (F) another spelling of the Irish name **Ciara** ('little dark-haired one').
ALTERNATIVE FORMS: **Keira, Kira**.

Kieran [KEER-un] (M) another spelling of the Irish name **Ciaran** ('little dark-haired one').
ALTERNATIVE FORMS: **Kieron, Keiran**.
FEMININE FORM: **Kiera**.

Killian (M) 'of the church'. Of Irish origin, the name was borne by a 7th-century saint who became Bishop of Würzburg in Germany.

Kim (F/M) a short form of **Kimberley**

(or another name beginning with these letters), often given as a name in its own right. Famous bearers include the young hero of Rudyard Kipling's novel *Kim* (1901) and the US actress Kim Basinger.
ALTERNATIVE FORM: **Kym.**

Kimberley (F/M) from the name of the South African city, a diamond-mining centre that was besieged during the Boer War.
ALTERNATIVE FORM: **Kimberly.**
RELATED NAME: **Kim.**

King (M) from the royal title *king*, or a short form of **Kingsley**. Famous bearers include the US film director King Vidor.

Kingsley (M) from a surname and place name meaning 'king's wood'. The 20th-century British novelist Kingsley Amis was a famous bearer of the name.
RELATED NAME: **King.**

Kip (M) short for **Christopher**.

Kira [KEER-a] (F) another spelling of **Kyra** ('lady') or **Kiera**.

Kiran (M) an Indian name meaning 'ray of light'.

Kirk (M) from the surname, meaning 'person who lives near a church'. It was popularized in the 20th century by the US actor Kirk Douglas (born Issur Demsky).

Kirsten (F) another form of **Christian**, of Scandinavian origin.

Famous bearers include the 20th-century Norwegian opera singer Kirsten Flagstad.
ALTERNATIVE FORM: **Kirstin.**
RELATED NAMES: **Kirsty, Kristen, Christine, Christina, Christiana, Tiana, Christie, Christa, Tina.**

Kirsty (F) another form of **Christie** ('Christian'), of Scottish origin. It has been borne in recent times by the US actress Kirstie Alley and the British singer and songwriter Kirsty MacColl.
ALTERNATIVE FORM: **Kirstie.**
RELATED NAMES: *see list at* **Kirsten.**

Kishore (M) an Indian name meaning 'young horse'.
FEMININE FORM: **Kishori.**

Kishori (F) the feminine form of **Kishore**.

Kit (M/F) short for **Christopher** or **Kitty**.

Kitty (F) a short form of **Catherine** ('pure'), sometimes given as a name in its own right.
SHORT FORM: **Kit.**

Kizzy (F) a short form of **Kezia**, sometimes given as a name in its own right.
ALTERNATIVE FORM: **Kizzie.**

Kris (M/F) short for any name beginning with these letters or this sound, such as **Kristen** or **Christopher**. Famous bearers include the US actor and singer Kris

Kristofferson (whose full name is Kristoffer).

Krishna (M) 'black, dark'. An Indian name borne by an important Hindu god.

Kristen (F) another form of **Christian**. The name was borne (in its alternative form) by a character in the US soap opera *Dallas*, who famously shot JR in a cliffhanging episode of 1980.
SHORT FORM: **Kris**.
ALTERNATIVE FORM: **Kristin**.
RELATED NAMES: **Kirsten, Kirsty, Christine, Christina, Christiana, Tiana, Christie, Christa, Tina**.

Kristian (M/F) another spelling of **Christian**. This form of the name is used in several countries of mainland Europe.

Kristina (F) another spelling of **Christina** ('Christian'). This form of the name is used in several countries of mainland Europe.

Kristine (F) another spelling of **Christine** ('Christian').

Kristy (F) another spelling of **Christie** ('Christian').
ALTERNATIVE FORMS: **Kristie, Christy**.

Krystal (F) another spelling of **Crystal**.

Kumar (M) 'boy, son, prince'. An Indian name that is sometimes given to one of the sons of Shiva.

Kumari (F) 'girl, daughter, princess'. The feminine form of **Kumar**, sometimes given to the wife of Shiva.

Kurt (M) another form of **Conrad**, of German origin. Famous modern bearers include the US novelist Kurt Vonnegut and the US singer Kurt Cobain.
ALTERNATIVE FORM: **Curt**.

Kyla (F) a feminine form of **Kyle**, another form of **Kylie**, or a short form of **Michaela**.

Kyle (M/F) from the Scottish surname, which comes from the word *kyle* meaning 'narrow channel'. It is now chiefly used as a boys' name, popularized by the US actor Kyle MacLachlan.
FEMININE FORM: **Kyla**.

Kylie (F) an Australian name, possibly from an Aboriginal word meaning 'boomerang' or a blend of **Kyle** and **Kelly**. It is chiefly associated with the Australian actress and singer Kylie Minogue.
ALTERNATIVE FORM: **Kyla**.

Kym (F) another spelling of **Kim**.

Kyra [KEER-a] (F) 'lady'. A name of Greek origin.
ALTERNATIVE FORM: **Kira**.

L

Lacey (F) from the surname, which comes from a French place name. It may also be associated with the word *lace*.

Lachlan (M) 'land of the lochs' or 'warlike'. A Scottish name that is also found in Australia, New Zealand, and Canada.
SHORT FORMS: **Lachie, Lockie, Lochie**.

Ladislas (M) 'glorious rule'. The English form of a name used in various central or Eastern European countries.
ALTERNATIVE FORM: **Ladislaus**.

Laelia (F) another spelling of **Lelia** (possibly meaning 'cheerful').

Laetitia (F) another spelling of **Letitia** ('joy').

Laila (F) another form of the Arabic name **Layla** ('night').

Laine (F) short for **Lorraine**.

Lakshman (M) an Indian name meaning 'having lucky marks'.
ALTERNATIVE FORM: **Laxman**.

Lakshmi (F) 'lucky omen'. An Indian name borne by Vishnu's wife, the goddess of beauty, good fortune, and wealth.
ALTERNATIVE FORM: **Laxmi**.

Lal (M) an Indian name meaning 'darling' or 'king'.

Lalage [LAL-a-jee, LAL-a-ghee] (F) 'chattering'. A name of classical origin that occurs in the *Odes* of the Roman poet Horace.
SHORT FORM: **Lallie**.

Lalita (F) an Indian name meaning 'amorous'.

Lallie (F) short for **Eulalia** or **Lalage**.
ALTERNATIVE FORM: **Lally**.

Lambert (M) 'famous land'. The name was borne by a 7th-century saint and by Lambert Simnel, a young impostor who tried to claim the English throne in the late 15th century.

Lana (F) possibly a short form of a name ending with these letters. It was made famous in the mid-20th

century by the US actress Lana
Turner (whose real name was Julia).

Lance (M) a name of uncertain
origin, possibly meaning 'land' or
referring to the weapon. It is also a
short form of **Lancelot**. Famous
modern bearers include the British
actor and comedian Lance Percival.

Lancelot (M) a name of uncertain
origin. It was borne by the most
famous knight of King Arthur's
Round Table, who became Queen
Guinevere's lover.
SHORT FORM: **Lance**.

Lara (F) a short form of **Larissa**,
given as a name in its own right. Of
Russian origin, it is borne by one of
the central characters of Boris
Pasternak's novel *Doctor Zhivago*
(1957), filmed in 1965.

Laraine (F) another spelling of
Lorraine, or from the French phrase
la reine meaning 'the queen'.

Larissa (F) a Russian name of
uncertain origin. It is usually found
in the short form **Lara** in English-
speaking countries.

Lark (F) from the name of the
songbird.

Larry (M) a short form of **Laurence**,
sometimes given as a name in its
own right. Famous modern bearers
include the US actor Larry Hagman.

Latasha (F) a blend of **Latisha** and
Natasha.

Latif (M) an Arabic name meaning
'gentle, kind'.
FEMININE FORM: **Latifa**.

Latifa (F) the feminine form of **Latif**.
ALTERNATIVE FORM: **Latifah**.

Latisha (F) another form of **Letitia**.

Laura (F) 'laurel'. The 14th-century
Italian poet Petrarch wrote love
poems to a woman of this name.
More recent famous bearers include
the 20th-century British fashion
designer Laura Ashley.
ALTERNATIVE FORM: **Lora**.
RELATED NAMES: **Laurie, Lowri,
Loretta, Laurel, Daphne**.

Lauraine (F) a blend of **Laura** and
Lorraine.

Laureen (F) a blend of **Laura** and the
name-ending *-een*.
ALTERNATIVE FORMS: **Laurene,
Loreen, Lorine**.

Laurel (F) from the name of the tree.
ALTERNATIVE FORM: **Laurelle**.
RELATED NAMES: **Laurie, Laura,
Daphne**.

Lauren (F) a feminine form of
Laurence. It was made famous in
the mid-20th century by the US
actress Lauren Bacall (born Betty
Perske) and became very popular in
the 1990s.
ALTERNATIVE FORMS: **Lauryn,
Loren, Lorin**.

Laurence (M) 'person from
Laurentum in Italy'. Famous bearers

of the name include the 3rd-century martyr St Laurence (who was burned to death on a gridiron) and, more recently, the British actor Sir Laurence Olivier.
ALTERNATIVE FORMS: **Lawrence, Loren, Lorin.**
FEMININE FORM: **Lauren.**
RELATED NAMES: **Larry, Laurie.**

Laurie (M/F) a short form of **Laurence, Laura, Lauren,** or **Laurel,** sometimes given as a name in its own right. Famous bearers include the 20th-century British writer Laurie Lee (whose full name was Laurence).
ALTERNATIVE FORMS: **Lawrie, Lauri, Lori** (F).
RELATED NAMES: **Larry** (M), **Lowri** (F), **Loretta** (F).

Laurina (F) a blend of **Laura** and the name-ending *-ina*.

Lauryn (F) another form of **Lauren.**

Lavender (F) from the name of the sweet-smelling plant.

Laverna (F) the name of the Roman goddess of thieves.
SHORT FORM: **Verna.**

Laverne (F) a name of uncertain origin, possibly another form of **Laverna** or **Verna.**

Lavinia (F) the name of the wife of Aeneas in classical mythology.
SHORT FORMS: **Vinnie, Vinny.**

Lawrence (M) another spelling of

Laurence, borne by the 20th-century British writer Lawrence Durrell.

Lawrie (M/F) another spelling of **Laurie.**

Laxman (M) another form of **Lakshman.**

Laxmi (F) another form of **Lakshmi.**

Layla (F) an Arabic name meaning 'night', borne in literature by the beloved of a 7th-century poet. It was popularized in the English-speaking world in the early 1970s by Eric Clapton's love song 'Layla'.
ALTERNATIVE FORMS: **Leila, Laila, Leyla, Lela, Lila, Lyla.**

Layton (M) another spelling of **Leighton.**

Lazarus (M) another form of **Eleazar** ('God is my help'). It is borne by two biblical characters: a sick man raised from the dead by Jesus and a beggar covered with sores.

Lea [LEE-a, lee] (F) another spelling of **Leah** or **Leigh.**

Leah [LEE-a] (F) 'languid, weary'. A biblical name borne by Rachel's elder sister, who became Jacob's first wife.
ALTERNATIVE FORMS: **Lea, Lia.**

Leander [lee-AND-a] (M) 'lion man'. The name of a character in Greek mythology and a 6th-century Spanish saint.

Leanne [lee-AN] (F) a blend of **Leigh**

and **Anne**, or another spelling of **Liane**.
ALTERNATIVE FORM: **Leanna**.

Leda [LEE-da] (F) the name of a character in Greek mythology. Zeus made love to Leda in the form of a swan and she gave birth to two sets of twins.

Lee (M/F) from a surname and place name meaning 'wood', 'clearing', or 'meadow'. This is the usual spelling of the boys' name in the UK. Famous modern bearers include the US actor Lee Marvin (male) and the US actress Lee Remick (female).
ALTERNATIVE FORMS: **Leigh, Lea** (F).

Leela (F) an Indian name meaning 'play'.
ALTERNATIVE FORM: **Lila**.

Leigh [lee] (F/M) another form of **Lee**. This is the usual spelling of the girls' name in the UK.
ALTERNATIVE FORM: **Lea** (F).

Leighton [LAY-t'n] (M) from a surname and place name meaning 'herb garden'.
ALTERNATIVE FORM: **Layton**.

Leila [LAY-la, LEE-la, LYE-la] (F) another form of the Arabic name **Layla** ('night'). Lord Byron used this form of the name in two of his poetic works.

Lelia (F) from a Roman family name, possibly meaning 'cheerful'.
ALTERNATIVE FORM: **Laelia**.

Lemuel (M) a biblical name, possibly meaning 'devoted to God'. It is the forename of the title character of Jonathan Swift's novel *Gulliver's Travels* (1726).

Len (M) short for **Leonard, Lionel, Lennox, Lennon**, or **Lenny**.

Lena (F) a short form of any name ending with these letters, such as **Helena**, given as a name in its own right.

Lennard (M) another spelling of **Leonard**.

Lennon (M) from the surname, which comes from an Irish name meaning 'sweetheart'. The surname is chiefly associated with the British singer and songwriter John Lennon.
SHORT FORM: **Len**.

Lennox (M) from a Scottish surname and place name. The British boxer Lennox Lewis is a famous bearer of the name.
SHORT FORM: **Len**.

Lenny (M) a short form of **Leonard** (or various names beginning with *Len-*), sometimes given as a name in its own right. The British comedian Lenny Henry was born Lenworth George Henry in 1958.
SHORT FORM: **Len**.
ALTERNATIVE FORM: **Lennie**.

Lenora (F) probably another form of **Eleanor**. The heroine of an 18th-century ballad, whose story was

retold by Edgar Allan Poe (among others), was called Lenore.
ALTERNATIVE FORM: **Lenore**.
RELATED NAMES: **Eleonora, Leonora, Nora, Ellie, Ella, Nell**.

Leo (M) 'lion'. The name was borne by a number of saints and popes. It was popularized in the UK in 2000 when the prime minister Tony Blair chose it for his son.
FEMININE FORMS: **Leona, Leonie**.
RELATED NAMES: **Leon, Lionel**.

Leon (M) another form of **Leo**. The British politician Leon Brittan is a famous bearer of the name.
RELATED NAME: **Lionel**.

Leona (F) a feminine form of **Leo**.
RELATED NAME: **Leonie**.

Leonard [LEN-ud] (M) 'brave as a lion'. Famous modern bearers include the US actor Leonard Nimoy and the British actor Leonard Rossiter.
SHORT FORM: **Len**.
ALTERNATIVE FORM: **Lennard**.
RELATED NAMES: **Leonardo, Lenny**.

Leonardo [lee-a-NAR-doe] (M) another form of **Leonard**, of Italian or Spanish origin. In the English-speaking world the name is chiefly associated with the Renaissance artist Leonardo da Vinci and (since the late 20th century) the US actor Leonardo DiCaprio.

Leonie [lee-OH-nee] (F) a feminine form of **Leo**, of French origin.

RELATED NAME: **Leona**.

Leonora (F) another form of Eleanor, of Italian origin. The name is borne by the heroine of Verdi's opera *Il Trovatore* (1853).
RELATED NAMES: **Eleonora, Lenora, Nora, Ellie, Ella, Nell**.

Leopold (M) 'bold people'. Famous royal bearers include three kings of Belgium and a son of Queen Victoria. Leopold Bloom is one of the central characters of James Joyce's novel *Ulysses* (1922).

Leroy (M) 'the king'. It was originally given as a nickname.
ALTERNATIVE FORMS: **Elroy, Delroy**.

Lesley (F) the usual spelling of **Leslie** as a girls' name. The British singer Lesley Garrett is a famous bearer of the name in this form.

Leslie (M/F) from a Scottish surname and place name, possibly meaning 'garden of hollies' or 'garden by the pool'. Famous bearers of the name in this form include the British actor Leslie Phillips (male) and the British actress Leslie Ash (female).
SHORT FORM: **Les**.
ALTERNATIVE FORM: **Lesley** (F).

Lester (M) from the surname, which comes from the place name Leicester. The British jockey Lester Piggott is a well-known bearer.
SHORT FORM: **Les**.

Letitia (F) 'joy'. The name is borne by the British actress Letitia Dean,

whose best-known role is Sharon Watts in the soap opera *EastEnders*, and by a character in the sitcom *The Vicar of Dibley*, played by Liz Smith.
SHORT FORMS: **Letty, Lettie, Tish.**
ALTERNATIVE FORMS: **Laetitia, Leticia, Latisha.**
RELATED NAMES: **Lettice, Tisha, Joy.**

Lettice (F) another form of **Letitia**. The British dramatist Peter Shaffer gave the name to one of the title characters of his play *Lettice and Lovage* (1987).
SHORT FORMS: **Letty, Lettie.**

Levi (M) 'attached'. A biblical name, borne by one of the sons of Jacob and Leah. In modern times it is chiefly associated with the US clothing manufacturer Levi Strauss and the jeans that his company first produced in the late 19th century.

Lewie (M) a short form of **Lewis** or another spelling of **Louis**.

Lewin (M) from the surname, meaning 'dear friend'.

Lewis [LOO-is] (M) an English form of **Louis** 'famous warrior' or **Llewellyn** (possibly meaning 'lion-like'). Its best-known bearer is the 19th-century writer Lewis Carroll, whose real name was Charles Lutwidge Dodson. The short form Lew was used by the 20th-century impresario Lew Grade (born Louis Winogradsky).
SHORT FORMS: **Lew, Lewie.**

RELATED NAMES: **Luis, Ludovic, Aloysius, Clovis.**

Lex (M) a short form of **Alexander** ('defender of men') or **Alexis** ('defender'), sometimes given as a name in its own right. A famous fictional bearer is the evil Lex Luthor, arch-enemy of Superman.
RELATED NAMES: **Alex, Alec, Lexie, Xander, Alistair, Sasha.**

Lexie (M/F) a short form of **Alexander** ('defender of men'), its feminine form **Alexandra**, or **Alexis** ('defender'), sometimes given as a name in its own right.
ALTERNATIVE FORMS: **Lexy, Lexine** (F).
RELATED NAMES: **Alex, Sasha, Alec** (M), **Lex** (M), **Xander** (M), **Alistair** (M), **Sandy** (F), **Sandra** (F), **Zandra** (F).

Leyla (F) another form of the Arabic name **Layla** ('night').

Lia [LEE-a] (F) another spelling of **Leah** ('languid, weary') or a short form of a name ending with these letters.

Liam [LEE-um] (M) a short form of **William** ('resolute protector'), of Irish origin, often given as a name in its own right. It has recently been popularized by the British actor Liam Neeson and the British rock singer Liam Gallagher.
RELATED NAMES: **Will, Billy, Gwilym, Wilkie.**

Liane [lee-AN] (F) a short form of a name ending with these letters, given in its own right, or another spelling of **Leanne**.
ALTERNATIVE FORMS: **Lianne, Liana**.

Libby (F) a short form of **Elizabeth** ('oath of God'), sometimes given as a name in its own right. Famous modern bearers include the radio presenter and journalist Libby Purves.
RELATED NAMES: **Liza, Lisa, Lizzie, Lizbeth, Lili, Lisette, Eliza, Elsa, Elsie, Elspeth, Elise, Eilis, Beth, Bethan, Betty, Betsy, Bess, Babette, Buffy, Isabel**.

Liddy (F) short for **Lydia**.

Lil (F) short for **Lilian** or **Lily**.

Lila [LEE-la, LYE-la] (F) another form of the Arabic name **Layla** ('night') or the Indian name **Leela** ('play'). It is also a short form of **Delilah**.

Lili (F) a short form of **Elizabeth** or another spelling of **Lily**.
ALTERNATIVE FORMS: **Lilian, Lilli, Lillie**.
RELATED NAMES: *see list at* **Libby**.

Lilian (F) another form of **Lili**. The name was popularized in the early 20th century by the US actress Lillian Gish.
SHORT FORM: **Lil**.
ALTERNATIVE FORM: **Lillian**.

Lilith (F) a biblical name meaning 'demon of the night'. It is now

sometimes regarded as another form of **Lily**.

Lily (F) from the name of the flower, which is a symbol of purity. It has recently been popularized by the British singer Lily Allen.
SHORT FORM: **Lil**.
ALTERNATIVE FORMS: **Lilly, Lili, Lilli, Lillie**.
RELATED NAMES: **Susannah, Shanna, Susan, Suzanne, Suzette, Susie**.

Lin (F) short for various names beginning with these letters, especially **Linda**, or another spelling of **Lynn**.

Lincoln (M) from a surname and place name meaning 'lake colony'.

Linda (F) 'pretty' or 'tender', or a short form of **Belinda** given as a name in its own right. It was popular in the mid-20th century, when the US singer Linda Ronstadt and the US photographer Linda Eastman (who later became Linda McCartney) were born.
SHORT FORM: **Lin**.
ALTERNATIVE FORM: **Lynda**.
RELATED NAMES: **Lindy, Lynn**.

Linden (F/M) from the name of the lime tree.
ALTERNATIVE FORM: **Lynden**.

Lindon (M) another spelling of **Lyndon**.

Lindsay [LIN-zi] (F/M) from the surname, which comes from the place name Lindsey. Famous modern bearers include the British film director Lindsay Anderson (male) and the British actress Lindsay Duncan (female).

ALTERNATIVE FORMS: **Lindsey, Lyndsay, Lynsey** (F), **Linsey** (F), **Linzi** (F).

Lindy (F) a short form of any name containing the letters-*lind*-, such as **Belinda, Linda**, or **Rosalind**, sometimes given as a name in its own right.

Linford (M) from a surname and place name meaning 'flax ford' or 'lime-tree ford'. The British athlete Linford Christie is a famous bearer of the name.

Linnet (F) another form of **Lynette**, influenced by the name of the songbird.

Linsey (F) another spelling of **Lindsay**.

Linton (M) from a surname and place name with various meanings.
ALTERNATIVE FORM: **Lynton**.

Linus [LINE-us] (M) the name of a musician in Greek mythology. It also occurs in the Bible, but is probably most familiar as the name of a little boy with a security blanket in Charles Schulz's cartoon strip *Peanuts*.

Linzi (F) another spelling of **Lindsay**.

Lionel (M) another form of **Leo** ('lion'), influenced by the English word *lion*. Famous modern bearers

include the British dancer and television presenter Lionel Blair.
SHORT FORM: **Len**.
RELATED NAME: **Leon**.

Lisa [LEE-sa, LEE-za] (F) a short form of **Elizabeth** ('oath of God'), often given as a name in its own right. The British singer Lisa Stansfield is a famous bearer.
RELATED NAMES: **Liza, Eliza, Elise, Lisette, Lizzie, Libby, Lizbeth, Lili, Elsa, Elsie, Elspeth, Eilis, Beth, Bethan, Betty, Betsy, Bess, Babette, Buffy, Isabel**.

Lisbeth (F) another spelling of **Lizbeth**.

Lisette (F) another form of **Elizabeth** ('oath of God'), of French origin.
ALTERNATIVE FORM: **Lysette**.
RELATED NAMES: *see list at* **Lisa**.

Lissa (F) short for **Melissa** or **Alissa**.

Liv (F) short for **Olivia** or **Livia**. It is also a Scandinavian name meaning 'protection' or 'life', made famous by the Norwegian actress Liv Ullmann.

Livia (F) from a Roman family name, possibly meaning 'bluish'. The name was borne by the ambitious and influential wife of the Roman emperor Augustus. It is sometimes regarded as a short form of **Olivia**.
SHORT FORMS: **Liv, Livvy**.

Livvy (F) short for **Olivia** or **Livia**.
ALTERNATIVE FORMS: **Livy, Livi**.

Liz (F) short for **Elizabeth**.

Liza [LIE-za, LEE-za] (F) a short form of **Elizabeth** ('oath of God'), often given as a name in its own right. The US actress Liza Minnelli is a famous bearer of the name.

RELATED NAMES: **Lisa, Eliza, Lizbeth, Lizzie, Lisette, Elise, Elsa, Elsie, Elspeth, Eilis, Libby, Lili, Beth, Bethan, Betty, Betsy, Bess, Babette, Buffy, Isabel.**

Lizbeth (F) a short form of **Elizabeth** ('oath of God'), sometimes given as a name in its own right.

ALTERNATIVE FORMS: **Lisbeth, Lizbet.**

RELATED NAMES: *see list at* **Liza.**

Lizzie (F) a short form of **Elizabeth**, sometimes given as a name in its own right. Lizzie Dripping, a fictional character created by the children's writer Helen Cresswell in the 1970s, is a young girl with a vivid imagination.

ALTERNATIVE FORM: **Lizzy.**

RELATED NAMES: *see list at* **Liza.**

Llewellyn (M) a Welsh name, possibly meaning 'lion-like'. In its original form *Llywelyn* it was borne by two Welsh princes of the 13th century.

SHORT FORM: **Llew.**

ALTERNATIVE FORM: **Llewelyn.**

RELATED NAMES: **Lewis, Lyn.**

Lloyd (M) from the Welsh surname, which means 'grey-haired'. Famous bearers of the forename include the 20th-century US actor Lloyd Bridges.

RELATED NAME: **Floyd.**

Lockie (M) short for **Lachlan.**

ALTERNATIVE FORM: **Lochie.**

Logan (M) from a Scottish surname and place name meaning 'little hollow'. The US-born writer Logan Pearsall Smith was a famous bearer of the name.

Lois [LOE-iss] (F) a biblical name, possibly meaning 'good' or 'better'. The name is borne by the fictional journalist Lois Lane, colleague of Clark Kent (alias Superman).

Lola (F) a short form of **Dolores** (or various other names containing the letters-*lo*-), sometimes given as a name in its own right. In the song 'Lola', recorded by the Kinks in 1970, the name is borne by a transvestite.

RELATED NAME: **Lolita.**

Lolita (F) a short form of **Dolores** (or various other names containing the letters -*lo*-), sometimes given as a name in its own right. It is chiefly associated with the title character of Vladimir Nabokov's novel *Lolita* (1955), a sexually attractive and precocious 12-year-old girl.

RELATED NAME: **Lola.**

Lora (F) another spelling of **Laura.**

Loraine (F) another spelling of **Lorraine.**

Lorcan (M) 'fierce'. An Irish name, borne by a 12th-century saint and archbishop of Dublin.

Loreen (F) another spelling of Laureen.

Loren (M/F) another form of Laurence or Lauren.

Loretta (F) another form of Laura ('laurel'), of Italian origin. The name is borne by the US singer Loretta Lynn.
RELATED NAMES: Laurie, Lowri, Laurel.

Lori (F) another spelling of Laurie or a short form of Lorraine.

Lorin (M/F) another form of Laurence or Lauren.
ALTERNATIVE FORM: Lorine (F).

Lorine (F) another spelling of Laureen or another form of Lorin.

Lorna (F) a name coined by the writer R. D. Blackmore for the title character of his novel *Lorna Doone* (1869).

Lorne (M) probably from the Scottish place name Lorn (or Lorne). The Canadian actor Lorne Greene popularized the name in the 1960s, when he starred in the US television series *Bonanza*.
ALTERNATIVE FORM: Lorn.

Lorraine (F) from the name of the French province. Famous bearers include the British actress Lorraine Chase.
SHORT FORMS: Lori, Lorri, Laine, Raine.

ALTERNATIVE FORMS: Loraine, Laraine, Lorrayne, Lorrain.

Lottie (F) a short form of Charlotte, which is a feminine form of Charles ('free man'), sometimes given as a name in its own right.
ALTERNATIVE FORM: Lotty.
RELATED NAMES: Charlie, Charlene, Carlotta, Carla, Carly, Carol, Caroline, Carolina, Carrie.

Louella (F) a compound of Lou (short for Louise) and Ella (or the name-ending -*ella*). The 20th-century US gossip columnist Louella Parsons was a famous bearer of the name.

Louis [LOO-ee] (M) 'famous warrior'. Of French origin, the name was borne by sixteen kings of France between the 8th and 18th centuries. Other famous bearers include the US jazz musician Louis Armstrong.
SHORT FORM: Lou.
ALTERNATIVE FORMS: Louie, Lewie.
FEMININE FORMS: Louise, Louisa, Luisa, Lulu, Aloysia.
RELATED NAMES: Lewis, Luis, Ludovic, Aloysius, Clovis.

Louise (F) a feminine form of Louis. The alternative form Louisa was more popular in the 19th century, when it was borne by the US writer Louisa M. Alcott, but Louise became fashionable again in the 20th century.
SHORT FORM: Lou.
ALTERNATIVE FORM: Louisa.

RELATED NAMES: **Luisa, Lulu, Aloysia.**

Lourdes (F) from the name of the place of pilgrimage in France, where St Bernadette had visions of the Virgin Mary. The US singer Madonna gave the name to her daughter, born in 1996.

Lowri (F) a Welsh form of **Laura** ('laurel'), made famous in the late 20th century by the television presenter Lowri Turner.
RELATED NAMES: **Laurie, Laurel, Daphne.**

Luca (M) another form of **Luke** or **Lucas**, of Italian origin.

Lucas (M) another form of **Luke**. It was more frequently found as a surname in the UK until the early 21st century, when it became increasingly popular as a forename.
RELATED NAMES: **Luke, Luca.**

Lucia (F) a feminine form of **Lucius**. The name was borne by St Lucia of Syracuse, martyred in the early 4th century.
RELATED NAMES: **Lucy, Lucille, Lulu.**

Lucian (M) another form of **Lucius**. Famous bearers include St Lucian, martyred in the late 3rd century, and the British painter Lucian Freud, born in Germany in 1922.

Lucie (F) another spelling of **Lucy**, of French origin.

Lucille (F) a feminine form of

Lucius, of French origin. The 20th-century US comic actress Lucille Ball was a famous bearer of the name.
RELATED NAMES: **Lucy, Lucia, Lulu.**

Lucinda (F) a blend of **Lucy** and the name-ending -*inda*. The Australian writer Peter Carey gave the name to one of the central characters of his novel *Oscar and Lucinda* (1988).
RELATED NAME: **Cindy.**

Lucius (M) 'light'. A Roman name that occurs in the Bible and in some of Shakespeare's plays.
FEMININE FORMS: **Lucia, Lucy, Lucille.**
RELATED NAMES: **Lucian.**

Lucretia (F) from a Roman family name of uncertain origin. It is chiefly associated with the Renaissance noblewoman Lucrezia Borgia, a well-respected patron of the arts who is rumoured to have been guilty of murder and incest.
ALTERNATIVE FORMS: **Lucrezia, Lucrece.**

Lucy (F) a feminine form of **Lucius**. It is also used as a short form of **Lucille** or **Lucinda**. Famous bearers include the zany housewife played by Lucille Ball in US sitcoms of the 1950s and 1960s such as *I Love Lucy* and *The Lucy Show*.
ALTERNATIVE FORM: **Lucie.**
RELATED NAMES: **Lucia, Lulu.**

Ludovic (M) another form of **Louis**

('famous warrior'). In Scotland it is also associated with a Gaelic name meaning 'devotee of the Lord'. Its best-known bearer is the British writer and broadcaster Ludovic Kennedy.

SHORT FORM: **Ludo**.
RELATED NAMES: **Lewis, Luis, Aloysius, Clovis**.

Luis (M) another form of **Louis** ('famous warrior'), of Spanish origin.

RELATED NAMES: **Lewis, Ludovic, Aloysius, Clovis**.

Luisa (F) a feminine form of **Louis** ('famous warrior'), of Spanish origin.

RELATED NAMES: **Louisa, Louise, Lulu, Aloysia**.

Luke (M) 'person from Lucania in Italy'. In the Bible, St Luke is the author of the third gospel, a doctor and a friend of St Paul. The name was popularized in the late 20th century by the fictional character Luke Skywalker in the *Star Wars* films.

RELATED NAMES: **Luca, Lucas**.

Lulu (F) a pet form of **Lucy** or **Louise**, sometimes given as a name in its own right. It is most familiar in modern times as the stage name of the Scottish singer Lulu, who was born Marie Lawrie in 1948.

RELATED NAMES: **Lucia, Lucille, Louisa, Luisa, Aloysia**.

Luther (M) 'warrior of the people'. As a German surname it was borne by the 16th-century religious reformer Martin Luther. Famous bearers of the forename include the US civil rights leader Martin Luther King, who was assassinated in 1968.

Lydia (F) 'woman from Lydia (an ancient region of Turkey)'. The name occurs in the Bible, borne by an early Christian convert. Famous fictional bearers include the title character of H. E. Bates's novel *Love for Lydia* (1952).

SHORT FORM: **Liddy**.

Lyla (F) another form of the Arabic name **Layla** ('night'). It is the title of a song by the band Oasis, which was a top ten hit single in 2005.

Lyle (M) from the Scottish surname, meaning 'of the island'.

Lyn (M/F) a short form of the Welsh boys' name **Llewellyn** (possibly meaning 'lion-like'), sometimes given as a name in its own right, or another spelling of the girls' name **Lynn**.

ALTERNATIVE FORM: **Lynn**.
RELATED NAMES: **Lewis** (M), **Lynette** (F).

Lynda (F) another spelling of **Linda**, borne by the British television writer Lynda La Plante.

Lynden (F/M) another spelling of **Linden**.

Lyndon (M) from a surname and

place name meaning 'lime-tree hill'. It was popularized in the 20th century by the US president Lyndon B. Johnson.

ALTERNATIVE FORM: **Lindon.**

Lyndsay (F/M) another spelling of **Lindsay.**

Lynette (F) another form of **Lynn** or of the Welsh name **Eluned** ('idol, image').

ALTERNATIVE FORMS: **Lynnette, Linnet.**

Lynn (F/M) a short form of **Linda** or **Lynette,** or of a name ending with -*lyn* or -*line*, given as a name in its own right. It was popularized in the 20th century by the British actress Lynn Fontanne (whose real name was Lillie). It is also an alternative spelling of the boys' name **Lyn.**

ALTERNATIVE FORMS: **Lynne, Lyn, Lin.**

RELATED NAME: **Lynette.**

Lynsey (F) another spelling of **Lindsay,** borne by the British singer and songwriter Lynsey de Paul.

Lynton (M) another form of **Linton.**

Lyra (F) 'lyre'. The name is borne by the young heroine of Philip Pullman's trilogy *His Dark Materials* (1995–2000).

Lysette (F) another spelling of **Lisette.**

Lyssa (F) short for **Alyssa.**

Lytton (M) from a surname and place name 'loud torrent'. It was the middle name of the British biographer known as Lytton Strachey.

M

Mab (F) short for **Mabel**. As the name of the queen of the fairies it is another form of **Maeve**.

Mabel (F) 'lovely, lovable'. It comes from the same origin as the rarer name **Amabel**, and used to rhyme with *rabble* rather than *table*. Famous bearers include Mabel Lucie Attwell, a 20th-century writer and illustrator of children's books.
SHORT FORM: **Mab**.
ALTERNATIVE FORMS: **Mabelle, Maybelle**.

Macey (F/M) from the surname, which comes from a French place name.
ALTERNATIVE FORM: **Macy**.

Mackenzie (M/F) from the surname, meaning 'son of Kenneth'. It is the middle name of the British actor known as Mackenzie Crook. The children's writer J. K. Rowling gave the name to her second daughter, born in 2005.
RELATED NAME: **Kenzie**.

Maddison (F/M) another spelling of Madison.

Maddy (F) a short form of **Madeleine, Madison,** or **Madonna**, sometimes given as a name in its own right. Famous bearers include the British singer Maddy Prior.
ALTERNATIVE FORM: **Maddie**.

Madeleine [MAD-lin, MAD-a-lin] (F) another form of **Magdalene**, of French origin. It is the usual form of the name in English-speaking countries in modern times.
ALTERNATIVE FORMS: **Madeline, Madelaine, Madelyn**.
RELATED NAMES: **Maddy, Madge**.

Madge (F) a short form of **Margaret** or **Madeleine**, given as a name in its own right. It is also used as a nickname for the US singer Madonna, although it is not normally associated with that name.
RELATED NAMES: **Maggie, Marguerite, Margarita, Rita, Margot, Margaux, Margery, Marjorie, Meg, Megan, Peggy, Greta, Gretchen, Gretel, Mairead, Maisie, May, Molly, Pearl, Maddy, Magdalene**.

Madhav (M) 'of the spring'. An Indian name sometimes given to the god Krishna.

Madhur (F) 'sweet'. An Indian name made famous in the latter half of the 20th century by the actress and cookery writer Madhur Jaffrey.

Madison (F/M) from the surname, meaning 'son of Maud', borne by the US president after whom Madison Square and Madison Avenue in New York were named. It was particularly popular as a girls' name in the early 21st century.
ALTERNATIVE FORM: **Maddison**.
RELATED NAME: **Maddy** (F).

Madonna (F) 'my lady'. An Italian title of the Virgin Mary. In modern times it is chiefly associated with the US singer of this name, born Madonna Ciccone in 1958.
SHORT FORM: **Maddy**.
RELATED NAMES: **Mary, Dolores, Mercedes, Concepta, Mona**.

Mae (F) another spelling of **May**, used by the US film star Mae West (whose full name was Mary).

Maeve [mayv] (F) another form of an Irish name meaning 'intoxicating', borne by a legendary queen of Connacht. The Irish writer Maeve Binchy is a famous bearer.
ALTERNATIVE FORM: **Mave**.
RELATED NAME: **Mab**.

Mag (F) short for **Margaret** or **Maggie**.

ALTERNATIVE FORM: **Mags**.

Magdalene [MAG-da-lin, MAUD-lin] (F) from the name given to the biblical character Mary Magdalene, meaning 'of Magdala (a village in Israel)', to distinguish her from other women called Mary who are mentioned in the Bible.
ALTERNATIVE FORMS: **Magdalen, Magdalena**.
RELATED NAMES: **Madeleine, Maddy, Madge**.

Maggie (F) a short form of **Margaret**, sometimes given as a name in its own right.
SHORT FORMS: **Mag, Mags**.
RELATED NAMES: **Marguerite, Margarita, Rita, Margot, Margaux, Margery, Marjorie, Madge, Meg, Megan, Peggy, Greta, Gretchen, Gretel, Mairead, Maisie, May, Molly, Pearl**.

Magnus (M) 'great'. The name of a number of Scandinavian saints and kings, it was imported to Scotland and Ireland in medieval times. The broadcaster Magnus Magnusson, born in Iceland, was a famous bearer of the name in the UK.

Mahavir (M) 'great hero'. An Indian name borne by the founder of Jainism.

Mahendra (M) an Indian name meaning 'great Indra (the god of the sky)'.
ALTERNATIVE FORM: **Mohinder**.

Mahmud (M) 'praiseworthy'. An Arabic name borne in the 11th century by the Muslim conqueror of India.

Mai (F) another spelling of **May**.

Maia [MY-a, MAY-a] (F) the name of a Greek or Roman goddess, the wife of Zeus or Jupiter.
ALTERNATIVE FORM: **Maya**.

Mair [mire] (F) a Welsh form of **Mary**.
RELATED NAMES: **Mari, Maire, Mairi, Maura, Maureen, Moira, Marie, Maria, Ria, Mia, Mimi, Mitzi, Marian, Marianne, May, Mariel, Mariella, Marietta, Miriam, Maryam**.

Maire [MY-ra, MAW-ra, MOY-ra] (F) the Irish form of **Mary**.
ALTERNATIVE FORM: **Máire**.
RELATED NAMES: *see list at* **Mair**.

Mairead [ma-RAID, MY-raid, MAW-raid] (F) a Gaelic form of **Margaret**, used in Ireland and Scotland.
RELATED NAMES: **Maisie, Maggie, Marguerite, Margarita, Rita, Margot, Margaux, Margery, Marjorie, Madge, Meg, Megan, Peggy, Greta, Gretchen, Gretel, May, Molly, Pearl**.

Mairi [MAH-ri] (F) the Scottish form of **Mary**.
ALTERNATIVE FORM: **Màiri**.
RELATED NAMES: *see list at* **Mair**.

Maisie (F) a short form of **Margaret**, of Scottish origin, now often given as a name in its own right. The name is borne (in its alternative form) by a white mouse in a series of books for young children by Lucy Cousins.
ALTERNATIVE FORM: **Maisy**.
RELATED NAMES: *see list at* **Mairead**.

Majid (M) an Arabic name meaning 'illustrious'.

Makram (M) an Arabic name meaning 'magnanimous'.

Malachi [MAL-a-kye] (M) 'my messenger'. The name of a biblical prophet and the book of the Bible containing his sayings.
ALTERNATIVE FORM: **Malachy**.

Malcolm (M) 'follower of St Columba'. Famous bearers of the name include four medieval kings of Scotland and, more recently, the British conductor Sir Malcolm Sargent.
SHORT FORM: **Mal**.

Maldwyn (M) another form of **Baldwin** ('brave friend'), of Welsh origin.

Mallory (F/M) from the surname, meaning 'unfortunate, unlucky'.
ALTERNATIVE FORMS: **Malory, Malerie** (F).

Malvina (F) a name coined by the 18th-century Scottish poet James Macpherson, possibly meaning 'smooth brow'. It has no connection with Malvinas, the Argentinian name for the Falkland Islands.

Mamie (F) a pet form of various names beginning with *Ma-*, such as **May**, sometimes given as a name in its own right. The short form is borne by the title character of Patrick Dennis's novel *Auntie Mame* (1955) and the musical based on it. SHORT FORM: **Mame.**

Manda (F) short for **Amanda**.

Mandy (F) a short form of **Amanda** ('lovable'), sometimes given as a name in its own right.
ALTERNATIVE FORMS: **Mandie, Mandi.**

Manfred (M) 'man of peace' or 'great peace'. Of German origin, the name is borne by an outcast tortured by guilt in Lord Byron's poetic drama *Manfred* (1817). It was popularized in the latter half of the 20th century by the musician Manfred Mann.

Mani (M) 'jewel'. An Indian name that is sometimes given to one of Shiva's sons.

Manley (M) from a surname and place name meaning 'common wood or meadow'. Its use as a forename may be influenced by the adjective *manly*. Famous bearers include the 19th-century British poet Gerard Manley Hopkins.

Manny (M) short for **Emmanuel**.

Mansur (M) an Arabic name meaning 'triumphant, victorious'.

Manu (M) 'wise'. An Indian name borne in Hindu mythology by the father of the human race.

Manuel [man-WEL] (M) another form of **Emmanuel** ('God with us'), of Spanish origin. It is chiefly associated with the hapless Spanish waiter in the television sitcom *Fawlty Towers*.
RELATED NAME: **Immanuel.**

Mara (F) 'bitter'. The biblical character Naomi suggests this as an alternative name for herself after the death of her husband and sons.
ALTERNATIVE FORM: **Marah.**

Marc (M) short for **Marcus**, or another spelling of **Mark**, of French origin. This form of the name was popularized in the 1960s and 1970s by the singer Marc Bolan (born Mark Feld).
RELATED NAME: **Marcel.**

Marcel (M) another form of **Marcus**, of French origin. Famous bearers include the French writer Marcel Proust and the French mime artist Marcel Marceau.
FEMININE FORM: **Marcella.**
RELATED NAME: **Mark.**

Marcella (F) a feminine form of **Marcus** or **Marcel**.
RELATED NAME: **Marcia.**

Marcia [MAR-si-a, MAR-sha] (F) a feminine form of **Marcus** or **Mark**, borne by a number of saints. Charles Schulz gave the short form

Marcie to a bespectacled character in his cartoon strip *Peanuts*.

SHORT FORMS: **Marcie, Marci, Marcy**.

ALTERNATIVE FORM: **Marsha**.

RELATED NAME: **Marcella**.

Marcus (M) a Roman name of uncertain origin. It may come from *Mars*, the name of the Roman god of war.

SHORT FORM: **Marc**.

FEMININE FORMS: **Marcia, Marcella**.

RELATED NAMES: **Mark, Marcel**.

Margaret (F) 'pearl'. There have been various royal bearers of the name, including Margaret Tudor (the sister of Henry VIII) in the 16th century and Princess Margaret (the sister of Elizabeth II) in the 20th century.

SHORT FORMS: **Marg, Marge, Margy, Margie, Margi, Mag, Mags, Peg**.

RELATED NAMES: **Maggie, Marguerite, Margarita, Rita, Margot, Margaux, Margery, Marjorie, Madge, Meg, Megan, Peggy, Greta, Gretchen, Gretel, Mairead, Maisie, May, Molly, Pearl**.

Margarita (F) another form of **Margaret**, of Spanish origin. It is also the name of a cocktail made with tequila.

RELATED NAMES: *see list at* **Margaret**.

Margaux [MAR-go] (F) another spelling of **Margot**, coined in honour of the French red wine with

this name and made famous by the US actress Margaux Hemingway.

RELATED NAMES: *see list at* **Margaret**.

Margery (F) another form of **Margaret**, which features in the nursery rhyme 'See-saw, Margery Daw'.

SHORT FORMS: **Marge, Margy, Margie, Margi**.

ALTERNATIVE FORM: **Marjorie**.

RELATED NAMES: *see list at* **Margaret**.

Margot [MAR-go] (F) another form of **Margaret**, of French origin. Famous British bearers include the ballerina Margot Fonteyn (whose real name was Margaret Hookham) and one of the central characters of the British television sitcom *The Good Life*.

ALTERNATIVE FORMS: **Margo, Margaux**.

RELATED NAMES: *see list at* **Margaret**.

Marguerite (F) another form of **Margaret**, of French origin. It is also the name of a type of daisy.

RELATED NAMES: *see list at* **Margaret**.

Mari (F) a Welsh form of **Mary** or another spelling of **Marie**.

RELATED NAMES: *see list at* **Maria**.

Maria [ma-REE-a, ma-RYE-a] (F) another form of **Mary**. It is borne by the central characters of two famous 20th-century musicals, *West Side Story* and *The Sound of Music*. The US singer Mariah Carey uses the alternative spelling of the name.

ALTERNATIVE FORM: **Mariah**.

RELATED NAMES: **Marie, Ria, Mia, Mimi, Mitzi, Marian, Marianne, May, Mair, Maire, Mairi, Mari, Maura, Maureen, Moira, Mariel, Mariella, Marietta, Miriam, Maryam**.

Mariam (F) another form of **Maryam** or **Miriam**.

RELATED NAMES: *see list at* **Marie**.

Marian [MARR-i-un] (F) another form of **Mary**. It is chiefly associated with Maid Marian, who features in the legend of Robin Hood.

ALTERNATIVE FORMS: **Marion, Marianne**.

RELATED NAMES: *see list at* **Marie**.

Marianne [marr-i-AN] (F) another form of **Mary** or **Marian**, of French origin, sometimes regarded as a blend of **Marie** and **Anne**. It was popularized in the 1960s by the British singer Marianne Faithfull.

RELATED NAMES: *see list at* **Marie**.

Marie [ma-REE, MAH-ri, MARR-i] (F) another form of **Mary**, of French origin. Famous bearers include the French queen Marie Antoinette, guillotined in 1793, and the British music-hall entertainer Marie Lloyd, born Matilda Wood in 1870.

ALTERNATIVE FORM: **Mari**.

RELATED NAMES: **Maria, Ria, Mia, Mimi, Mitzi, Marian, Marianne, May, Mair, Maire, Mairi, Mari, Maura, Maureen, Moira, Mariel,**

Mariella, Marietta, Miriam, Maryam.

Mariel (F) another form of **Mary** or **Muriel** ('bright as the sea'). It is also the name of a Cuban port, after which the US actress Mariel Hemingway was named.

RELATED NAMES: **Meriel, Merrill;** *see also list at* **Marie**.

Mariella (F) another form of **Mary**, of Italian origin. Famous bearers include the journalist and broadcaster Mariella Frostrup.

ALTERNATIVE FORM: **Marielle**.

RELATED NAMES: *see list at* **Marie**.

Marietta (F) another form of **Mary**, of Italian origin.

RELATED NAMES: *see list at* **Marie**.

Marigold (F) from the name of the flower, so called in honour of the Virgin Mary and because of its orange or yellow colour. The British statesman Sir Winston Churchill gave the name to one of his daughters, who died in early childhood.

Marilyn (F) a blend of **Mary** and **Lynn**. It is chiefly associated with the US film star Marilyn Monroe (whose real first name was Norma).

ALTERNATIVE FORMS: **Marylin, Marylyn, Merilyn, Merrilyn**.

Marina (F) originally from a Roman family name related to **Marius**, but now chiefly associated with the sea. Famous royal bearers include the

mother and daughter of Elizabeth II's cousin Princess Alexandra.
RELATED NAME: **Marnie**.

Mario (M) another form of **Marius**, of Italian or Spanish origin. Famous bearers include the US writer Mario Puzo, author of *The Godfather* (1969), and a video-game character created by Nintendo.
RELATED NAME: **Marion**.

Marion (F/M) another form of **Marian** or **Marius**. It was the real name of the US actor known as John Wayne, but is now rarely given to boys.
RELATED NAME: **Mario** (M).

Marisa (F) a blend of **Mary** and the name-ending *-isa*.

Marissa (F) a blend of **Mary** and the name-ending *-issa*.

Marius (M) a Roman name of uncertain origin. It may come from *Mars* (the name of the Roman god of war) or from a Latin word meaning 'virile'. The 20th-century British actor Marius Goring was a famous bearer.
RELATED NAMES: **Mario, Marion**.

Marjorie (F) the usual spelling of **Margery** in modern times, possibly influenced by the herb name *marjoram*.
SHORT FORMS: **Marje, Marji, Marjie**.
ALTERNATIVE FORM: **Marjory**.
RELATED NAMES: **Margaret, Marguerite, Margarita, Rita,** **Margot, Margaux, Maggie, Madge, Meg, Megan, Peggy, Greta, Gretchen, Gretel, Mairead, Maisie, May, Molly, Pearl**.

Mark (M) another form of **Marcus**, borne in the Bible by the author of the second gospel. In the case of King Mark of Cornwall in Arthurian legend, it may be another form of a Celtic name.
ALTERNATIVE FORM: **Marc**.
FEMININE FORM: **Marcia**.
RELATED NAME: **Marcel**.

Marlene (F) a blend of **Mary** and **Magdalene**, of German origin. The German-born actress and singer Marlene Dietrich (born Maria Magdalena von Losch) popularized the name in the 20th century.

Marlon (M) a name of uncertain origin, made famous in the mid-20th century by the US actor Marlon Brando.

Marmaduke (M) possibly from an Irish name meaning 'follower of Maedoc (an Irish saint)'. The name is chiefly given to cats and dogs. Famous human bearers include Marmaduke Hussey, a former chairman of the BBC's board of governors.
RELATED NAME: **Duke**.

Marnie (F) another form of **Marina**, of Scandinavian origin. It is borne by a compulsive thief in the Alfred

Hitchcock film *Marnie* (1964), based on a novel of the same name by Winston Graham.
ALTERNATIVE FORM: **Marni**.

Marsha (F) another spelling of **Marcia**, borne by the singer and actress Marsha Hunt, who made her name in the 1960s musical *Hair*.

Marshall (M) from the surname, meaning 'horse servant'. It was the middle name of the 20th-century Canadian writer known as Marshall McLuhan and is the real name of the rap singer known as Eminem.
ALTERNATIVE FORM: **Marshal**.

Martha (F) 'lady'. The name of a biblical character who offers Jesus hospitality but complains about having to do all the work while her sister Mary sits at his feet and listens to him.
ALTERNATIVE FORM: **Marta**.

Marti (F) a short form of **Martina**, sometimes given as a name in its own right. Famous bearers include the British comedian Marti Caine and the British singer and actress Marti Webb.

Martin (M) probably from *Mars*, the name of the Roman god of war. The name was borne in the 4th century by St Martin of Tours, who is remembered for the generous act of dividing his cloak in half to share it with a beggar.
ALTERNATIVE FORM: **Martyn**.

FEMININE FORM: **Martina**.
RELATED NAME: **Marty**.

Martina (F) the feminine form of **Martin**. Famous modern bearers include the Czech-born tennis player Martina Navratilova.
ALTERNATIVE FORM: **Martine**.
RELATED NAME: **Marti**.

Marty (M) a short form of **Martin**, sometimes given as a name in its own right. Famous bearers include the British comedian Marty Feldman (whose full name was Martin) and the British singer Marty Wilde (whose real name is Reginald Smith).

Marvin (M) 'famous friend'. Alternatively, it may be another form of **Mervyn**. The name is borne by a depressed robot in *The Hitchhiker's Guide to the Galaxy* by Douglas Adams.
SHORT FORM: **Marv**.

Mary (F) a biblical name of uncertain meaning that comes from the same origin as **Miriam**. It is chiefly associated with the Virgin Mary, mother of Jesus Christ. There have also been many royal bearers, including Mary Tudor and Mary, Queen of Scots in the 16th century.
RELATED NAMES: **Marie, Maria, Ria, Mia, Mimi, Mitzi, Marian, Marianne, May, Mair, Maire, Mairi, Mari, Maura, Maureen, Moira, Mariel, Mariella,**

Marietta, Maryam, Madonna, Concepta, Dolores, Mercedes.

Maryam (F) the Arabic form of **Mary** or **Miriam**.
ALTERNATIVE FORM: **Mariam**.
RELATED NAMES: *see list at* **Mary**.

Marylin (F) another spelling of **Marilyn**.
ALTERNATIVE FORM: **Marylyn**.

Mason (M) from the surname, referring to somebody who works with stone.

Masud (M) an Arabic name meaning 'lucky'.

Matilda (F) 'mighty in battle'. The name was borne in the 11th century by the wife of William the Conqueror. Roald Dahl gave the name to a young genius with paranormal powers in his children's book *Matilda* (1988).
SHORT FORMS: **Mattie, Matty**.
ALTERNATIVE FORM: **Mathilda**.
RELATED NAMES: **Tilly, Tilda, Maud**.

Matt (M) a short form of **Matthew** or **Matthias**, sometimes given as a name in its own right. Famous modern bearers include the singer Matt Monro (whose real name was Terry Parsons) and the US actor Matt Damon (whose full name is Matthew).

Matthew (M) 'gift of God'. A biblical name borne by one of Jesus Christ's apostles, a former tax collector and the author of the first gospel.
ALTERNATIVE FORM: **Mathew**.

RELATED NAMES: **Matt, Matthias**.

Matthias (M) another form of **Matthew**, of Greek origin. In the Bible, Matthias is the apostle chosen to replace Judas Iscariot after the death of Jesus Christ.
ALTERNATIVE FORM: **Mathias**.
RELATED NAME: **Matt**.

Maud (F) a short form of **Matilda**, given as a name in its own right. It is the title of a poem by Tennyson, published in 1855, which contains the famous line 'Come into the garden, Maud'.
ALTERNATIVE FORMS: **Maude, Maudie**.
RELATED NAMES: **Tilly, Tilda**.

Maura (F) another spelling of **Maire**, the Irish form of **Mary**.
RELATED NAMES: *see list at* **Maureen**.

Maureen (F) another form of **Mary**, of Irish origin. Famous modern bearers include the US actress Maureen O'Hara and the British actress Maureen Lipman.
SHORT FORMS: **Mo, Reenie**.
RELATED NAMES: **Maire, Maura, Moira, Mairi, Mair, Mari, Marie, Maria, Ria, Mia, Mimi, Mitzi, Marian, Marianne, May, Mariel, Mariella, Marietta, Miriam, Maryam**.

Maurice [MORR-iss] (M) 'dark-skinned'. Famous bearers include the 20th-century French singer Maurice Chevalier and the gay hero

of E. M. Forster's novel *Maurice* (published posthumously in 1971).
SHORT FORM: **Mo.**
ALTERNATIVE FORM: **Morris.**

Mave (F) short for **Mavis**, or another spelling of **Maeve** ('intoxicating').

Mavis (F) 'song thrush'. The name was popular in the first half of the 20th century. From the 1970s it was chiefly associated with a character played by Thelma Barlow in the soap opera *Coronation Street*.
SHORT FORM: **Mave.**

Max (M) a short form of **Maximilian, Maxwell, Maxim** or **Maximus**, now often given in its own right. Famous modern bearers include the British writer Sir Max Beerbohm (whose full name was Maximilian), the British comedian Max Wall (whose full name was Maxwell), and the British singer Max Bygraves (whose real name was Walter).
FEMININE FORM: **Maxine.**

Maxie (F) short for **Maxine.**

Maxim (M) another form of **Maximus**, of Russian origin, or a short form of **Maximilian**. Maxim de Winter is the principal male character of Daphne du Maurier's novel *Rebecca* (1938).

Maximilian (M) another form of **Maximus**, borne by a 3rd-century saint.
RELATED NAMES: **Max, Maxim.**

Maximus (M) 'greatest'. A Roman name, borne by the character played by Russell Crowe in the film *Gladiator* (2000).
RELATED NAMES: **Max, Maxim, Maximilian.**

Maxine (F) the feminine form of **Max.**
SHORT FORM: **Maxie.**

Maxwell (M) from a Scottish surname and place name meaning 'Magnus's well'.
RELATED NAME: **Max.**

May (F) a short form of **Mary** or **Margaret**, now usually given as a name in its own right. It may also be associated with the month name or the plant name.
ALTERNATIVE FORMS: **Mae, Mai.**
RELATED NAME: **Mamie.**

Maya [MY-a, MAY-a] (F) another spelling of **Maia**, possibly influenced by **May**, or an Indian name meaning 'illusion'. The US writer Maya Angelou was born Marguerite Johnson in 1928.

Maybelle (F) another form of **Mabel.**

Maynard (M) from the surname, meaning 'brave and strong'. Famous bearers include the 20th-century British economist John Maynard Keynes.

Meena (F) 'fish'. An Indian name borne by the daughter of the goddess of the dawn.
ALTERNATIVE FORM: **Mina.**

Meera (F) 'sea'. An Indian name borne by the actress, writer, and comedian Meera Syal.

Meg (F) a short form of **Margaret** ('pearl'), sometimes given as a name in its own right. As a short form it is used by one of the heroines of Louisa M. Alcott's novel *Little Women* (1868) and by the US actress Meg Ryan.
RELATED NAMES: **Megan, Peggy, Maggie, Marguerite, Margarita, Rita, Margot, Margaux, Margery, Marjorie, Madge, Greta, Gretchen, Gretel, Mairead, Maisie, May, Molly, Pearl**.

Megan (F) a Welsh form of **Margaret** ('pearl').
ALTERNATIVE FORMS: **Meghan, Meagan, Meaghan**.
RELATED NAMES: *see list at* **Meg**.

Meir (M) a Jewish name meaning 'giving light'.

Mel (M/F) short for various names beginning with or containing these letters, such as **Melvin, Melanie**, or **Imelda**. It is also a traditional Irish boys' name, borne by the actor Mel Gibson.

Melanie (F) 'dark, black'. Famous bearers include two members of the Spice Girls, Melanie Chisholm (Mel C) and Melanie Brown (Mel B), who were born in the mid-1970s, when the name was particularly popular in the UK.
SHORT FORM: **Mel**.
ALTERNATIVE FORMS: **Mellony, Melony, Melany**.

Melchior (M) 'king of the city'. Melchior was one of the three Magi who brought gifts to the young Jesus.

Melinda (F) a blend of **Melanie** or **Melissa** and the name-ending -*inda*. The British model and television presenter Melinda Messenger is a famous bearer of the name.

Melissa (F) 'honey bee'. The name became fashionable in the UK in the late 20th century.
SHORT FORMS: **Mel, Lissa**.

Mellony (F) another spelling of **Melanie**.
ALTERNATIVE FORM: **Melony**.

Melody (F) from the word *melody*, meaning 'tune'.
ALTERNATIVE FORM: **Melodie**.

Melville (M) from the surname, which comes from a French place name meaning 'bad settlement'.

Melvin (M) a name of uncertain origin, possibly another form of **Melville** or of a Gaelic name meaning 'smooth brow'. The British writer and television presenter Melvyn Bragg is a famous bearer of the name in its alternative form.
SHORT FORM: **Mel**.
ALTERNATIVE FORM: **Melvyn**.

Menahem (M) 'comforter'. A biblical

name, borne by a cruel king of Israel. The alternative form was made famous by the 20th-century Israeli statesman Menachem Begin.
ALTERNATIVE FORM: **Menachem**.

Mercedes [mer-SAY-deez] (F) 'mercies' or 'ransom'. From a Spanish title of the Virgin Mary. It is chiefly associated with the large expensive cars manufactured by Mercedes-Benz, originally named after a girl called Mercedes.
RELATED NAMES: **Mary, Madonna, Dolores, Concepta**.

Mercy (F) from the word *mercy*, especially in the sense 'forgiveness' or 'compassion'. Charles Dickens gave the name to a character in his novel *Martin Chuzzlewit* (1844).
ALTERNATIVE FORMS: **Mercia, Merry**.

Meredith (F/M) another form of a Welsh boys' name, possibly meaning 'great chief'. It was popularized as a girls' name by a character in Edith Bagnold's novel *National Velvet* (1935).
SHORT FORM: **Merry**.

Meriel (F) another form of **Muriel** ('bright as the sea').
RELATED NAMES: **Mariel, Merrill**.

Merilyn (F) another form of **Marilyn**.
ALTERNATIVE FORM: **Merrilyn**.

Merle (F) possibly another form of **Meriel**, influenced by the French word *merle*, meaning 'blackbird'.

The name was made famous in the 1930s by the actress Merle Oberon.

Merlin (M) the English form of a Welsh name meaning 'sea hill' or 'sea fort'. It is chiefly associated with the magician Merlin in Arthurian legend.
ALTERNATIVE FORM: **Merlyn**.

Merlyn (M/F) another spelling of **Merlin** that may be given to boys or girls.

Merrill (M/F) another form of **Muriel** ('bright as the sea'), which became a surname and was later readopted as a forename for boys or girls.
RELATED NAMES: **Meriel** (F), **Mariel** (F).

Merrilyn (F) another form of **Marilyn**.
ALTERNATIVE FORM: **Merilyn**.

Merry (F/M) from the word *merry*, meaning 'jolly'. It may also be a short or alternative form of various other names beginning with *Mer-*, such as **Mercy** or **Meredith**.

Mervyn (M) a name of Welsh origin and uncertain meaning. Alternatively, it may be another form of **Marvin**. Famous bearers include the 20th-century British writer Mervyn Peake, author of the *Gormenghast* trilogy.
SHORT FORM: **Merv**.
ALTERNATIVE FORM: **Mervin**.

Meryl (F) a name of uncertain origin, possibly another form of **Mary**,

Meriel, or **Merrill**. The US actress Meryl Streep was born Mary Louise Streep in 1949.

Mia [MEE-a] (F) a short form of **Maria**, now often given as a name in its own right. The US actress Mia Farrow (whose full name is Maria) popularized the name in the latter half of the 20th century.
RELATED NAMES: **Mary, Ria, Mimi, Mitzi, Marie, Marian, Marianne, May, Mair, Maire, Mairi, Mari, Maura, Maureen, Moira, Mariel, Mariella, Marietta, Miriam, Maryam.**

Micah (M) another form of **Michael**. The name of a biblical prophet and the book of the Bible containing his sayings.
RELATED NAMES: **Mickey, Mitchell.**

Michael (M) 'who is like God?'. St Michael, patron saint of soldiers, was a biblical archangel who led the angels in a battle against Satan. The British actor Michael Caine (born Maurice Micklewhite) and the US singer Michael Jackson are famous modern bearers of the name.
SHORT FORMS: **Mick, Mike, Mikey, Mitch.**
FEMININE FORMS: **Michaela, Michelle.**
RELATED NAMES: **Mickey, Mitchell, Micah.**

Michaela [mik-AY-la, mik-EYE-la] (F) a feminine form of **Michael**. The name has been borne by two

presenters of popular television wildlife shows: Michaela Denis (in the 1950s) and Michaela Strachan (since the 1990s).
SHORT FORMS: **Mickey, Kayla, Kyla.**
RELATED NAME: **Michelle.**

Michal (F) 'brook'. A biblical name, borne by a daughter of Saul and wife of King David.

Michelle [mish-ELL] (F) a feminine form of **Michael**, of French origin. The US actress Michelle Pfeiffer is a famous bearer of the name.
SHORT FORMS: **Mickey, Chelle, Shell.**
ALTERNATIVE FORM: **Michele.**
RELATED NAME: **Michaela.**

Mick (M/F) short for **Michael** or **Mickey**.

Mickey (M/F) a short form of **Michael, Michaela**, or **Michelle**, sometimes given to boys as a name in its own right. Famous male bearers include the US actor Mickey Rooney (whose real name is Joe Yule) and the cartoon character Mickey Mouse.
SHORT FORM: **Mick.**
ALTERNATIVE FORM: **Micky.**
RELATED NAMES: **Mitchell, Micah.**

Mike (M) short for **Michael**.
ALTERNATIVE FORM: **Mikey.**

Mildred (F) 'gentle strength'. The name was borne by a 7th-century abbess and saint. Famous fictional bearers include the title character of

James M. Cain's novel *Mildred Pierce* (1941), filmed in 1945.

Miles (M) a name of uncertain origin, possibly meaning 'soldier' or 'grace, favour'.
ALTERNATIVE FORMS: **Myles, Milo.**

Milla (F) a short form of **Camilla** (possibly meaning 'attendant at a pagan ceremony'), sometimes given as a name in its own right. In the case of the Ukrainian-born actress Milla Jovovich, it is short for Militza.
RELATED NAME: **Millie.**

Millicent (F) 'hard worker'. Famous modern bearers include the British singer and actress Millicent Martin.
RELATED NAME: **Millie.**

Millie (F) a short form of **Millicent** or **Camilla**, sometimes given as a name in its own right. It was popularized in the mid-20th century by Milly-Molly-Mandy, the fictional heroine of a series of children's books by the British writer Joyce Lankester Brisley.
ALTERNATIVE FORM: **Milly.**
RELATED NAME: **Milla.**

Milo (M) another form of **Miles.**

Milton (M) from a surname and place name meaning 'settlement with a mill'. Famous modern bearers include US economist Milton Friedman and the Ugandan politician Milton Obote.
SHORT FORM: **Milt.**

Mimi [MEE-mee] (F) a short form of **Maria**, of Italian origin. It is borne by the tragic heroine of Puccini's opera *La Bohème* (1896).
RELATED NAMES: **Mary, Ria, Mia, Mitzi, Marie, Marian, Marianne, May, Mair, Maire, Mairi, Mari, Maura, Maureen, Moira, Mariel, Mariella, Marietta, Miriam, Maryam.**

Mina (F) a short form of various names ending with these letters, especially **Wilhelmina** ('resolute protector'), sometimes given as a name in its own right. It is also another spelling of the Indian name **Meena.**
ALTERNATIVE FORM: **Minna.**
RELATED NAMES: **Minnie, Billie, Wilma, Willa.**

Mindy (F) probably a blend of **Mandy** and **Cindy**. The name was borne by one of the title characters of the US sitcom *Mork and Mindy* (1978–82).

Minerva (F) the name of the Roman goddess of wisdom.

Minnie (F) a short form of **Wilhelmina** ('resolute protector'), sometimes given as a name in its own right. Famous bearers include the cartoon character Minnie Mouse and the British actress Minnie Driver (whose real name is Amelia).
RELATED NAMES: **Mina, Billie, Wilma, Willa.**

Minta (F) short for **Araminta**.
ALTERNATIVE FORM: **Minty**.

Mirabelle (F) 'admirable, lovely'.
ALTERNATIVE FORM: **Mirabella**.

Miranda (F) 'wonderful, lovely'. A
name coined by Shakespeare for the
heroine of *The Tempest*. The British
actress Miranda Richardson is a
famous modern bearer.
SHORT FORMS: **Mira, Randa, Randi**.

Miriam (F) a biblical name of
uncertain meaning that comes from
the same origin as **Mary**. In the Bible,
Miriam is the sister of Moses and
Aaron. A more recent famous bearer
is the British doctor and television
presenter Miriam Stoppard.
RELATED NAMES: **Marie, Maria, Ria,
Mia, Mimi, Mitzi, Marian,
Marianne, May, Mair, Maire,
Mairi, Mari, Maura, Maureen,
Moira, Mariel, Mariella,
Marietta, Maryam**.

Mirza (M) an Indian name meaning
'prince'.

Mitch (M) short for **Mitchell** or
Michael.

Mitchell (M) another form of
Michael, which became a surname
and was later readopted as a
forename.
SHORT FORM: **Mitch**.
RELATED NAMES: **Mickey, Micah**.

Mitzi (F) a short form of **Maria**, of
German origin. The US actress,

singer, and dancer Mitzi Gaynor is a
famous bearer of the name.
RELATED NAMES: **Mary, Ria, Mia,
Mimi, Marie, Marian, Marianne,
May, Mair, Maire, Mairi, Mari,
Maura, Maureen, Moira, Mariel,
Mariella, Marietta, Miriam,
Maryam**.

Mo (M/F) short for **Maurice, Moses**,
or **Maureen**.

Mohammed (M) another form of the
Arabic name **Muhammad**
('praiseworthy'). It is the most
common form of the boys' name in
the UK in modern times.
ALTERNATIVE FORM: **Mohammad**.

Mohan (M) 'enchanting'. An Indian
name sometimes given to the gods
Shiva and Krishna.

Mohinder (M) another form of the
Indian name **Mahendra** ('great
Indra').

Mohini (F) 'enchanting woman'. An
Indian name given to the god
Vishnu in the form of a beautiful
woman.

Moira (F) another form of **Mary**, of
Irish or Scottish origin. The British
ballerina Moira Shearer was a
famous bearer of the name.
ALTERNATIVE FORM: **Moyra**.
RELATED NAMES: **Mairi, Maire,
Maura, Maureen, Mair, Mari,
Marie, Maria, Ria, Mia, Mimi,
Mitzi, Marian, Marianne, May,**

Mariel, Mariella, Marietta, Miriam, Maryam.

Molly (F) a short form of **Margaret** or **Mary**, now often given as a name in its own right.
ALTERNATIVE FORMS: **Mollie, Polly**.
RELATED NAMES: **Maggie, Peggy, Meg, Megan, Marguerite, Margarita, Rita, Margot, Margaux, Margery, Marjorie, Madge, Greta, Gretchen, Gretel, Mairead, Maisie, May, Pearl**; *see also list at* **Moira**.

Mona (F) another form of an Irish name meaning 'noble'. In the title of the painting *Mona Lisa* by Leonardo da Vinci, it is short for **Madonna**.

Monica (F) the name of St Augustine's mother, possibly meaning 'adviser'. More recent famous bearers include the 20th-century British novelist Monica Dickens and one of the central characters of the US television series *Friends*.

Montague (M) from a surname and place name meaning 'pointed hill'.
ALTERNATIVE FORM: **Montagu**.
RELATED NAME: **Monty**.

Montgomery (M) from a surname and place name meaning 'Gomeric's hill'. It was the middle name of the 20th-century US actor known as Montgomery Clift.
RELATED NAME: **Monty**.

Monty (M) a short form of various names beginning with *Mont-*, such

as **Montague** or **Montgomery**, sometimes given as a name in its own right. Famous bearers include the television gardener Monty Don (whose full name is Montagu).

Morag (F) 'great'. A name of Gaelic origin that is particularly popular in Scotland.

Mordecai [MOR-di-kye] (M) 'devotee of Marduk (a Babylonian god)'. A biblical name, borne by Esther's cousin and foster father. More recent famous bearers include the Canadian novelist Mordecai Richler.

Morgan (M/F) another form of a Welsh boys' name, possibly meaning 'sea circle'. Famous male bearers include the US actor Morgan Freeman. As a girls' name it may be associated with the legendary sorceress Morgan le Fay, half-sister of King Arthur.
ALTERNATIVE FORM: **Morgana** (F).

Morna (F) another form of **Myrna** (possibly meaning 'beloved').

Morris (M) another spelling of **Maurice** ('dark-skinned'). The name is more frequently found as a surname in this form.

Mortimer (M) from the surname, which comes from a French place name meaning 'dead sea'. The 20th-century British archaeologist Sir Mortimer Wheeler was a famous bearer of the name.
SHORT FORM: **Mort**.

Morwenna (F) 'maiden'. The name of a 5th-century Cornish saint. The British comedian Morwenna Banks was born in Cornwall in 1964.
ALTERNATIVE FORM: **Morwen**.

Moses (M) a biblical name, possibly meaning 'child' or 'saved'. In the Bible, Moses is the patriarch who leads the Israelites out of Egypt.
SHORT FORM: **Mo**.
RELATED NAMES: **Moshe, Moss**.

Moshe (M) a Jewish form of **Moses**, borne by the 20th-century Israeli politician Moshe Dayan.
RELATED NAME: **Moss**.

Moss (M) from the surname, which is another form of **Moses**. The 20th-century US dramatist Moss Hart was a famous bearer of the name.

Moyra (F) another spelling of **Moira**.

Muhammad (M) 'praiseworthy'. The name of the Prophet of Islam. The 20th-century US boxer Cassius Clay adopted the name Muhammad Ali when he became a Muslim.
ALTERNATIVE FORMS: **Mohammed, Mohammad**.

Muhsin (M) an Arabic name meaning 'beneficent'.
FEMININE FORM: **Muhsina**.

Muhsina (F) the feminine form of **Muhsin**.

Mukhtar (M) an Arabic name meaning 'chosen'.

Muna (F) an Arabic name meaning 'hope, desire'.

Mungo (M) a Scottish name, possibly meaning 'dear'. It was the nickname of a 6th-century saint, whose real name was Kentigern. Other famous bearers include the 18th-century Scottish explorer Mungo Park.

Munir (M) an Arabic name meaning 'bright, shining'.
FEMININE FORM: **Munira**.

Munira (F) the feminine form of **Munir**.

Murdo (M) another form of a Scottish name meaning 'lord' or 'mariner'.
ALTERNATIVE FORM: **Murdoch**.

Murgatroyd (M) from the surname, which comes from a place name meaning 'Margaret's meadow'.

Muriel (F) 'bright as the sea'. Of Gaelic origin, the name was borne by the 20th-century Scottish-born writer Muriel Spark.
RELATED NAMES: **Meriel, Merrill, Mariel**.

Murray (M) from the surname, which comes from the Scottish place name Moray. It is the middle name of the British motor-racing commentator known as Murray Walker.

Mustafa (M) an Arabic name meaning 'chosen'. Al-Mustafa is a title of Muhammad.

Mya (F) possibly another form of Maia or Mia, influenced by Myra.

Myfanwy [mi-VAN-wee] (F) a Welsh name meaning 'my dear woman'.

Myles (M) another spelling of Miles.

Myra (F) a name coined by the 16th-century English poet Fulke Greville. Notorious bearers in the latter half of the 20th century include the murderer Myra Hindley and the fictional transsexual Myra Breckinridge, created by Gore Vidal.

Myrna (F) an English form of an Irish name, possibly meaning 'beloved', borne by the mother of the legendary Irish hero Fionn MacCool. Other famous bearers include the 20th-century US actress Myrna Loy.
ALTERNATIVE FORM: **Morna**.

Myron (M) 'myrrh'. The name of a Greek sculptor of the 5th century BC.

Myrtle (F) from the plant name.
RELATED NAMES: **Hadassah, Dassah, Esther, Hester.**

N

Nada (F) another form of **Nadia**, or an Arabic name meaning 'dew'.
RELATED NAME: **Nadine**.

Nadia (F) 'hope'. Of Russian origin, the name was popularized in the 1970s by the Romanian gymnast Nadia Comaneci.
RELATED NAMES: **Nada, Nadine**.

Nadim (M) an Arabic name meaning 'drinking companion'.

Nadine (F) another form of **Nadia**, of French origin. The South African novelist Nadine Gordimer is a famous bearer of the name.
RELATED NAME: **Nada**.

Nadiyya (F) an Arabic name meaning 'moist with dew'.

Nahum (M) 'comforter'. The name of a biblical prophet and the book of the Bible containing his sayings. Other famous bearers include the 17th-century dramatist Nahum Tate.

Nan (F) short for **Nancy** or **Nanette**.

Nancy (F) another form of **Anne** ('favour' or 'grace'). It was borne by a woman who met a violent end in Charles Dickens' novel *Oliver Twist* (1838). Famous 20th-century bearers include the British politician Nancy Astor and the British writer Nancy Mitford.
SHORT FORM: **Nan**.
RELATED NAMES: **Nanette, Annette, Annie, Hannah, Anna, Anya, Anita, Anneka, Anouska, Anais**.

Nanda (F) a feminine form of **Ferdinand** ('ready to travel'), of Spanish origin. The name is borne by the heroine of Antonia White's novel *Frost in May* (1933).

Nanda (M) 'joy'. An Indian name borne by Krishna's foster father and the Buddha's stepbrother.

Nanette (F) another form of **Anne** ('favour' or 'grace'), given as a name in its own right. It was popularized in the early 20th century by the musical *No, No, Nanette*. The British actress Nanette Newman is a famous bearer of the name.
SHORT FORM: **Nan**.

ALTERNATIVE FORM: **Nannette**.

RELATED NAMES: **Nancy, Annie, Annette, Hannah, Anna, Anya, Anita, Anneka, Anouska, Anais**.

Naomi [nay-OH-mee, NAY-oh-mee] (F) 'pleasantness'. A biblical name, borne by Ruth's mother-in-law. It was popularized in the late 20th century by the British model Naomi Campbell.

Narayan (M) 'son of man'. An Indian name sometimes given to Brahma, the god of creation.

Narendra (M) an Indian name meaning 'mighty man' or 'doctor'.
ALTERNATIVE FORM: **Narinder**.

Nasir (M) an Arabic name meaning 'helper, supporter'.

Nat (M/F) short for **Nathan, Nathaniel, Natalie**, or **Natasha**.

Natalie (F) 'Christmas'. The 20th-century US actress Natalie Wood was a famous bearer of the name.
SHORT FORM: **Nat**.
ALTERNATIVE FORM: **Nathalie**.
RELATED NAMES: **Natasha, Noel**.

Natasha (F) another form of **Natalie**, of Russian origin. The name is borne by the vivacious heroine of Leo Tolstoy's novel *War and Peace* (1863–9). Other famous bearers include the British actress Natasha Richardson.
SHORT FORM: **Nat**.
RELATED NAMES: **Tasha, Noel**.

Nathan (M) 'gift'. A biblical name, borne by a prophet and by one of the sons of David. It was particularly popular in the late 20th and early 21st centuries.
SHORT FORM: **Nat**.

Nathaniel (M) 'gift of God'. A biblical name, borne (in its alternative form) by one of Jesus Christ's apostles in St John's gospel. It was also the full name of the US jazz musician known as Nat King Cole.
SHORT FORM: **Nat**.
ALTERNATIVE FORM: **Nathanael**.

Navin (M) an Indian name meaning 'new'.
ALTERNATIVE FORM: **Naveen**.

Ned (M) a short form of any name beginning with *Ed-*, especially **Edward** ('guardian of wealth'), sometimes given as a name in its own right. Famous modern bearers include the British broadcaster and writer Ned Sherrin.
ALTERNATIVE FORMS: **Neddy, Neddie**.
RELATED NAMES: **Eddie, Ted, Teddy**.

Neil (M) another form of **Niall**. Famous modern bearers of the name include the US astronaut Neil Armstrong, who was the first person to set foot on the moon.
ALTERNATIVE FORMS: **Neal, Neale, Neill**.
RELATED NAME: **Nigel**.

Nell (F) a short form of **Eleanor**,

Ellen, or **Helen**, sometimes given as a name in its own right. It was famously borne in the 17th century by Charles II's mistress Nell Gwyn (whose full name was Eleanor). The alternative form Nellie is also used as a short form of **Cornelia**.
ALTERNATIVE FORMS: **Nellie, Nelly**.
RELATED NAMES: **Ella, Ellie**.

Nella (F) short for **Fenella**.

Nelson (M) from the surname, meaning 'son of Neil' or 'son of Nell', made famous by the 18th-century British admiral Horatio Nelson. The forename is now chiefly associated with the 20th-century South African statesman Nelson Mandela.

Nena (F) another form of **Nina**.

Nerissa (F) 'sea nymph'. A name coined by Shakespeare for a character in his play *The Merchant of Venice*.

Nerys (F) a Welsh name, probably meaning 'lady'. The Welsh actress Nerys Hughes is a famous bearer.

Nessa (F) a short form of **Vanessa** (or another name ending with these letters), sometimes given as a name in its own right. It is also an Irish name, borne by the powerful and ambitious mother of the legendary king Conchobar.

Nessie (F) short for **Agnes** or **Vanessa**. It is also used as a

nickname for the Loch Ness monster.

Nesta (F) another form of **Agnes** ('pure, holy'), of Welsh origin.
RELATED NAMES: **Annis, Ines**.

Nestor (M) 'homecoming'. In Greek legend, Nestor was a wise old king who fought in the Trojan War.

Nettie (F) short for various names ending in *-nette* or *-netta*, such as **Annette** or **Jeanette**.
ALTERNATIVE FORM: **Netta**.

Neve (F) another form of the Irish name **Niamh** ('radiance'), spelt as it sounds.

Neville (M) from the surname, which comes from a French place name meaning 'new town'. It was the middle name of the 20th-century British statesman known as Neville Chamberlain.
ALTERNATIVE FORMS: **Nevil, Nevill, Nevile**.

Newton (M) from a surname and place name meaning 'new town'. The surname is chiefly associated with the 17th-century English scientist Sir Isaac Newton. The US politician known as Newt Gingrich is a famous bearer of the forename.
SHORT FORM: **Newt**.

Ngaio [NYE-oh] (F) a New Zealand name, probably from a Maori word meaning 'clever'. It was made famous by the 20th-century New Zealand novelist Ngaio Marsh, creator of the fictional detective Roderick Alleyn.

Ngaire [NYE-ree] (F) a New Zealand name, possibly from a Maori word meaning 'flaxen'.
ALTERNATIVE FORM: **Nyree**.

Nia (F) the Welsh form of **Niamh**, or an African name meaning 'purpose'.

Niall [NYE-ul] (M) a Gaelic name, possibly meaning 'cloud', 'passionate', or 'champion'. It was borne by a 4th-century Irish king known as Niall of the Nine Hostages.
RELATED NAMES: **Neil, Nigel**.

Niamh [neev, NEE-iv] (F) 'radiance'. An Irish name borne by the daughter of the sea god, who carried off Oisin to the land of eternal youth. Famous modern bearers include the Irish actress Niamh Cusack.
ALTERNATIVE FORM: **Neve**.
RELATED NAME: **Nia**.

Nicci (F/M) another spelling of **Nicky**.

Nichol (M) another spelling of **Nicol**.

Nichola (F) another spelling of **Nicola**.

Nicholas (M) 'the people's victory'. The name was borne in the 4th century by St Nicholas, patron saint of Greece and Russia, on whom the figure of Santa Claus is based. Other famous bearers include the title

character of Charles Dickens' novel *Nicholas Nickleby* (1839).
ALTERNATIVE FORMS: **Nicolas, Nickolas**.
FEMININE FORMS: **Nicola, Nicole, Nicky, Nicolette, Colette**.
RELATED NAMES: **Nick, Nicky, Nico, Nicol, Colin, Coll, Nicodemus**.

Nichole (F) another spelling of **Nicole**.

Nick (M) a short form of **Nicholas** or **Nicodemus**, sometimes given as a name in its own right.
ALTERNATIVE FORM: **Nik**.
RELATED NAMES: **Nicky, Nico, Nicol, Colin, Coll**.

Nicky (F/M) a short form of **Nicola, Nicole, Nicholas** or **Nicodemus**, sometimes given as a name in its own right. The girls' name is usually found in one of the alternative spellings, which are less frequently used for boys.
ALTERNATIVE FORMS: **Nickie, Nicki, Nikki, Niki, Nicci**.
RELATED NAMES: **Nick** (M), **Nico** (M), **Nicol** (M), **Colin** (M), **Coll** (M), **Nicolette** (F), **Colette** (F).

Nico (M) a short form of **Nicholas** or **Nicodemus**, sometimes given as a name in its own right.
RELATED NAMES: **Nick, Nicky, Nicol, Colin, Coll**.

Nicodemus (M) 'the people's victory'. A biblical name, borne by a man who helped Joseph of Arimathea

prepare Jesus Christ's body for burial.
RELATED NAMES: **Nicholas, Nick, Nicky, Nico, Nicol, Colin, Coll.**

Nicol (M) another form of **Nicholas**. The actor Nicol Williamson was born in Scotland, where this form of the name is particularly popular.
ALTERNATIVE FORM: **Nichol.**
RELATED NAMES: **Nick, Nicky, Nico, Colin, Coll, Nicodemus.**

Nicola (F) a feminine form of **Nicholas**. Famous modern bearers of the name include the British actress Nicola Pagett.
ALTERNATIVE FORM: **Nichola.**
RELATED NAMES: **Nicole, Nicky, Nicolette, Colette.**

Nicolas (M) another spelling of **Nicholas**.

Nicole (F) a feminine form of **Nicholas**, of French origin. It was popularized in the late 20th century by a character in a series of car commercials and by the US actress Nicole Kidman.
ALTERNATIVE FORM: **Nichole.**
RELATED NAMES: **Nicola, Nicky, Nicolette, Colette.**

Nicolette (F) a feminine form of **Nicholas**, of French origin.
RELATED NAMES: **Colette, Nicole, Nicola, Nicky.**

Nigel (M) another form of **Niall**, sometimes associated with a Latin word meaning 'black'. Famous modern bearers include the British actor Nigel Hawthorne and the British racing driver Nigel Mansell.
FEMININE FORM: **Nigella.**
RELATED NAME: **Neil.**

Nigella (F) the feminine form of **Nigel**, sometimes associated with the plant name. It was made famous in the late 20th century by the television cook and food writer Nigella Lawson.

Nik (M) another spelling of **Nick**.

Nikki (F/M) another spelling of **Nicky**.
ALTERNATIVE FORM: **Niki.**

Nile (M) from the name of the river, possibly influenced by **Niall**, which sounds similar.

Nina (F) a short form of various Russian names ending with these letters, given as a name in its own right in English-speaking countries. The British writer Nina Bawden is a famous bearer.
ALTERNATIVE FORM: **Nena.**

Ninette (F) another form of **Nina**, of French origin. It was used as a stage name by the 20th-century Irish-born ballerina Ninette de Valois (whose real name was Edris Stannus).

Ninian (M) a name of uncertain origin, borne by a 5th-century British saint who brought Christianity to the Picts of southern Scotland.

Nita (F) short for **Anita**.

Noah (M) a biblical name of uncertain origin, possibly meaning 'rest' or 'comfort'. In the Bible, Noah builds an ark to escape the great flood sent by God to punish humankind. The name became fashionable in the UK in the early 21st century.

Noam (M) a Jewish name meaning 'pleasantness'. The US linguist Noam Chomsky is the best-known bearer of the name.

Noel (M/F) 'Christmas'. Famous 20th-century bearers include the British dramatist and actor Noël Coward (male) and the British children's writer Noel Streatfeild (female).
ALTERNATIVE FORMS: **Noël, Noelle** (F), **Noele** (F), **Noeleen** (F), **Noelene** (F).
RELATED NAMES: **Natalie** (F), **Natasha** (F).

Nola (F) a short form of **Finola** (which is an English form of the Gaelic name **Fionnuala**, meaning 'fair-shouldered'), given as a name in its own right. It is also regarded as a feminine form of **Nolan**.
RELATED NAMES: **Nuala, Finola, Fenella**.

Nolan (M) from the Irish surname, meaning 'son of a champion'.
FEMININE FORMS: **Nola, Noleen**.

Noleen (F) a feminine form of **Nolan**.

ALTERNATIVE FORM: **Nolene**.

Nona (F) 'ninth'. In the days of large families, the name was sometimes given to the ninth-born child.

Nora (F) a short form of **Honora** ('honour') given as a name in its own right, especially in Ireland. It may also be regarded as a short form of **Eleonora, Leonora**, or **Lenora**. Famous modern bearers include the US singer Norah Jones.
ALTERNATIVE FORMS: **Norah, Noreen, Norene**.

Norbert (M) 'illustrious northerner'. Borne by a 12th-century saint, the name is most frequently seen in modern times on the side of trucks belonging to the transport company Norbert Dentressangle.

Norma (F) the name of the title character of Bellini's opera *Norma* (1831). It is sometimes associated with the Latin word *norma*, meaning 'rule, standard', or regarded as a feminine form of **Norman**.

Norman (M) 'man from the north'. The word *Norman* originally referred to the Vikings who settled in northern France in the 9th century, and the inhabitants of that region who invaded England in the 11th century. Famous modern bearers of the name include the British comic actor Norman Wisdom.
SHORT FORM: **Norm**.

Norris (M) from the surname, meaning 'northerner'. The writer and television presenter Norris McWhirter, co-founder of the *Guinness Book of Records*, was a famous bearer of the name.

Nuala [NOO-la] (F) a short form of the Gaelic name **Fionnuala** ('fair-shouldered'), given as a name in its own right, especially in Ireland.
RELATED NAMES: **Nola, Finola, Fenella.**

Nur (M/F) an Arabic name meaning 'light'.
ALTERNATIVE FORM: **Nura** (F).

Nye (M) short for **Aneurin.**

Nyree (F) another form of the New Zealand name **Ngaire**, spelt as it sounds. It was made famous in the 1960s by the New-Zealand-born actress Nyree Dawn Porter.

O

Obadiah (M) 'servant of God'. The name of a biblical prophet and the book of the Bible containing his prophecies. The oily chaplain Obadiah Slope, a character in Anthony Trollope's novel *Barchester Towers* (1857), is a famous fictional bearer.

Oberon (M) another spelling of Auberon ('noble bear'), borne by the king of the fairies in Shakespeare's play *A Midsummer Night's Dream*.

Ocean (M/F) from the word *ocean*, which comes from the name of the Greek sea god Oceanus.

Octavia (F) the feminine form of Octavius, borne in the 1st century BC by a wife of Mark Antony. Other famous bearers include the 19th-century social reformer Octavia Hill.

Octavian (M) another form of Octavius. It was one of the names by which the Roman emperor Augustus was formerly known.

Octavius (M) 'eighth'. From a Roman family name. It was sometimes given to the eighth-born child in the days of large families.
ALTERNATIVE FORM: **Octavian**.
FEMININE FORM: **Octavia**.

Oded (M) 'supporter'. The name of a biblical prophet.

Odette (F) 'prosperity'. Of French origin, the name is borne by the central character of Tchaikovsky's ballet *Swan Lake* (1877), a princess who is turned into a swan. The film *Odette* (1950) tells the story of Odette Sansom, a real-life heroine of the Second World War.
RELATED NAMES: **Odile, Ottilie, Ottoline**.

Odhran [OH-ran, OR-an] (M) 'sallow'. An Irish name borne by an abbot who accompanied St Columba to Scotland.
ALTERNATIVE FORMS: **Odran, Oran, Orin**.

Odile (F) 'prosperity'. The name of an 8th-century saint who founded a convent in Alsace.

RELATED NAMES: **Odette, Ottilie, Ottoline.**

Ofra (F) another form of **Ophrah**.

Ogden (M) from a surname and place name meaning 'oak valley'. It was the middle name of the 20th-century US poet known as Ogden Nash.

Oisin [oh-SHEEN] (M) 'little deer'. An Irish name borne by a legendary poet and warrior, the son of Fionn MacCool.
ALTERNATIVE FORMS: **Osheen, Ossian.**

Olga (F) another form of **Helga** ('prosperous, successful'), of Russian origin. The name was borne in the 10th century by St Olga of Kiev and in the 20th century by the Soviet gymnast Olga Korbut.

Olive (F) from the name of the tree, which is a symbol of peace. The cartoon character Olive Oyl, the skinny girlfriend of Popeye, is a famous bearer of the name.
RELATED NAME: **Olivia.**

Oliver (M) from a French name of uncertain origin, possibly meaning 'olive tree', 'elf army', or 'ancestral relic'. It was borne by the 17th-century English statesman Oliver Cromwell, the young hero of Charles Dickens' novel *Oliver Twist* (1838), and the 20th-century British actor Oliver Reed.
SHORT FORM: **Ollie.**

Olivia (F) probably another form of Olive, given by Shakespeare to one of the central characters of his play *Twelfth Night*. Famous modern bearers include the actress Olivia de Havilland and the singer Olivia Newton-John.
SHORT FORMS: **Liv, Livvy, Livia.**

Olwen (F) a Welsh name meaning 'white footprint'. According to legend, Olwen was a beautiful maiden in whose footprints white flowers sprang up. The name was popularized in the mid-20th century by a piece of music called 'The Dream of Olwen', written by Charles Williams.
ALTERNATIVE FORM: **Olwyn.**

Olympia (F) from the place name Olympus, the mountain home of the gods in Greek mythology. The US actress Olympia Dukakis is a famous bearer of the name.

Omar (M) an Arabic name meaning 'prosperous' or a biblical name meaning 'talkative'. Famous bearers of the Arabic name include the 11th-century Persian poet Omar Khayyám and the 20th-century Egyptian-born actor Omar Sharif.
ALTERNATIVE FORM: **Umar.**

Oona (F) an Irish form of **Una** ('lamb' or 'one'), borne by the wife of the legendary Irish hero Fionn MacCool.
ALTERNATIVE FORM: **Oonagh.**
RELATED NAMES: **Juno, Unity.**

Opal (F) from the name of the gemstone.
ALTERNATIVE FORM: **Opaline**.

Ophelia (F) 'help'. It is chiefly associated with the beautiful young woman of this name in Shakespeare's play *Hamlet*, who goes mad and drowns.

Ophrah (F) 'fawn'. A biblical boys' name that is now given to girls.
ALTERNATIVE FORMS: **Ophra, Ofra**.

Oprah (F) a name made famous by the US television personality Oprah Winfrey, who was originally named Orpah.

Oran (M) another form of the Irish name **Odhran** ('sallow'), spelt as it sounds.
ALTERNATIVE FORM: **Orin**.

Oren (M) a biblical name meaning 'pine tree'.
ALTERNATIVE FORM: **Orin**.

Oriana (F) 'sunrise' or 'golden'. The name was sometimes given to Elizabeth I, for example in a book of madrigals called *The Triumphs of Oriana* (1601).

Orin (M) another form of **Oran** or **Oren**.

Orla (F) another form of **Orlaith**, spelt as it sounds. The name has been made famous in recent times by the television journalist Orla Guerin.
ALTERNATIVE FORM: **Orlagh**.

Orlaith [OR-la] (F) 'golden princess'. An Irish name borne by the sister and daughter of Brian Boru, High King of Ireland.
ALTERNATIVE FORMS: **Orla, Orlagh**.

Orlando (M) another form of **Roland** ('famous land'), of Italian origin. The title character of Virginia Woolf's novel *Orlando* (1928) lives through four centuries, initially as a man and later as a woman. Other famous bearers include the British actor Orlando Bloom. The name may also be associated with the city of Orlando in Florida.

Orpah (F) 'deer'. A biblical name, borne by Ruth's sister-in-law.

Orrell (M) from a surname and place name meaning 'hill where ore is found'.

Orson (M) 'bear cub'. The name is chiefly associated with the 20th-century US film director and actor Orson Welles.

Orville (M) a name coined by Fanny Burney for a character in her novel *Evelina* (1778). In the late 20th century it was more familiar as the name of a large green nappy-wearing duck in Keith Harris's ventriloquist act.

Osbert (M) 'illustrious god'. The name was borne in the 20th century by the British cartoonist Osbert

Lancaster and the British writer Osbert Sitwell.

Oscar (M) 'deer lover', 'gentle friend', or 'divine spearman'. Famous bearers include the 19th-century Irish writer Oscar Wilde. The name is also associated with the statuettes awarded annually in the USA by the Academy of Motion Picture Arts and Sciences.

Osheen (M) another form of the Irish name Oisin ('little deer'), spelt as it sounds.

Osmond (M) 'divine protector'. The name was borne by an 11th-century saint. It is now more often found as a surname.
ALTERNATIVE FORM: **Osmund**.

Ossian (M) another form of the Irish name Oisin ('little deer'), used by the 18th-century Scottish poet James Macpherson when he published various supposed translations of the legendary poet's works.
ALTERNATIVE FORM: **Osian**.

Oswald (M) 'divine rule'. The name was borne by two English saints: a 7th-century king of Northumbria and a 10th-century archbishop of York. More recent famous bearers include Sir Oswald Mosley, who founded the British Union of Fascists in 1932.
SHORT FORM: **Ozzie**.

Otis (M) from the surname, which is another form of **Otto**. The US soul singer Otis Redding, who died in a plane crash in 1967 at the age of 26, was a famous bearer of the name.

Ottilie (F) another form of **Odile** ('prosperity').

Otto (M) 'prosperity'. The name was borne by the 19th-century German statesman Prince Otto von Bismarck and the 20th-century US film director Otto Preminger.
RELATED NAME: **Otis**.

Ottoline (F) another form of **Odile** ('prosperity'). The name was made famous in the early 20th century by the British society hostess Lady Ottoline Morrell.

Owen (M) a Welsh name of uncertain origin, possibly related to **Eugene** ('well-born'). The 15th-century Welsh rebel Owen Glendower was a famous bearer of the name. In Ireland it is sometimes regarded as an English form of **Eoghan** ('born of the yew tree'), spelt as it sounds.
ALTERNATIVE FORM: **Owain**.

Ozzie (M) short for various names beginning with *Os-*, especially **Oswald**.
ALTERNATIVE FORM: **Ozzy**.

P

Paddy (M) short for **Patrick**. It is also used as a nickname for an Irishman, as in the case of the British politician Paddy Ashdown (born Jeremy Ashdown in 1941), who lived in Northern Ireland as a child.

Padma (M/F) an Indian name meaning 'lotus'.

Padraig [PAH-drig, PAH-drik] (M) the Gaelic form of **Patrick**.
ALTERNATIVE FORM: **Padraic**.

Paige (F) from the surname, which comes from the word *page* referring to the young servant of a great lord. It became a fashionable girls' name throughout the English-speaking world in the 1990s.
ALTERNATIVE FORM: **Page**.

Pamela (F) a name invented by the 16th-century poet Sir Philip Sidney and later used by Samuel Richardson for the title character of his novel *Pamela* (1740). It was particularly popular in the mid-20th century, when the comedian and psychologist Pamela Stephenson/Connolly and the humorous poet Pam Ayres were born.
SHORT FORMS: **Pam, Pammy**.
ALTERNATIVE FORM: **Pamella**.

Pandora (F) 'all gifts'. In Greek mythology, Pandora had a box that she was forbidden to open. When she did so, all kinds of trouble were released into the world and only hope remained in the box. In Sue Townsend's early *Adrian Mole* books, a girl called Pandora is the object of the hero's adolescent desires.

Paris (F) from the name of the capital city of France. The US model and socialite Paris Hilton is a famous modern bearer of the name.

Paris (M) the name of a Trojan prince in Greek mythology.

Parker (M) from the surname, meaning 'park keeper'.

Parry (M) from the Welsh surname, meaning 'son of Harry'.

Parvati (F) 'daughter of the mountain'. An Indian name

sometimes given to the wife of Shiva.

Pascal (M) 'of Easter'. A French name that is occasionally found in English-speaking countries, given to children born at Easter or in honour of the 17th-century French mathematician Blaise Pascal.
FEMININE FORM: **Pascale**.

Pascale (F) the feminine form of **Pascal**.

Pat (M/F) short for **Patrick**, **Patricia**, **Patsy**, or **Patty**.

Patience (F) from the word *patience*, referring to the virtue of enduring hardship without complaint. Famous bearers of the name include the title character of the Gilbert and Sullivan opera *Patience* (1881) and the 20th-century inspirational poet Patience Strong (born Winifred May).

Patrice (M/F) another form of **Patrick** or **Patricia**, of French origin.
RELATED NAMES: **Patty** (F), **Patsy** (F), **Trisha** (F), **Tisha** (F).

Patricia (F) 'noble'. The name was particularly popular in the mid-20th century. Famous modern bearers include the British actresses Patricia Routledge and Patricia Hodge.
SHORT FORMS: **Pat**, **Trish**, **Tish**.
RELATED NAMES: **Patty**, **Patsy**, **Trisha**, **Tisha**, **Patrice**.

Patrick (M) 'noble'. An Irish name borne in the 5th century by the patron saint of Ireland. More recent famous bearers include the British astronomer Patrick Moore and the US actor Patrick Swayze.
SHORT FORMS: **Pat**, **Paddy**.
ALTERNATIVE FORMS: **Padraig**, **Padraic**.
RELATED NAME: **Patrice**.

Patsy (F) a short form of **Patricia**, sometimes given as a name in its own right. It was popularized in the late 20th century by the British actress Patsy Kensit and the fictional character Patsy Stone (played by Joanna Lumley) in the television sitcom *Absolutely Fabulous*.
SHORT FORM: **Pat**.
RELATED NAMES: **Patty**, **Trisha**, **Tisha**, **Patrice**.

Patty (F) a short form of **Patricia**, sometimes given as a name in its own right.
SHORT FORM: **Pat**.
ALTERNATIVE FORMS: **Pattie**, **Patti**.
RELATED NAMES: **Patsy**, **Trisha**, **Tisha**, **Patrice**.

Paul (M) 'small'. From a Roman family name that originated as a nickname. The name is borne in the Bible by St Paul, formerly called Saul, who was converted to Christianity on the road to Damascus. Famous modern bearers include the US actor Paul Newman and the British singer and songwriter Paul McCartney.
FEMININE FORMS: **Paula**, **Pauline**, **Paulette**.

Paula (F) a feminine form of **Paul**. The British television presenter Paula Yates was a famous bearer of the name.
SHORT FORM: **Polly**.
RELATED NAMES: **Pauline, Paulette**.

Paulette (F) a feminine form of **Paul**, of French origin.
SHORT FORM: **Polly**.
RELATED NAMES: **Paula, Pauline**.

Pauline (F) a feminine form of **Paul**. In recent times the name has been chiefly associated with the fictional character Pauline Fowler (played by Wendy Richard) in the soap opera *EastEnders*.
SHORT FORM: **Polly**.
ALTERNATIVE FORM: **Paulina**.
RELATED NAMES: **Paula, Paulette**.

Payton (M/F) another form of **Peyton**.

Pearce (M) another spelling of **Pierce**, which ultimately comes from **Peter** ('rock, stone').

Pearl (F) from the name of the jewel. The 20th-century US writer Pearl Buck was a famous bearer of the name.
ALTERNATIVE FORM: **Perle**.
RELATED NAMES: *see list at* **Peggy**.

Peg (F) short for **Peggy** or **Margaret**.

Peggy (F) a short form of **Margaret** ('pearl'), sometimes given as a name in its own right. Famous modern bearers include the British actress Dame Peggy Ashcroft and the

fictional character Peggy Mitchell in the soap opera *EastEnders*.
SHORT FORM: **Peg**.
RELATED NAMES: **Maggie, Marguerite, Margarita, Rita, Margot, Margaux, Margery, Marjorie, Madge, Meg, Megan, Greta, Gretchen, Gretel, Mairead, Maisie, May, Molly, Pearl**.

Pelham (M) from the surname, which comes from an English place name. It was the first name of the 20th-century British novelist known as P. G. Wodehouse, creator of humorous characters such as Bertie Wooster and his valet Jeeves.

Penelope [pi-NELL-a-pee] (F) the name of the patient, loving, and faithful wife of Odysseus in Greek mythology, possibly meaning 'duck' or 'thread'. Famous modern bearers include the British actress Penelope Keith.
SHORT FORM: **Pen**.
RELATED NAME: **Penny**.

Penn (M) from the surname, sometimes given as a forename in honour of William Penn, the 17th-century founder of Pennsylvania in the USA.

Penny (F) a short form of **Penelope**, sometimes given as a name in its own right.
SHORT FORM: **Pen**.

Percival (M) the name of one of the knights of King Arthur's Round Table, of uncertain origin.
SHORT FORM: **Perce.**

Percy (M) from a surname of French aristocratic origin. The forename was popularized in the early 19th century by the British poet Percy Bysshe Shelley. More recent famous bearers include the British television gardener Percy Thrower.
SHORT FORM: **Perce.**

Perdita [PER-dit-a] (F) 'lost'. A name coined by Shakespeare for the young heroine of his play *The Winter's Tale*. It is also borne by one of the canine characters in Dodie Smith's novel *The Hundred and One Dalmatians* (1956), filmed in 1961 and 1996.
RELATED NAME: **Purdy.**

Peregrine (M) 'stranger, foreigner'. The name is borne by the title character of Tobias Smollett's novel *The Adventures of Peregrine Pickle* (1751).
RELATED NAME: **Perry.**

Perle (F) a Jewish form of **Pearl.**

Perry (M) a short form of **Peregrine**, sometimes given as a name in its own right. Alternatively, it may be from the surname, which means 'pear tree'. Famous modern bearers include the singer Perry Como (whose full name was Pierino) and the fictional detective Perry Mason (created by Erle Stanley Gardner), as well as Kevin's friend (an adolescent boy played by Kathy Burke) in Harry Enfield's television comedy shows.

Pet (F) short for **Petula.**

Peta (F) a feminine form of **Peter.**
RELATED NAME: **Petra.**

Peter (M) 'rock, stone'. The name of one of Jesus Christ's apostles, formerly called Simon, who is regarded as the founder of the Christian Church. Famous bearers in children's fiction include Peter Rabbit, created by Beatrix Potter, and Peter Pan, created by J. M. Barrie.
SHORT FORM: **Pete.**
FEMININE FORMS: **Petra, Peta.**
RELATED NAMES: **Piers, Pierce.**

Petra (F) a feminine form of **Peter.** In the early 1960s the name was chosen by viewers of the children's television programme *Blue Peter* for the presenters' first pet dog, who made regular appearances until her death in 1977.
RELATED NAME: **Peta.**

Petronella (F) from a Roman family name of uncertain origin. In its alternative form the name was borne by St Petronilla, an early Christian martyr.
ALTERNATIVE FORM: **Petronilla.**

Petula (F) a name of uncertain origin, made famous in the mid-20th century by the British singer Petula Clark.
SHORT FORM: **Pet.**

Peyton (M/F) from the surname, which comes from an English place name. In the 1950s and 1960s it was chiefly associated with *Peyton Place*, the title of a novel by Grace Metalious (set in a fictional US town) and its television adaptation.
ALTERNATIVE FORM: **Payton**.

Phelan (M) an English form of an Irish name meaning 'little wolf'.

Phelim (M) an English form of an Irish name meaning 'ever virtuous'.

Phemie (F) short for **Euphemia**.

Phil (M/F) short for various names beginning with *Phil-* or *Phyl-*.

Philbert (M) 'very illustrious'. St Philbert (or Philibert) was a 7th-century French monk and abbot.
SHORT FORM: **Phil**.
ALTERNATIVE FORMS: **Filbert, Philibert**.

Philemon [fye-LEE-mun] (M) 'kiss'. The name of a character in Greek mythology and of an early Christian to whom one of St Paul's epistles is addressed.

Philip (M) 'lover of horses'. The name of Alexander the Great's father and of one of Jesus Christ's apostles. More recent famous bearers include the British poet Philip Larkin and Elizabeth II's husband Prince Philip.
SHORT FORMS: **Phil, Pip**.
ALTERNATIVE FORM: **Phillip**.
FEMININE FORM: **Philippa**.

Philippa (F) the feminine form of **Philip**. The British television presenter Philippa Forrester is a famous bearer of the name.
SHORT FORMS: **Phil, Pip**.
ALTERNATIVE FORMS: **Phillipa, Philipa, Phillippa**.
RELATED NAME: **Pippa**.

Phillida (F) another spelling of **Phyllida**.

Philo (M) 'loved'. The name was borne by a 1st-century Jewish philosopher.

Philomena (F) 'greatly beloved'. The name became popular after the discovery in Italy of the remains of a young woman said to have been an early Christian martyr called St Philomena.
SHORT FORM: **Phil**.

Phineas (M) a biblical name, probably meaning 'person from Nubia in Africa'. The 19th-century US showman Phineas T. Barnum was a famous bearer.
ALTERNATIVE FORM: **Phinehas**.
RELATED NAME: **Pinchas**.

Phoebe [FEE-bee] (F) 'bright'. A name sometimes given to the Greek goddess of the moon. It has recently been popularized by a character in the US television series *Friends*.

Phoenix [FEE-niks] (M/F) from the name of the mythological bird that is said to rise from its own ashes after burning to death. It may also be associated with the US city of this name, the capital of Arizona.

Phylicia (F) a blend of **Phyllis** and **Felicia**.
SHORT FORMS: **Phyl, Phil**.
ALTERNATIVE FORM: **Phyllicia**.

Phyllida (F) another form of **Phyllis**. The British actress Phyllida Law is a famous bearer of the name.
ALTERNATIVE FORM: **Phillida**.

Phyllis (F) 'foliage'. The name of a princess in Greek mythology who committed suicide when her lover left her and was changed by the gods into an almond tree.
SHORT FORMS: **Phyl, Phil**.
RELATED NAME: **Phyllida**.

Pia (F) 'pious'. The name is borne by the US actress Pia Zadora.

Pierce (M) from the surname, which is another form of **Piers**. The Irish-born actor Pierce Brosnan is probably the best-known bearer of the name.
ALTERNATIVE FORM: **Pearce**.
RELATED NAME: **Peter**.

Piers (M) another form of **Peter** ('rock, stone'), of Old French origin. The name is borne by the title character of the medieval poem *Piers Plowman* by William Langland.
RELATED NAME: **Pierce**.

Pinchas (M) a Jewish form of

Phineas, made famous by the Israeli violinist Pinchas Zukerman.

Pip (M/F) short for **Philip, Philippa**, or **Pippa**.

Piper (F) from the surname, meaning 'person who plays the pipes'. Famous bearers include the US actress Piper Laurie (whose real name is Rosetta Jacobs) and one of the central characters of the US television series *Charmed*, a young woman with magical powers.

Pippa (F) a short form of **Philippa**, the feminine form of **Philip** ('lover of horses'), sometimes given as a name in its own right. It is borne by the young heroine of Robert Browning's poetic drama *Pippa Passes* (1841), who utters the famous words 'God's in his heaven – All's right with the world!'
SHORT FORM: **Pip**.

Polly (F) another form of **Molly** or a short form of **Pauline, Paula**, or **Paulette**. It is a name traditionally given to parrots, and also features in the nursery rhyme 'Polly put the kettle on'.
SHORT FORM: **Poll**.

Pollyanna (F) a compound of **Polly** and **Anna**, borne by the eternally optimistic young heroine of Eleanor Porter's novel *Pollyanna* (1913).

Poppy (F) from the flower name. The name is borne by the heroine of Mary Wesley's novel *The Vacillations* *of Poppy Carew* (1986), filmed in 1994.

Portia [POR-sha] (F) from a Roman family name meaning 'pig'. Shakespeare gave the name to the heroine of his play *The Merchant of Venice*, who proves to be a skilful amateur lawyer.

Posy (F) from the word *posy*, meaning 'bunch of flowers'. It is also sometimes used as a childish alternative to **Josie** or **Rosie**. Famous bearers include the British cartoonist Posy Simmonds (whose real name is Rosemary).

Pradeep (M) an Indian name meaning 'lantern'.
ALTERNATIVE FORM: **Pradip**.

Prakash (M) an Indian name meaning 'light' or 'famous'.

Prasad (M) an Indian name meaning 'brightness'.

Precious (M/F) from the word *precious*, meaning 'valuable, treasured'.

Prem (M) an Indian name meaning 'love'.
FEMININE FORM: **Prema**.

Prema (F) the feminine form of **Prem**.

Prentice (M) from the surname, meaning 'apprentice'. It is borne by Prentice McHoan, the hero of Iain Banks' novel *The Crow Road* (1992).
ALTERNATIVE FORM: **Prentiss**.

Presley (M) from the surname, usually given in honour of the US singer Elvis Presley. It ultimately comes from a place name meaning 'priest's wood'.

Preston (M) from a surname and place name meaning 'priest's settlement'. It was popularized in the early 21st century by the British singer and celebrity Samuel Preston, who is generally known by his surname alone.

Price (M) from the Welsh surname, meaning 'son of Rhys'.
ALTERNATIVE FORM: **Pryce**.

Primrose (F) from the flower name, which means 'first rose' and is associated with the spring.

Prince (M) from the royal title *prince*. It was popularized in the late 20th century by the US singer and songwriter who was initially known by this name alone.

Priscilla (F) 'ancient'. The name of a minor biblical character, also called Prisca, from a Roman family name. More recent famous bearers include the US actress Priscilla Presley.
SHORT FORM: **Prissy**.
RELATED NAME: **Cilla**.

Priya (F) an Indian name meaning 'beloved'.

Prosper (M) 'fortunate, prosperous'. The 5th-century theologian St Prosper of Aquitaine and the 19th-century French writer Prosper

Mérimée were famous bearers of the name.

Prudence (F) 'good judgement'. The cookery writer known as Prue Leith was born Prudence Margaret Leith in South Africa in 1940.
SHORT FORMS: **Pru, Prue**.
RELATED NAME: **Purdy**.

Prunella (F) 'little plum'. The best-known modern bearer of the name is the British actress Prunella Scales.
SHORT FORMS: **Pru, Prue**.

Pryce (M) another form of **Price**.

Psyche [SYE-kee] (F) 'soul' or 'butterfly'. The name of Cupid's beloved in classical mythology.

Ptolemy [TOL-a-mee] (M) 'warlike'. The name of a number of kings of Egypt, and of a 2nd-century Greek astronomer.
SHORT FORM: **Tolly**.

Purdy (F) a short form of **Perdita** ('lost') or **Prudence** ('good judgement'), sometimes given as a name in its own right. Alternatively, it may come from the surname, meaning 'by God!', borne by the gunmaker James Purdey (as in the case of the character played in the mid-1970s by Joanna Lumley in the television series *The New Avengers*).
ALTERNATIVE FORMS: **Purdey, Purdie**.

Q

Queenie (F) from a nickname sometimes given to girls called **Regina** or bearing the name of the reigning queen.

Quentin (M) another form of **Quintus**, borne by a 3rd-century saint. Famous modern bearers include the British writer and gay icon Quentin Crisp (whose real name was Denis Pratt) and the US film director Quentin Tarantino.
RELATED NAMES: **Quintin, Quincy.**

Quincy (M) from a surname of French aristocratic origin, which ultimately comes from the Roman name **Quintus**. It was borne in the 19th century by the US president John Quincy Adams.

RELATED NAMES: **Quentin, Quintin.**

Quinn (M) from the Irish surname, meaning 'descendant of Conn'.

Quintin (M) another form of **Quintus**. The 20th-century British politician Quintin Hogg was a famous bearer of the name.
RELATED NAMES: **Quentin, Quincy.**

Quinton (M) from a surname and place name meaning 'queen's settlement'.

Quintus (M) 'fifth'. A name of Roman origin, sometimes given to the fifth-born child of a family.
RELATED NAMES: **Quentin, Quintin, Quincy.**

R

Rab (M) a Scottish short form of **Robert**.

Rabbie (M) a Scottish short form of **Robert**, chiefly associated with the 18th-century Scottish poet Robert Burns.

Rachel (F) 'ewe'. A biblical name, borne by the wife of Jacob and mother of Joseph and Benjamin. More recent famous bearers include the British cricketer Rachael Heyhoe-Flint and a character in the US television series *Friends*.
ALTERNATIVE FORMS: **Rachael, Rachelle**.
RELATED NAMES: **Raquel, Rae**.

Radha (F) 'success'. An Indian name borne by Krishna's favourite female companion.

Rae (F) a short form of **Rachel**, sometimes given as a name in its own right. It may also be regarded as a feminine form of **Ray**.
RELATED NAME: **Raquel**.

Raelene (F) a compound of **Rae** and the name-ending *-lene*. It is particularly popular in Australia.

Rafe (M) another form of **Ralph**, spelt as it sounds in what is now the less common pronunciation of the name.

Rafiq (M) an Arabic name meaning 'friend' or 'kind'.

Raghav (M) an Indian name meaning 'descendant of Raghu'.

Raghu (M) an Indian name meaning 'swift'.

Raine (F) possibly from the French word *reine*, meaning 'queen'. It is also a short form of **Lorraine**. The name is borne by the former Countess Spencer, stepmother of Diana, Princess of Wales.

Raj (M) an Indian name meaning 'king'. It is also a short form of various names beginning with these letters.
ALTERNATIVE FORMS: **Raja, Rajan**.

Raja (F) an Arabic name meaning 'hope'.

Raja (M) another form of **Raj**.

Rajani (F) 'night'. An Indian name sometimes given to the wife of Shiva.

Rajendra (M) an Indian name meaning 'mighty king'.
ALTERNATIVE FORM: **Rajinder**.

Rajesh (M) an Indian name meaning 'ruler of kings'.

Rajiv (M) 'striped'. An Indian name borne by the 20th-century Indian statesman Rajiv Gandhi.

Rakesh (M) 'ruler of the day of the full moon'. An Indian name sometimes given to the god Shiva.

Ralph [ralf, rafe] (M) 'wolf counsel'. Famous modern bearers include the British actors Sir Ralph Richardson and Ralph Fiennes.
ALTERNATIVE FORMS: **Ralf, Rafe**.

Rama (M) 'pleasing'. An Indian name borne by the god Vishnu in various forms.
ALTERNATIVE FORM: **Ram**.

Ramesh (M) an Indian name meaning 'lord of Lakshmi (Vishnu's wife)'.

Ramona (F) a feminine form of **Raymond**, of Spanish origin. The name was popularized in the UK by a song with this title that was a top ten hit single in 1964.

Ramsay (M) from the surname, which comes from the place name Ramsey. It was the middle name of the British statesman known as Ramsay MacDonald, who became the first Labour prime minister in 1924.
ALTERNATIVE FORM: **Ramsey**.

Ran (M) short for various names beginning with these letters, such as **Randolph** or **Ranulph**.

Rana (F) an Arabic name meaning 'eye-catching'.

Ranald (M) a Scottish form of **Ronald**.
RELATED NAMES: **Ronnie, Reginald, Reggie, Reynold**.

Randa (F) short for **Miranda**.
ALTERNATIVE FORM: **Randi**.

Randall (M) another form of **Randolph** that is more frequently found as a surname in modern times.
RELATED NAMES: **Randy, Ranulph**.

Randolph (M) 'wolf shield'. The name was borne by the father and son of the British statesman Sir Winston Churchill.
SHORT FORM: **Ran**.
ALTERNATIVE FORM: **Randolf**.
RELATED NAMES: **Randy, Randall, Ranulph**.

Randy (M) a short form of **Randolph** or **Randall**, sometimes given as a name in its own right, despite the sexual connotations of the word *randy*. As a short form it is used by the US singer and songwriter Randy Newman (whose full name is Randall).

Rani (F) an Indian name meaning 'queen'.
ALTERNATIVE FORM: **Ranee**.

Ranjit (M) 'coloured' or 'delighted'. An Indian name borne by Ranjit Singh, who founded a Sikh kingdom in the 19th century.

Ranulph (M) another form of **Randolph**. The British explorer Sir Ranulph Fiennes is probably the best-known bearer of the name in modern times.
SHORT FORM: **Ran**.
ALTERNATIVE FORM: **Ranulf**.
RELATED NAMES: **Randall, Randy**.

Raphael (M) 'God heals'. Raphael was one of the archangels, mentioned by name in the Apocrypha. Other famous bearers include the Renaissance painter known as Raphael (whose real name was Raffaello Santi).

Raquel [rak-EL] (F) another form of **Rachel**, of Spanish origin. Famous bearers include the US film star Raquel Welch and a character in the British television sitcom *Only Fools and Horses*.
RELATED NAME: **Rae**.

Rashid (M) an Arabic name meaning 'rightly guided'.
ALTERNATIVE FORM: **Rasheed**.
FEMININE FORM: **Rashida**.

Rashida (F) the feminine form of **Rashid**.
ALTERNATIVE FORM: **Rasheeda**.

Rastus (M) a short form of **Erastus** ('beloved'), sometimes given as a name in its own right.

Ravi (M) 'sun'. An Indian name borne by the sun god and made internationally famous by the sitar-player Ravi Shankar.

Ray (M) a short form of **Raymond**, sometimes given as a name in its own right. The US science-fiction writer Ray Bradbury is a famous bearer.
FEMININE FORM: **Rae**.

Raymond (M) 'decisive protector'. Famous bearers of the name include the 20th-century US crime writer Raymond Chandler.
FEMININE FORM: **Ramona**.
RELATED NAME: **Ray**.

Reanna (F) another spelling of the Welsh name **Rhianna** ('maiden' or 'great queen').
ALTERNATIVE FORM: **Rianna**.

Reanne (F) another spelling of the Welsh name **Rhian** ('maiden').
ALTERNATIVE FORMS: **Rianne, Rian**.

Rebecca (F) a biblical name, possibly meaning 'binding'. In the Bible, Rebekah is Isaac's wife, the mother of Esau and Jacob. The name was popularized by Daphne du Maurier's novel *Rebecca* (1938) and became particularly fashionable in the late 20th century.
SHORT FORM: **Becca**.
ALTERNATIVE FORM: **Rebekah**.

RELATED NAMES: **Becky, Rivka.**

Reece (M/F) another form of the Welsh boys' name **Rhys** ('ardour'), spelt as it sounds. It is occasionally given to girls, perhaps from its use as a surname, as in the case of the US actress Reese Witherspoon (it was her mother's maiden name).
ALTERNATIVE FORMS: **Reese, Rees.**

Reed (M) another form of **Reid.**

Reenie (F) short for **Doreen** or **Maureen**, or another form of the girls' name **Rene.**

Reg (M) short for **Reginald** or **Reggie.**

Regan [REE-gun] (F) a name of uncertain origin, possibly meaning 'queen' or 'princess'. It is borne by one of the king's heartless daughters in Shakespeare's play *King Lear.*

Reggie (M) a short form of **Reginald**, sometimes given as a name in its own right.
SHORT FORM: **Reg.**
RELATED NAMES: **Reynold, Ronald, Ronnie, Ranald.**

Regina (F) 'queen'. The name was borne by an early Christian martyr. It was fashionable during the reign of Queen Victoria, but not during the reign of Elizabeth II (perhaps because it sounds similar to the word *vagina*).

Reginald (M) 'decisive ruler'. The name is borne by the fictional character Reginald Perrin, created in

the 1970s by the writer David Nobbs and immortalized by the comic actor Leonard Rossiter in *The Fall and Rise of Reginald Perrin.*
SHORT FORMS: **Reg, Rex.**
RELATED NAMES: **Reggie, Reynold, Ronald, Ronnie, Ranald.**

Reid (M) from the surname, meaning 'red, ruddy'.
ALTERNATIVE FORM: **Reed.**

Remus (M) the name of one of the legendary founders of Rome. It is also borne by the narrator of Joel Chandler Harris's 'Uncle Remus' stories, based on African–American folk tales.

Rena (F) another form of **Renee**, a short form of **Serena**, or another spelling of **Rina.**
RELATED NAME: **Renata.**

Renata [ruh-NAH-ta] (F) another form of **Renee**. The original Latin form of the name, it is now found in many European countries.
RELATED NAME: **Rena.**

Rene [REE-nee] (F) a short form of **Irene** ('peace'), sometimes given as a name in its own right, or another form of **Renee.**
ALTERNATIVE FORM: **Reenie.**

Rene [REN-ay, ruh-NAY] (M) 'reborn'. The name was popularized in North America by the French missionary St René Goupil, who was martyred there in 1642. In the UK it is chiefly associated with the hapless French

café-owner René Artois in the television sitcom 'Allo 'Allo.
ALTERNATIVE FORM: **René.**
FEMININE FORM: **Renee.**

Renee [REN-ay, ruh-NAY, REE-nee] (F) the feminine form of the boys' name **Rene**. Famous modern bearers include the US actress Renée Zellweger.
ALTERNATIVE FORMS: **Renée, René, Rene.**
RELATED NAMES: **Renata, Rena.**

Reuben [ROO-b'n] (M) 'behold, a son'. A biblical name, borne by one of the sons of Jacob.
SHORT FORM: **Rube.**
ALTERNATIVE FORM: **Ruben.**

Reuel [ROO-ul, rool] (M) 'friend of God'. The name of a minor biblical character, it was also the third forename of the British writer J. R. R. Tolkien, author of *The Lord of the Rings* (1954–5).

Rex (M) 'king'. It is also used as a short form of **Reginald**, as in the case of the 20th-century British actor Rex Harrison.

Reynard (M) 'decisive and strong'. In fables and folk tales it is a traditional name for a fox.

Reynold (M) another form of **Reginald**, of Old French origin.
RELATED NAMES: **Reggie, Ronald, Ronnie, Ranald.**

Rhea (F) the name of the mother of Zeus in Greek mythology. In Roman legend Rhea Silvia is the mother of Romulus and Remus, the founders of Rome.

Rhett (M) from the surname, probably meaning 'advice'. It is chiefly associated with Rhett Butler, one of the central characters in Margaret Mitchell's novel *Gone with the Wind* (1936), played by Clark Gable in the 1939 film adaptation.

Rhian [ree-AN] (F) a Welsh name meaning 'maiden'.
ALTERNATIVE FORMS: **Rian, Rianne, Reanne, Rhianna.**

Rhianna (F) another form of **Rhian** or **Rhiannon**.
ALTERNATIVE FORMS: **Rianna, Reanna.**

Rhiannon [ree-AN-on] (F) 'great queen'. A Welsh name borne in legend by a goddess associated with the moon and horses, who married a mortal prince and was falsely accused of killing their baby son.
ALTERNATIVE FORM: **Rhianna.**

Rhoda (F) 'rose' or 'woman from Rhodes'. The name is borne by a minor biblical character. It was popularized in the 1970s by the US television sitcom *Rhoda*.

Rhodri (M) 'wheel king'. A Welsh name borne by a 9th-century king and, more recently, by the politician Rhodri Morgan, who became First Minister of the Welsh Assembly in 2000.

Rhona (F) another spelling of **Rona**, influenced by **Rhoda**.

Rhonda (F) possibly a blend of **Rhona** and **Rhoda**. Alternatively, it may be a Welsh name meaning 'good lance', influenced by Rhondda, the name of a river and valley associated with coal mining. The 20th-century US actress Rhonda Fleming is a famous bearer of the name.

Rhys [reece] (M) 'ardour'. A Welsh name borne by two medieval rulers (Rhys ap Tewdur and Rhys ap Gruffudd) and, more recently, by the actor Rhys Ifans.
ALTERNATIVE FORMS: **Reece, Reese, Rees**.

Ria [REE-a] (F) a short form of **Maria**, sometimes given as a name in its own right. It was popularized in the late 1970s by the central character of the sitcom *Butterflies*, a bored housewife played by Wendy Craig.
RELATED NAMES: **Mary, Mia, Mitzi, Mimi, Marie, Marian, Marianne, May, Mair, Maire, Mairi, Mari, Maura, Maureen, Moira, Mariel, Mariella, Marietta, Miriam, Maryam**.

Rian [ree-AN] (F) another spelling of the Welsh name **Rhian** ('maiden').
ALTERNATIVE FORMS: **Rianne, Reanne**.

Rian [RYE-un] (M) an Irish name meaning 'king'.
RELATED NAME: **Ryan**.

Rianna (F) another spelling of the Welsh name **Rhianna** ('maiden' or 'great queen').
ALTERNATIVE FORM: **Reanna**.

Riaz (M) an Arabic name meaning 'meadows, gardens'.

Ricci (M/F) another spelling of **Ricki** or **Ricky**.

Richard (M) 'powerful ruler'. The name has been borne by three kings of England, including the popular Richard the Lionheart in the 12th century and the much-maligned Richard III in the 15th century. More recent famous British bearers include the actor Richard Burton and the entrepreneur Richard Branson.
SHORT FORMS: **Rich, Dick, Dickie, Dicky**.
FEMININE FORMS: **Richenda, Richelle**.
RELATED NAMES: **Rick, Ricky, Richie, Dickon**.

Richelle (F) a feminine form of **Richard**.
RELATED NAMES: **Ricki, Richenda**.

Richenda (F) a feminine form of **Richard**.
RELATED NAMES: **Ricki, Richelle**.

Richie (M) a short form of **Richard**, sometimes given as a name in its own right. As a short form it is used by the Australian cricketer Richie Benaud.

ALTERNATIVE FORM: **Ritchie**.

RELATED NAMES: **Rick, Ricky, Dickon**.

Rick (M) a short form of **Richard** or **Ricky**, sometimes given as a name in its own right. As a short form it is used by the British rock musician Rick Wakeman and the British chef Rick Stein.

ALTERNATIVE FORM: **Rik**.

RELATED NAMES: **Ricky, Richie, Dickon**.

Ricki (F) a short form of **Richenda**, **Richelle**, or various names containing the letters -ric- (such as **Frederica**), sometimes given as a name in its own right.

ALTERNATIVE FORMS: **Rikki, Rickie, Ricky, Ricci**.

Ricky (M) a short form of **Richard**, sometimes given as a name in its own right. Famous modern bearers include the British comic actor and writer Ricky Gervais.

ALTERNATIVE FORMS: **Rikki, Rickie, Ricki, Ricci**.

RELATED NAMES: **Rick, Richie, Dickon**.

Ridley (M) from a surname and place name meaning 'reedy meadow'. The British film director Ridley Scott is a famous modern bearer of the name.

Rik (M) another spelling of **Rick**,

borne by the British comedian Rik Mayall.

Rikki (M/F) another spelling of **Ricki** or **Ricky**.

Riley (M/F) from an English surname and place name meaning 'rye meadow', or from the Irish surname Reilly, possibly meaning 'valiant'.

Rina (F) another form of an Irish name meaning 'queenly', or a short form of various names ending with these letters, such as **Carina**.

ALTERNATIVE FORM: **Rena**.

Riordan [REAR-dun] (M) an Irish name meaning 'royal poet'.

Rita (F) a short form of **Margarita** ('pearl'), now usually given as a name in its own right. It was popularized in the mid-20th century by the US film star Rita Hayworth (born Margarita Cansino).

RELATED NAMES: **Marguerite, Margaret, Greta, Gretel, Gretchen, Margot, Margaux, Margery, Marjorie, Madge, Maggie, Meg, Megan, Peggy, Mairead, Maisie, May, Molly, Pearl**.

Ritchie (M) another spelling of **Richie**.

Rivka (F) a Jewish form of **Rebecca** (possibly meaning 'binding').

RELATED NAME: **Becky**.

Roald (M) 'famous ruler'. A

Norwegian name, made famous in English-speaking countries by the 20th-century British writer Roald Dahl (whose parents were Norwegian).

Rob (M) short for **Robert** or **Robin**. The real name of the 18th-century Scottish outlaw known as Rob Roy was Robert MacGregor.

Robbie (M/F) a short form of **Robert, Roberta**, or **Robin**, sometimes given as a name in its own right. Famous male bearers include the Scottish actor Robbie Coltrane and the English singer Robbie Williams.
ALTERNATIVE FORM: **Robby**.

Robert (M) 'great fame'. The name was borne by the 14th-century Scottish king Robert the Bruce and, more recently, the US actors Robert Redford and Robert De Niro.
SHORT FORMS: **Bob, Rob, Rab, Rabbie**.
FEMININE FORMS: **Roberta, Robin, Bobbie**.
RELATED NAMES: **Bobby, Robbie, Robin, Rupert**.

Roberta (F) a feminine form of **Robert**. The children's writer Edith Nesbit gave the name to the eldest of the three title characters of her book *The Railway Children* (1906), filmed in 1970 and again in 2000.
RELATED NAMES: **Bobbie, Robbie, Robin**.

Robin (M/F) another form of **Robert**, now often given to girls as well as boys through association with the bird of this name. The best-known male bearer is the legendary outlaw Robin Hood.
SHORT FORM: **Rob** (M).
ALTERNATIVE FORMS: **Robyn** (F), **Robina** (F).
RELATED NAMES: **Robbie, Bobby** (M), **Rupert** (M), **Bobbie** (F), **Roberta** (F).

Rocco (M) 'rest, repose'. Of Italian origin, the name was borne by a 14th-century saint who healed victims of the plague. The US singer Madonna gave the name to her son, born in 2000.
FEMININE FORM: **Rochelle**.
RELATED NAME: **Rocky**.

Rochelle (F) possibly a feminine form of **Rocco**, of French origin. Alternatively, it may be from the French place name La Rochelle, meaning 'the little rock'.

Rocky (M) a pet form of **Rocco** (as in the case of the 20th-century US boxer Rocky Marciano), or a nickname for a tough person. It was popularized as a name in its own right by the film *Rocky* (1976) and its sequels, in which Sylvester Stallone played the fictional boxer Rocky Balboa.

Roddy (M) a short form of **Roderick** or **Rodney**, sometimes given as a name in its own right. The Irish writer Roddy Doyle is a well-known bearer.

SHORT FORM: **Rod**.

Roderick (M) 'famous and powerful'. The name is chiefly found in literature, such as Tobias Smollett's novel *The Adventures of Roderick Random* (1748). The short form is used by the Scottish singer Rod Stewart.

SHORT FORM: **Rod**.
RELATED NAME: **Roddy**.

Rodney (M) from a surname and place name of uncertain origin. The name is borne by the fictional character Rodney Trotter, the put-upon younger brother of 'Del Boy' in the television sitcom *Only Fools and Horses*. The short form was used by the US actor Rod Steiger.

SHORT FORM: **Rod**.
RELATED NAME: **Roddy**.

Roger (M) 'famous spearman'. The British actor Roger Moore is a famous bearer of the name. The word *roger* is sometimes used in radio communications to indicate that a message has been received and understood. As a verb it has sexual connotations.

ALTERNATIVE FORM: **Rodger**.

Rohan [ROE-un, ROE-han] (M) an Indian name meaning 'ascending', or another form of the boys' name **Rowan** ('little red one'). It is also a place name in France and in the

fictional world of J. R. R. Tolkien's *The Lord of the Rings* (1954–5).

Roisin [roe-SHEEN] (F) 'little rose'. An Irish name borne by the heroine of the Gaelic poem and song 'Roisin Dubh' ('Dark Rosaleen').

ALTERNATIVE FORM: **Rosheen**.
RELATED NAME: **Rosaleen**.

Roland (M) 'famous land'. The name of a legendary French hero who fought and died in the service of Charlemagne.

SHORT FORM: **Roly**.
ALTERNATIVE FORM: **Rowland**.
RELATED NAME: **Orlando**.

Rolf (M) another form of **Rudolph** ('famous wolf'). The Australian artist and entertainer Rolf Harris is a famous bearer of the name.

RELATED NAMES: **Rollo, Rudy**.

Rollo (M) another form of **Rolf**, borne by a Viking who became the first Duke of Normandy in the early 10th century.

RELATED NAMES: **Rudolph, Rudy**.

Roman (M) 'person from Rome'. Of Russian, Polish, or Czech origin, the name was made internationally famous in the latter half of the 20th century by the film director Roman Polanski.

Romeo (M) 'pilgrim to Rome'. Borne by the young hero of Shakespeare's play *Romeo and Juliet*, it entered the English language as a name for any male lover. The British footballer

David Beckham and his wife Victoria chose it for their second son in 2002.

Romy (F) a short form of **Rosemary**, sometimes given as a name in its own right. It was borne by the Austrian actress Romy Schneider (whose full name was Rosemarie).

Rona (F) from the name of a Scottish island, or a feminine form of **Ronald**.
ALTERNATIVE FORM: **Rhona**.

Ronald (M) 'decisive ruler'. The 20th-century US actor and president Ronald Reagan was a famous bearer of the name.
SHORT FORM: **Ron**.
FEMININE FORM: **Rona**.
RELATED NAMES: **Ronnie, Ranald, Reginald, Reggie, Reynold**.

Ronan (M) 'little seal'. An Irish name borne by a 5th-century saint who worked as a missionary in Cornwall. The name has recently been popularized by the Irish singer Ronan Keating.

Ronni (F) a short form of **Veronica** ('true image'), sometimes given as a name in its own right. As a short form it is used by the British impressionist Ronni Ancona.
ALTERNATIVE FORM: **Roni**.

Ronnie (M) a short form of **Ronald**, sometimes given as a name in its own right. The short form is chiefly associated with 'The Two Ronnies': the British comedians and actors Ronnie Barker and Ronnie Corbett.
ALTERNATIVE FORM: **Ronny**.
RELATED NAMES: **Ranald, Reginald, Reggie, Reynold**.

Rory (M) another form of the Irish or Scottish name **Ruairi** ('red king' or 'fiery'). Famous modern bearers include the British impressionist Rory Bremner.

Ros (F) short for **Rosalind, Rosamund, Rosalie**, or **Rosaleen**.

Rosa (F) another form of **Rose**. It is the usual form of the name in several European countries, such as Spain and Italy.
RELATED NAMES: **Rosie, Rosalie, Rosina, Rosita**.

Rosaleen (F) another form of **Rosalind** or an English form of the Irish name **Roisin** ('little rose').
SHORT FORM: **Ros**.
RELATED NAMES: **Rosheen, Lindy**.

Rosalie (F) another form of **Rose** (the flower name), of French origin. The 20th-century British actress Rosalie Crutchley was a famous bearer of the name.
SHORT FORM: **Ros**.
RELATED NAMES: **Rosa, Rosie, Rosina, Rosita**.

Rosalind (F) 'pretty rose' or 'tender horse'. Shakespeare gave the name to one of the central characters of his play *As You Like It*.
SHORT FORM: **Ros**.

ALTERNATIVE FORMS: **Rosalinda, Rosalyn, Rosaline, Rosaleen.**
RELATED NAME: **Lindy.**

Rosamund (F) 'pure rose' or 'horse protection'. The 20th-century British novelist Rosamond Lehmann was a famous bearer of the name.
SHORT FORM: **Ros.**
ALTERNATIVE FORM: **Rosamond.**

Rosanne (F) a compound of **Rose** and **Anne**. The alternative forms of the name were made famous in the late 20th century by the US actresses Roseanne Barr and Rosanna Arquette.
ALTERNATIVE FORMS: **Roseanne, Rosanna.**

Roscoe (M) from a surname and place name meaning 'roe-deer wood'.

Rose (F) from the flower name, or from a Germanic name meaning 'horse'. It was the middle name of Elizabeth II's sister Princess Margaret.
RELATED NAMES: **Rosa, Rosie, Rosalie, Rosina, Rosita.**

Rosemary (F) from the name of the herb, meaning 'sea dew', or a compound of **Rose** and **Mary**. Famous modern bearers include the US singer Rosemary Clooney.
ALTERNATIVE FORM: **Rosemarie.**
RELATED NAMES: **Rosie, Romy.**

Roshan (M) a Muslim name meaning 'light, bright, shining'.

Roshanara (F) a Muslim name meaning 'light of the assembly'.

Rosheen (F) another form of the Irish name **Roisin** ('little rose'), spelt as it sounds.

Rosie (F) a pet form of **Rose** or a short form of **Rosemary**, now often given as a name in its own right. It is borne by the title character of Laurie Lee's autobiographical novel *Cider with Rosie* (1959).
RELATED NAMES: **Rosa, Rosalie, Rosina, Rosita, Romy.**

Rosina (F) another form of **Rose**, of Italian origin.
RELATED NAMES: **Rosa, Rosie, Rosalie, Rosita.**

Rosita (F) another form of **Rose**, of Spanish origin.
RELATED NAMES: **Rosa, Rosie, Rosalie, Rosita.**

Ross (M) from a Scottish surname and place name meaning 'headland'. It has recently been popularized by a character in the US television series *Friends*.

Rowan (F) from the name of the tree, noted for its bright red berries.

Rowan (M) an English form of an Irish name meaning 'little red one'. Famous modern bearers include the British comic actor Rowan Atkinson and the British churchman Rowan Williams, who became Archbishop of Canterbury in 2002.
ALTERNATIVE FORM: **Rohan.**

Rowena (F) a name of uncertain origin, possibly meaning 'fame and joy'. Sir Walter Scott gave the name to one of the heroines of his novel *Ivanhoe* (1819).

Rowland (M) another spelling of **Roland**, borne in the 19th century by Sir Rowland Hill, who introduced the penny post. This form of the name is more often found as a surname.

Roxana (F) 'dawn' or 'star'. In its various forms the name has been borne by Alexander the Great's wife, the woman loved by Cyrano de Bergerac in the play and film based on his life, and the title character of the song 'Roxanne' (1979) by the Police.
SHORT FORM: **Roxy**.
ALTERNATIVE FORMS: **Roxanne, Roxane, Roxanna**.

Roy (M) 'red' or 'king'. Famous modern bearers of the name include the US singer and cowboy actor Roy Rogers (born Leonard Slye) and the US singer and songwriter Roy Orbison.

Royston (M) from a surname and place name meaning 'Royce's settlement'. Royston Vasey, the name of the fictional setting for the television comedy series *The League of Gentlemen*, is the real name of the controversial comedian Roy 'Chubby' Brown.

Ruairi [ROR-ee, ROO-a-ee] (M) another form of an Irish or Scottish name meaning 'red king' or 'fiery'. It was borne by a 12th-century High King of Ireland.
ALTERNATIVE FORMS: **Ruari, Rory**.

Rube (M/F) short for **Reuben, Ruben,** or **Ruby**.

Ruben (M) another form of **Reuben** ('behold, a son'), of Spanish origin.

Ruby (F) from the name of the gemstone. The US comedian Ruby Wax is a famous modern bearer of the name, which became particularly popular in the UK in the early 21st century.
SHORT FORM: **Rube**.

Rudolph (M) 'famous wolf'. Well-known bearers of the name include the silent-film star Rudolph Valentino (whose real name was Rodolfo) and the title character of the Christmas song 'Rudolph the Red-Nosed Reindeer'.
ALTERNATIVE FORM: **Rudolf**.
RELATED NAMES: **Rudy, Rolf, Rollo**.

Rudy (M) a short form of **Rudolph**, sometimes given as a name in its own right. The 20th-century US singer Rudy Vallee (whose real name was Hubert) was a famous bearer.
ALTERNATIVE FORM: **Rudi**.
RELATED NAMES: **Rolf, Rollo**.

Rufus (M) 'red-haired or ruddy'. The name occurs in the Bible and was given as a nickname to William II in the 11th century. It is borne by the British actor Rufus Sewell.

Rupert (M) another form of **Robert**, of German origin. Famous bearers include the Australian media tycoon Rupert Murdoch and the children's cartoon character Rupert Bear.

Rupinder (F) an Indian name meaning 'very beautiful'.

Russ (M) a short form of **Russell**, sometimes given as a name in its own right. It was borne in the 20th century by the British pianist Russ Conway (whose real name was Trevor Stanford).

Russell (M) from the surname, meaning 'little red one'. Famous modern bearers of the name include the British television presenter

Russell Harty and the New Zealand-born actor Russell Crowe.

RELATED NAME: **Russ**.

Ruth (F) a biblical name of uncertain origin, possibly meaning 'friend'. The story of Ruth, a Moabite widow who left her own people to be with her grieving mother-in-law Naomi, is told in the book of the Bible that bears her name.

RELATED NAME: **Ruthie**.

Ruthie (F) a pet form of **Ruth**, sometimes given as a name in its own right.

Ryan (M) from the surname, which ultimately comes from the Irish name **Rian** ('king'). The US actor Ryan O'Neal and the British footballer Ryan Giggs are famous modern bearers.

S

Sabah (F) an Arabic name meaning 'morning'.
ALTERNATIVE FORM: **Saba**.

Sabina (F) 'Sabine woman'. The Sabines were a race of people whose women were carried off by the Romans. St Sabina was an early Christian martyr.
SHORT FORM: **Bina**.

Sabri (M) an Arabic name meaning 'patient'.

Sabrina (F) the name of a legendary character (the illegitimate daughter of a Welsh king) associated with the River Severn. In the late 20th century it was borne by the heroine of the US television series *Sabrina, the Teenage Witch*.
SHORT FORM: **Brina**.

Sacha (M/F) another spelling of **Sasha**, of French origin. Famous male bearers include the French singer Sacha Distel and the British comedian Sacha Baron Cohen.

Sadie (F) a short form of **Sarah** ('princess'), now usually given as a name in its own right.

ALTERNATIVE FORM: **Zadie**.
RELATED NAMES: **Sally, Zara**.

Saffron (F) from the name of the yellow food additive, which comes from a type of crocus. The name is borne by the sensible but frumpy teenage daughter played by Julia Sawalha in the British sitcom *Absolutely Fabulous*.
SHORT FORM: **Saffy**.

Salah (M) an Arabic name meaning 'goodness'. Salah al-Din was the real name of the 12th-century sultan known in English-speaking countries as Saladin.
ALTERNATIVE FORM: **Saleh**.

Salha (F) the feminine form of **Salih**.

Salih (M) an Arabic name meaning 'virtuous'.
FEMININE FORM: **Salha**.

Salim (M) an Arabic name meaning 'safe'.
ALTERNATIVE FORMS: **Saleem, Selim**.
FEMININE FORM: **Salma**.

Sally (F) a short form of **Sarah** ('princess'), now usually given as a

name in its own right. It is borne by the heroine of the film *When Harry Met Sally* (1989), played by Meg Ryan.
SHORT FORM: **Sal**.
RELATED NAMES: **Sadie, Zara, Zadie**.

Salma (F) the feminine form of **Salim**.

Salome [sa-LOE-mee] (F) 'peace'. In the Bible, Salome danced for her stepfather King Herod and asked for the head of John the Baptist in return.

Sam (M/F) a short form of various names beginning with these letters, especially **Samuel** or **Samantha**, now often given to boys as a name in its own right.
RELATED NAME: **Sammy**.

Samantha (F) a name of uncertain origin, possibly coined as a feminine form of **Samuel**, influenced by **Anthea**. It was popularized in the 1960s by the central character of the US television series *Bewitched*, and remained fashionable for the rest of the century.
SHORT FORM: **Sam**.
RELATED NAME: **Sammy**.

Sami (M) an Arabic name meaning 'sublime'.
FEMININE FORM: **Samya**.

Samir (M) an Arabic name meaning 'companion in night talk'.
ALTERNATIVE FORM: **Sameer**.
FEMININE FORM: **Samira**.

Samira (F) the feminine form of **Samir**.

Sammy (M/F) a short form of various names beginning with *Sam-*, especially **Samuel** or **Samantha**, sometimes given as a name in its own right.
ALTERNATIVE FORMS: **Sammie, Sammi** (F).

Samson (M) 'sun'. A biblical name borne by a man of great strength who was tricked by his lover Delilah and blinded by the Philistines.
ALTERNATIVE FORM: **Sampson**.

Samuel (M) a biblical name, possibly meaning 'God has listened' or 'asked of God'. Samuel, the longed-for son of Hannah, was an important Hebrew judge and prophet. The name has been borne by a number of famous English men of letters, including the 17th-century diarist Samuel Pepys and the 18th-century lexicographer Samuel Johnson.
SHORT FORM: **Sam**.
RELATED NAME: **Sammy**.

Samya (F) the feminine form of **Sami**.

Sandhya (F) an Indian name meaning 'twilight'.

Sandra (F) a short form of **Alexandra** ('defender of men'), from the Italian form of the name. It may also be regarded as a short form of **Cassandra**, but is usually given as a name in its own right.

RELATED NAMES: **Alex, Lexie, Sandy, Zandra, Sasha, Cassie.**

Sandy (F) a short form of **Sandra** or **Alexandra** ('defender of men'), sometimes given as a name in its own right. Famous modern bearers include the British singer Sandie Shaw, the Danish-born comedian Sandi Toksvig, and the fictional heroine of the musical *Grease*, Sandy Olsson.
ALTERNATIVE FORMS: **Sandie, Sandi.**
RELATED NAMES: **Alex, Lexie, Zandra, Sasha.**

Sandy (M) short for **Alexander.**

Sanjay (M) 'triumphant'. An Indian name borne by the younger son of the 20th-century Indian stateswoman Indira Gandhi.

Sanjeev (M) 'reviving'. An Indian name borne by the comedian and actor Sanjeev Bhaskar.
ALTERNATIVE FORM: **Sanjiv.**

Saoirse [SAIR-sha] (F) an Irish name meaning 'freedom'.

Sapphire (F) from the name of the gemstone.

Sara [SAR-a, SAIR-a] (F) another form of **Sarah.**
ALTERNATIVE FORM: **Zara.**

Sarah [SAIR-a, SAR-a] (F) 'princess'. A biblical name borne by the wife of Abraham and mother of Isaac. Princess Margaret gave the name to her daughter, born in 1964, and it was particularly popular in the UK in the 1970s and 1980s.
ALTERNATIVE FORM: **Sara.**
RELATED NAMES: **Sadie, Sally, Zara, Zadie.**

Sasha (M/F) another form of **Alexander** ('defender of men') or its feminine form **Alexandra**, of Russian origin.
ALTERNATIVE FORM: **Sacha.**
RELATED NAMES: **Alex, Lexie, Alec** (M), **Lex** (M), **Xander** (M), **Alistair** (M), **Sandy** (F), **Sandra** (F), **Zandra** (F).

Saskia (F) a name of Dutch origin, possibly meaning 'Saxon'. Famous modern bearers include the British actresses Saskia Wickham and Saskia Reeves.

Saul (M) 'prayed for'. A biblical name, borne by an early king of Israel. It was also the original name of St Paul. More recent famous bearers include the US novelist Saul Bellow.

Savannah (F) from the word *savannah*, referring to open grassland. In the USA it may be associated with a city or river of this name.
ALTERNATIVE FORM: **Savanna.**

Sayyid (M) an Arabic name meaning 'lord, master'.

Scarlett (F) from the surname, meaning 'wearer of scarlet clothes' or 'maker or seller of scarlet cloth'. It was popularized by Scarlett O'Hara, the heroine of Margaret Mitchell's

novel *Gone with the Wind* (1936), played by Vivien Leigh in the 1939 film adaptation. More recent famous bearers include the US actress Scarlett Johansson.
ALTERNATIVE FORM: **Scarlet**.

Scott (M) from the surname, meaning 'person from Scotland'. The US ragtime composer and musician Scott Joplin was a famous bearer of the name, which was further popularized in the 1980s by a character in the Australian soap opera *Neighbours*, played by Jason Donovan.

Seamus [SHAY-mus] (M) a Gaelic form of **James** ('supplanter'), chiefly used in Ireland. Famous bearers include the poet Seamus Heaney, who won the Nobel Prize for literature in 1995.
ALTERNATIVE FORMS: **Seumas, Seamas, Shamus**.
RELATED NAMES: **Hamish, Jamie, Jim, Jimmy, Jem, Jacob, Jake, Jago**.

Sean [shawn] (M) an Irish form of **John** ('God is gracious'). Famous modern bearers include the British actors Sean Connery and Sean Bean.
ALTERNATIVE FORMS: **Seán, Shaun, Shawn, Shane**.
FEMININE FORMS: **Shauna, Sinead, Siobhan**.
RELATED NAMES: **Eoin, Sion, Evan, Ian, Ivan, Juan, Johnny, Jack, Jackie, Jake, Jock, Hank**.

Sebastian (M) 'person from Sebaste (a place name meaning 'venerable')'.

St Sebastian was an early Christian martyr, said to have been shot with arrows and beaten to death. More recent famous bearers include the British athlete Sebastian Coe.
SHORT FORM: **Seb**.

Selim (M) another form of the Arabic name **Salim** ('safe').

Selima (F) possibly a feminine form of **Selim** or another form of **Selina**. The name was borne by a cat that 'drowned in a tub of gold fishes', according to a poem by the 18th-century poet Thomas Gray.
ALTERNATIVE FORM: **Selma**.

Selina (F) from the name of a Greek goddess of the moon.
ALTERNATIVE FORMS: **Selena, Celina**.

Selwyn (M) from a surname of uncertain origin. It was borne by the 20th-century British politician Selwyn Lloyd (whose first name was John).

Septima (F) the feminine form of **Septimus**.

Septimus (M) 'seventh'. In the days of large families, the name was sometimes given to the seventh-born child. Famous fictional bearers include Septimus Harding, the title character of Anthony Trollope's novel *The Warden* (1855).
FEMININE FORM: **Septima**.

Seraphina (F) from the word *seraphim*, which literally means 'fiery ones' and refers to an order of

angels. Serafina Pekkala is a witch queen in Philip Pullman's trilogy *His Dark Materials* (1995–2000).
SHORT FORM: **Fina**.
ALTERNATIVE FORM: **Serafina**.

Serena (F) 'calm, serene'. The US tennis player Serena Williams is a famous bearer of the name.
SHORT FORM: **Rena**.

Seth (M) 'appointed'. A biblical name, borne by the third son of Adam and Eve. It is also the name of various rustic characters in literature, such as Seth Starkadder in Stella Gibbons' novel *Cold Comfort Farm* (1932).

Seumas (M) another spelling of Seamus.

Sextus (M) 'sixth'. In former times the name was sometimes given by parents to their sixth child, but it is now rarely needed for this purpose.

Seymour (M) from a surname of French aristocratic origin, which comes from the place name Saint-Maur. It is borne by the unlikely hero of the film and musical *The Little Shop of Horrors*.

Shadi (M) an Arabic name meaning 'singer'.
FEMININE FORM: **Shadya**.

Shadya (F) the feminine form of Shadi.

Shakir (M) an Arabic name meaning 'thankful'.
FEMININE FORM: **Shakira**.

Shakira (F) the feminine form of Shakir, borne by the wife of the British actor Michael Caine.

Shakti (F) 'power'. An Indian name sometimes given to the wife of Shiva.

Shamus (M) another form of the Irish name **Seamus** (which is a Gaelic form of **James**, meaning 'supplanter'), spelt as it sounds.

Shana [SHAH-na] (F) another form of the Welsh name **Sian** ('God is gracious').
ALTERNATIVE FORM: **Shanna**.
RELATED NAMES: **Jane, Jean, Shona, Siobhan, Shevaun, Sinead, Joan, Joanna, Joni, Janet, Jeanette, Janine, Juanita**.

Shandy (F) from the name of the drink, a mixture of beer and lemonade.

Shane (M) another form of **Sean**, the Irish form of **John** ('God is gracious'). It was popularized by the gunfighter hero of the classic western film *Shane* (1953).
RELATED NAMES: **Shaun, Eoin, Sion, Evan, Ian, Ivan, Juan, Johnny, Jack, Jackie, Jake, Jock, Hank**.

Shanelle (F) another spelling of Chanel.
ALTERNATIVE FORMS: **Shanel, Chanelle**.

Shania [sha-NYE-a] (F) 'on my way'.

A name of American Indian origin, made famous in the late 20th century by the Canadian singer and songwriter Shania Twain. It is sometimes regarded as another form of **Shana** or **Shayna**.

Shankar (M) 'bringer of good fortune'. An Indian name sometimes given to the god Shiva.

Shanna (F) another form of Susannah (from the Hebrew form of the name), **Shannon, Shana**, or an Irish name meaning 'old, wise'.
ALTERNATIVE FORM: **Shannah**.

Shannon (F/M) possibly from the name of a river in Ireland. Its use as a forename may be influenced by **Shane** or **Sharon**.
ALTERNATIVE FORM: **Shanna**.

Shanta (F) an Indian name meaning 'calm'.

Shanti (F) an Indian name meaning 'tranquillity'.

Shari (F) a short form of **Sharon**, sometimes given as a name in its own right. The 20th-century US puppeteer Shari Lewis was a famous bearer of the name.

Sharif (M) an Arabic name meaning 'honourable'.
FEMININE FORM: **Sharifa**.

Sharifa (F) the feminine form of **Sharif**.

Sharmila (F) an Indian name meaning 'modest'.

Sharon (F) from a biblical place name. It was particularly popular in the UK in the 1960s and 1970s. Famous bearers include the US actress Sharon Stone.
ALTERNATIVE FORMS: **Sharron, Sharona**.
RELATED NAME: **Shari**.

Shashi (M/F) an Indian name referring to the moon.

Shaun (M) another spelling of **Sean**, the Irish form of **John** ('God is gracious').
ALTERNATIVE FORM: **Shawn**.
FEMININE FORM: **Shauna**.
RELATED NAMES: **Shane, Eoin, Sion, Evan, Ian, Ivan, Juan, Johnny, Jack, Jackie, Jake, Jock, Hank**.

Shauna (F) a feminine form of **Shaun**.
ALTERNATIVE FORM: **Shawna**.
RELATED NAMES: **Sian, Shana, Shona, Siobhan, Shevaun, Sinead, Sheena, Joan, Joanna, Joni, Jane, Jean, Janet, Jeanette, Janine, Juanita**.

Shaw (M) from the surname, meaning 'wood, copse'.

Shayna (F) a Jewish name meaning 'beautiful'.

Shea [shay] (M/F) from the Irish surname, possibly meaning 'hawk-like'.
ALTERNATIVE FORM: **Shay**.

Sheba (F) short for **Bathsheba**.

Sheela (F) an Indian name meaning 'good character, piety', or another spelling of **Sheila**.

Sheena (F) a feminine form of **John** ('God is gracious'), of Irish or Scottish origin.
RELATED NAMES: **Jane, Jean, Sian, Shana, Shona, Shauna, Siobhan, Shevaun, Sinead, Joan, Joanna, Joni, Janet, Jeanette, Janine, Juanita.**

Sheila (F) another form of **Cecilia**, of Irish origin. In Australia it is used as a slang term for any girl or woman. Famous British bearers of the name include the actress Sheila Hancock and the dramatist Shelagh Delaney.
ALTERNATIVE FORMS: **Sheela, Sheelagh, Shelagh.**
RELATED NAMES: **Cecile, Cecily, Cicely, Cissie, Celia.**

Shelby (F/M) from the surname, of uncertain origin.

Sheldon (M) from a surname and place name meaning 'steep-sided valley' or 'flat-topped hill'.

Shell (F) short for **Shelley** or **Michelle**.

Shelley (F) from the surname of the British poet Percy Bysshe Shelley. Famous modern bearers include the US actress Shelley Winters (whose real name was Shirley).
ALTERNATIVE FORM: **Shelly.**

Sher (M) a Muslim name meaning 'lion'.

Sheridan (M/F) from the surname of the Irish dramatist Richard Brinsley Sheridan. Famous modern bearers include the British critic and broadcaster Sheridan Morley (male) and the British actress Sheridan Smith (female).
SHORT FORM: **Sherry.**

Sherilyn (F) another form of **Cherilyn**.

Sherman (M) from the surname, which originally referred to a person whose job involved the use of shears. The forename is borne by the title character of the film *The Nutty Professor* (1996), played by Eddie Murphy.
SHORT FORM: **Sherm.**

Sherry (F) another form of **Cherie**, influenced by the name of the fortified wine. The British actress Sherrie Hewson is a famous bearer.
ALTERNATIVE FORMS: **Sherri, Sherrie.**

Sherry (M/F) short for **Sheridan**.

Sherwin (M) from the surname, meaning 'loyal friend' or 'fast runner'.

Sheryl (F) another form of **Cheryl**.

Shevaun (F) another form of the Irish name **Siobhan** ('God is gracious'), spelt as it sounds.
ALTERNATIVE FORM: **Chevonne.**

RELATED NAMES: **Joan, Joanna, Joni, Shona, Shauna, Sinead, Sheena, Sian, Shana, Jane, Jean, Janet, Jeanette, Janine, Juanita.**

Shifra (F) a Jewish name meaning 'beauty, grace'.

Shilpa (F) 'stone'. An Indian name borne by the actress Shilpa Shetty.

Shirin [shi-reen] (F) 'sweet, charming'. A Muslim name borne by the Iranian lawyer and human-rights activist Shirin Ebadi, who won the Nobel Peace Prize in 2003.
ALTERNATIVE FORM: **Shireen.**

Shirley (F) from a surname and place name meaning 'bright clearing'. Formerly given to boys, it became a girls' name after Charlotte Brontë used it for the heroine of her novel *Shirley* (1849). It was popularized in the 1930s by the US child star Shirley Temple.
SHORT FORM: **Shirl.**

Shiva (M) 'benign' or 'auspicious'. An Indian name borne by an important Hindu god.

Shlomo (M) a Jewish form of Solomon ('peace').
RELATED NAME: **Suleiman.**

Shobha (F) an Indian name meaning 'beautiful'.

Sholto (M) a Scottish name meaning 'sower'.

Shona (F) a feminine form of **John** ('God is gracious'), of Scottish origin. It is also the name of a Scottish island, and of a southern African people and their language.
RELATED NAMES: **Joan, Joanna, Joni, Janet, Shauna, Siobhan, Shevaun, Sheena, Sinead, Sian, Shana, Jane, Jean, Jeanette, Janine, Juanita.**

Shula (F) a short form of **Shulamit.** In the UK the name is chiefly associated with a fictional character in the BBC radio soap opera *The Archers*, in whose case it was coined from a random selection of letters.

Shulamit (F) a Jewish name meaning 'peacefulness'.
SHORT FORM: **Shula.**
ALTERNATIVE FORMS: **Shulamith, Shulamite.**

Shyam (M) 'dark' or 'beautiful'. An Indian name sometimes given to the god Krishna.
FEMININE FORM: **Shyama.**

Shyama (F) the feminine form of **Shyam**, sometimes given to the wife of Shiva.

Shyanne (F) another form of **Cheyenne.**

Si (M) short for **Simon** or **Silas.**

Sian [shahn] (F) the Welsh form of **Jane** ('God is gracious'). The Welsh actress Siân Phillips was born Jane Phillips in 1934.
ALTERNATIVE FORMS: **Siân, Shana.**
RELATED NAMES: **Jean, Shona, Siobhan, Shevaun, Sinead, Joan,**

Joanna, Joni, Janet, Jeanette, Janine, Juanita.

Sibyl (F) another form of Sybil ('prophetess').
ALTERNATIVE FORMS: **Sibylla, Sibella.**

Siddartha (M) 'he who has accomplished his goal'. An Indian name borne by the Buddha.

Sidney (M/F) another spelling of Sydney or another form of **Sidonie.**
SHORT FORM: **Sid.**

Sidonie (F) 'person from Sidon (a city in ancient Phoenicia)'. Of French origin, it was the first name of the French writer known by her surname Colette.
ALTERNATIVE FORMS: **Sidony, Sydney, Sidney.**

Siegfried [SEEG-freed] (M) 'peace after victory'. A German name, borne by a legendary hero whose story is told in the 19th-century composer Richard Wagner's *Ring* cycle of operas. Famous British bearers include the 20th-century poet Siegfried Sassoon.

Sienna (F) from the word *sienna*, referring to a reddish-brown colour that is named after the Italian city of Siena. The US-born British actress and model Sienna Miller has recently popularized the name.
ALTERNATIVE FORM: **Siena.**

Sierra (F) from the word *sierra*, referring to mountain ranges in Spain, the USA, and Mexico.

Sigmund (M) 'victorious defender'. The Austrian psychiatrist Sigmund Freud was a famous bearer of the name.

Sigourney (F) from a surname of uncertain origin. The US writer F. Scott Fitzgerald gave it to a character in his novel *The Great Gatsby* (1925), and the US actress Sigourney Weaver (whose real name is Susan) adopted it in the 1960s.

Sigrid (F) 'beautiful victory'. A name of Scandinavian origin.

Silas (M) 'woodlander'. From *Silvanus*, the name of the Roman god of the woods. In the Bible, Silas (or Silvanus) is a companion of St Paul. The name is also borne by the title characters of two 19th-century novels: George Eliot's *Silas Marner* (a lonely weaver) and Sheridan Le Fanu's *Uncle Silas* (a murderous villain).
SHORT FORM: **Si.**

Silvester (M) another spelling of Sylvester.

Silvestra (F) another spelling of Sylvestra.

Silvia (F) another spelling of Sylvia.

Simon (M) 'listening'. A biblical name borne by various characters, notably two of Jesus Christ's apostles, one of whom is usually known as Peter. It

also features in the nursery rhyme 'Simple Simon'. Famous modern bearers include the British conductor Simon Rattle.
SHORT FORMS: **Si, Sim.**
ALTERNATIVE FORM: **Simeon.**
FEMININE FORM: **Simone.**

Simone [si-MOAN] (F) a feminine form of **Simon**, of French origin. It was borne by the 20th-century French feminist writer Simone de Beauvoir.

Sinclair (M) from a surname of French aristocratic origin, which comes from the place name Saint-Clair. It was the middle name of the 20th-century US novelist known as Sinclair Lewis.

Sindy (F) another spelling of **Cindy**, chiefly associated with a brand of doll.

Sinead [shi-NAID] (F) the Irish form of **Janet** ('God is gracious'). Famous modern bearers include the Irish actress Sinéad Cusack and the Irish singer Sinéad O'Connor.
ALTERNATIVE FORM: **Sinéad.**
RELATED NAMES: **Shona, Siobhan, Shevaun, Sheena, Sian, Shana, Jane, Jean, Joan, Joanna, Joni, Jeanette, Janine, Juanita.**

Siobhan [shi-VAWN] (F) the Irish form of **Joan** ('God is gracious'). Famous modern bearers include the Irish actress Siobhán McKenna.

ALTERNATIVE FORMS: **Siobhán, Shevaun, Chevonne.**
RELATED NAMES: **Joanna, Joni, Shona, Shauna, Sinead, Sheena, Sian, Shana, Jane, Jean, Janet, Jeanette, Janine, Juanita.**

Sion [shon] (M) a Welsh form of **John** ('God is gracious').
ALTERNATIVE FORM: **Siôn.**
FEMININE FORM: **Sian.**
RELATED NAMES: **Evan, Sean, Shaun, Shane, Eoin, Ian, Ivan, Juan, Johnny, Jack, Jackie, Jake, Jock, Hank.**

Sissy (F) another spelling of **Cissie**, which is a short form of **Cecilia** or Cicely. In the case of the US actress Sissy Spacek (whose real name is Mary), it originated as a nickname meaning 'sister', given by her brothers.
ALTERNATIVE FORMS: **Sissie, Cissy.**

Sita (F) 'furrow'. An Indian name borne by the goddess of agriculture and the wife of Rama.

Skye (F) from the name of the Scottish island, or from the word *sky*.
ALTERNATIVE FORM: **Sky.**

Skylar (M/F) from a Dutch surname meaning 'scholar'.

Sloan (M/F) 'raider'. Of Irish origin, the name is more often found as a surname in modern times. The alternative form Sloane is more frequently given to girls and may be

associated with the phrase *Sloane Ranger*, coined in the 1970s to describe upper-class young women living in the fashionable area around Sloane Square in London.
ALTERNATIVE FORM: **Sloane**.

Sly (M) short for **Sylvester**.

Sofia [so-FYE-a] (F) another spelling of **Sophia**.

Sofie (F) another spelling of **Sophie**.

Solomon (M) 'peace'. A biblical name, borne by a king of Israel who was renowned for his wisdom. It also features in the nursery rhyme 'Solomon Grundy'.
SHORT FORMS: **Sol, Solly**.
RELATED NAMES: **Shlomo, Suleiman**.

Somerled (M) 'summer traveller'. A Scottish name borne by a 12th-century warlord.

Sonia [SONN-ya] (F) another form of **Sophia**, of Russian origin.
ALTERNATIVE FORMS: **Sonya, Sonja**.

Sophia [so-FYE-a] (F) 'wisdom'. The name was popularized in the latter half of the 20th century by the Italian-born film star Sophia Loren (whose real name is Sofia Scicolone).
ALTERNATIVE FORMS: **Sofia, Sophie**.
RELATED NAME: **Sonia**.

Sophie (F) another form of **Sophia**, of French origin. It is the most fashionable form of the name in modern times. Famous bearers

include the Countess of Wessex, wife of Prince Edward.
ALTERNATIVE FORMS: **Sophy, Sofie**.
RELATED NAME: **Sonia**.

Sorcha [SOR-ka, SOR-sha] (F) 'brightness'. Of Gaelic origin, the name is borne by the Irish actress Sorcha Cusack.

Sorrel (F/M) from the plant name, probably meaning 'sour'.
ALTERNATIVE FORMS: **Sorrell, Sorel**.

Spencer (M) from the surname, which originally referred to a person who dispensed supplies in a manor house. Famous modern bearers include the US actor Spencer Tracy and the British rock musician Spencer Davis.

Stacey (F) a short form of **Anastasia** ('resurrection') or **Eustacia** ('good harvest'), given as a name in its own right.
ALTERNATIVE FORMS: **Stacy, Stacie, Staci**.

Stacy (M/F) a short form of **Eustace** ('good harvest'), given as a name in its own right. Famous bearers include two US actors called Stacy Keach, father and son. It is also an alternative spelling of the girls' name **Stacey**, which is more frequent in modern times.

Stafford (M) from a surname and place name meaning 'ford by a landing-place'. It was the middle name of the 20th-century British politician known as Stafford Cripps.

Stanislas (M) 'government glory'. The name was borne in the 11th century by the Polish bishop and martyr St Stanislas.
ALTERNATIVE FORM: **Stanislaus**.

Stanley (M) from a surname and place name meaning 'stony meadow'. It was popular in the late 19th and early 20th centuries, when it was given to the British comedian Stanley Holloway and the British footballer Stanley Matthews.
SHORT FORM: **Stan**.

Stefan (M) another form of **Stephen**, found in various countries of mainland Europe and sometimes in the English-speaking world.
RELATED NAMES: **Steffan, Steve, Stevie**.

Steffan (M) the Welsh form of **Stephen**.
RELATED NAMES: **Stefan, Steve, Stevie**.

Stella (F) 'star'. The name occurs in literature in Sir Philip Sidney's sonnets *Astrophel and Stella* (1582) and Jonathan Swift's *Journal to Stella* (1710–13).
RELATED NAMES: **Estelle, Astra, Esther**.

Stephanie (F) a feminine form of **Stephen**. In the alternative form Stefanie the name is borne by the US actress known as Stefanie Powers (whose real name is Stefania) and the German tennis player known as Steffi Graf.
SHORT FORMS: **Steph, Steff, Steffi, Steffie**.
ALTERNATIVE FORMS: **Stefanie, Steffany**.
RELATED NAME: **Stevie**.

Stephen (M) 'crown'. The name of the first Christian martyr, who was stoned to death. Famous modern bearers include the British comedian and writer Stephen Fry and the US film director Steven Spielberg.
ALTERNATIVE FORM: **Steven**.
FEMININE FORM: **Stephanie**.
RELATED NAMES: **Steve, Stevie, Steffan, Stefan**.

Steve (M) a short form of **Stephen, Steven**, or **Stevie**, sometimes given as a name in its own right. As a short form it was used by the 20th-century US actor Steve McQueen.
RELATED NAMES: **Stevie, Steffan, Stefan**.

Stevie (M/F) a short form of **Stephen, Steven**, or **Stephanie**, sometimes given as a name in its own right. Famous bearers include the US singer Stevie Wonder (male), whose full name is Steveland, and the British poet Stevie Smith (female), whose real name was Florence.
RELATED NAMES: **Steve** (M), **Steffan** (M), **Stefan** (M).

Stewart (M) another spelling of **Stuart**.
SHORT FORM: **Stew**.

Stirling (M) from the surname and

place name, of uncertain origin. The British racing driver Stirling Moss is probably the best-known bearer. In its alternative form the name may be associated with the word *sterling*, meaning 'excellent'.
ALTERNATIVE FORM: **Sterling**.

Storm (M/F) from the word *storm*, referring to the weather.

Struan (M) a Scottish name meaning 'stream'.

Stuart (M) from the surname, meaning 'steward', borne by the Scottish and English royal families in the 16th and 17th centuries. **Stewart**, the usual spelling of the surname before and after this time, is a less common spelling of the forename.
SHORT FORM: **Stu**.

Sue (F) short for various names beginning with *Su-*, especially **Susan**.
ALTERNATIVE FORM: **Su**.

Suha (F) an Arabic name meaning 'star'.

Sukie (F) short for various names beginning with *Su-*, especially **Susan**.
ALTERNATIVE FORM: **Suky**.

Suleiman (M) the Arabic form of **Solomon** ('peace'). The name was borne in the 16th century by the Ottoman emperor Suleiman the Magnificent.
ALTERNATIVE FORMS: **Suleyman**, **Sulayman**.
RELATED NAME: **Shlomo**.

Suman (M) an Indian name meaning 'cheerful' or 'wise'.

Summer (F) from the name of the season. It was popularized in the early 21st century by a character in the Australian soap opera *Neighbours*.

Sundar (M) an Indian name meaning 'beautiful'.
ALTERNATIVE FORM: **Sunder**.

Sunil (M) an Indian name meaning 'dark blue'.

Sunita (F) an Indian name meaning 'of good conduct'.

Surendra (M) an Indian name meaning 'the mightiest of gods'.
ALTERNATIVE FORM: **Surinder**.

Suresh (M) an Indian name meaning 'ruler of the gods'.

Surya (M) 'sun'. An Indian name borne by the sun god.

Susan (F) another form of **Susannah** that was particularly popular in the mid-20th century. Famous bearers include the British actress Susan Hampshire and the US actress Susan Sarandon.
SHORT FORMS: **Sue, Sukie**.
ALTERNATIVE FORM: **Suzan**.
RELATED NAMES: **Susie, Suzanne, Suzette, Shanna, Lily**.

Susannah (F) a biblical name meaning 'lily'. In the Apocrypha, Susannah is a woman falsely accused of adultery. The British actress

Susannah York is a famous modern bearer of the name.

ALTERNATIVE FORMS: **Susanna, Suzanna**.

RELATED NAMES: **Susan, Suzanne, Susie, Suzette, Shanna, Lily**.

Susie (F) a short form of various names beginning with *Su-*, such as **Susan** or **Susannah**, sometimes given as a name in its own right.

ALTERNATIVE FORMS: **Suzie, Suzy**.

RELATED NAMES: **Suzanne, Suzette, Shanna, Lily**.

Suzanne (F) another form of **Susannah**, of French origin. It is the title of a song by the Canadian musician Leonard Cohen.

ALTERNATIVE FORM: **Susanne**.

RELATED NAMES: **Susan, Suzette, Susie, Shanna, Lily**.

Suzette (F) another form of **Susannah**, of French origin. It also occurs in the name of the dessert *crêpe suzette*, a pancake flavoured with orange juice and liqueur.

RELATED NAMES: **Suzanne, Susan, Susie, Shanna, Lily**.

Sven (M) 'boy'. Of Swedish origin, the name was made famous in the UK in the early 21st century by the football manager Sven Göran Eriksson.

Sybil (F) 'prophetess'. Famous modern bearers of the name include the British actress Dame Sybil Thorndike and the fictional character Sybil Fawlty, wife of Basil, in the television sitcom *Fawlty Towers*.

ALTERNATIVE FORMS: **Sibyl, Cybill, Sybilla, Sibylla, Sibella**.

Sydney (M/F) from the surname, which may be from the French place name Saint-Denis or an English place name meaning 'wide island'. (The Australian city of Sydney was named after the 18th-century British politician Lord Sydney.) Famous male bearers include Sydney Carton, the hero of Charles Dickens' novel *A Tale of Two Cities* (1859). As a girls' name it is also another form of **Sidonie**.

SHORT FORMS: **Syd, Sid**.

ALTERNATIVE FORM: **Sidney**.

Sylvester (M) 'of the woods'. The name was borne by a 4th-century saint whose feast day is 31 December. More recent famous bearers include the US actor Sylvester Stallone.

SHORT FORM: **Sly**.

ALTERNATIVE FORM: **Silvester**.

FEMININE FORM: **Sylvestra**.

Sylvestra (F) the feminine form of **Sylvester**. The name is borne by the British actress Sylvestra Le Touzel.

ALTERNATIVE FORM: **Silvestra**.

Sylvia (F) 'wood, forest'. In Roman legend Rhea Silvia is the mother of Romulus and Remus, the founders of Rome. Famous modern bearers include the US poet Sylvia Plath and the British actress Sylvia Syms.

ALTERNATIVE FORM: **Silvia**.

T

Tabitha (F) 'doe, gazelle'. An alternative name for the biblical character known as **Dorcas**. It is also a popular name for cats, by association with the word *tabby* or the Beatrix Potter character Tabitha Twitchit.
SHORT FORM: **Tabby**.

Tacy (F) 'be silent'.
ALTERNATIVE FORMS: **Tacey, Taci, Tacie**.

Tad (M) a short form of **Thaddeus**, sometimes given as a name in its own right.

Tahir (M) an Arabic name meaning 'pure, virtuous'.

Talbot (M) from the surname, which is of uncertain origin.

Talfryn (M) from a Welsh place name meaning 'high hill'. The name was borne by the 20th-century Welsh actor Talfryn Thomas.

Talia [TAHL-i-a, TAL-i-a] (F) a Jewish name meaning 'dew from God', another form of **Thalia**, or a short form of *Natalia* (the Russian form of **Natalie**).

Talitha (F) a biblical name meaning 'little girl'.

Tallulah (F) from the US place name Tallulah Falls, in the state of Georgia, which is of American Indian origin and means 'leaping water'. The name is chiefly associated with the 20th-century US actress Tallulah Bankhead.

Talulla (F) an Irish name meaning 'abundance'.

Tamar [TAY-mar] (F) 'date palm'. A biblical name, borne by Absalom's sister and daughter. It is more frequently found in the alternative form **Tamara**.

Tamara [ta-MAR-a, TAM-a-ra] (F) another form of **Tamar**, of Russian origin. Famous modern bearers include the British celebrity Tamara Beckwith.
RELATED NAME: **Tammy**.

Tammy (F) a short form of **Tamara** or **Tamsin**, sometimes given as a name in its own right. The US singer Tammy Wynette was born Virginia Wynette Pugh in 1942.

Tamsin (F) another form of **Thomasina** ('twin'). The name is borne by the British actresses Tamsin Greig and Tamzin Outhwaite.
ALTERNATIVE FORM: **Tamzin**.
RELATED NAME: **Tammy**.

Tanith (F) the name of the Phoenician goddess of love.

Tansy (F) from the flower name, which means 'immortal'.

Tanya (F) another form of **Tatiana**. In the 1960s the name was borne by a famous performing elephant.
ALTERNATIVE FORM: **Tania**.

Tara (F) from an Irish place name meaning 'hill', associated with the High Kings of Ireland in former times. It is also the name of Scarlett O'Hara's home in Margaret Mitchell's novel *Gone with the Wind* (1936). Famous modern bearers include the British actress Tara Fitzgerald and the British celebrity Tara Palmer-Tomkinson. Tara is also an Indian name, meaning 'star', sometimes given to the wives of Shiva and Buddha.

Tariq (M) 'nocturnal visitor' or 'morning star'. An Arabic name borne by the writer and political campaigner Tariq Ali.

Tarquin (M) from the Roman name

Tarquinius, borne by two kings of Rome in the 6th century BC.

Tasha (F) a short form of **Natasha** ('Christmas'), sometimes given as a name in its own right.

Tasmin (F) a blend of **Tamsin** and **Jasmine**. The British violinist Tasmin Little is a famous bearer of the name.

Tate (M/F) from the surname, meaning 'cheerful'.

Tatiana (F) from a Roman family name of uncertain origin. A Russian name that is sometimes found in English-speaking countries.
RELATED NAME: **Tanya**.

Taylor (M/F) from the surname, meaning 'tailor'. It was particularly fashionable in the late 20th and early 21st centuries.
ALTERNATIVE FORMS: **Tayler**, **Tayla** (F).

Teal (F) from the word *teal*, referring to a type of duck or a dark greenish-blue colour.
ALTERNATIVE FORM: **Teale**.

Ted (M) a short form of **Teddy**, **Theodore**, or **Edward**, sometimes given as a name in its own right. As a short form it was used with reference to the 20th-century British statesman Edward Heath.
RELATED NAMES: **Theo, Eddie, Ned**.

Teddy (M) a short form of **Theodore** ('gift of God') or **Edward** ('guardian of wealth'), sometimes given as a name in its own right. It was the nickname of the 20th-century US president Theodore Roosevelt, after whom the teddy bear is named.

SHORT FORM: **Ted.**

ALTERNATIVE FORM: **Teddie.**

RELATED NAMES: **Ted, Eddie, Ned, Theo.**

Tegan (F) a Welsh name meaning 'lovely'.

ALTERNATIVE FORM: **Teagan.**

Tel (M) short for **Terry** or **Terence.**

Terence (M) from the Roman name *Terentius*, borne in the 2nd century BC by the Roman dramatist known as Terence. Famous modern bearers include the British dramatist Terence Rattigan and the British actor Terence Stamp.

SHORT FORM: **Tel.**

ALTERNATIVE FORMS: **Terrence, Terrance.**

RELATED NAME: **Terry.**

Teresa (F) a name of uncertain origin, possibly meaning 'harvest' or from the name of the Greek island of Thera. It was borne by two famous nuns: St Teresa of Avila in the 16th century and Mother Teresa of Calcutta in the 20th century.

ALTERNATIVE FORM: **Theresa.**

RELATED NAMES: **Terri, Tess, Tessa, Tessie.**

Terri (F) a short form of **Teresa,** sometimes given as a name in its own right. The US actress Teri Hatcher is a famous bearer of the name in its alternative form.

ALTERNATIVE FORM: **Teri.**

RELATED NAMES: **Tess, Tessa, Tessie.**

Terry (M) another form of **Theodoric** 'ruler of the people' or a short form of **Terence.** As a short form it is used by the Irish-born broadcaster Terry Wogan and the English football manager Terry Venables.

SHORT FORM: **Tel.**

RELATED NAMES: **Derek, Dirk, Theodoric.**

Tertius (M) 'third'. A name of Roman origin, sometimes given to the third-born child of a family. The name is borne by a character in George Eliot's novel *Middlemarch* (1872).

Tess (F) a short form of **Tessa** or **Teresa,** sometimes given as a name in its own right. The heroine of Thomas Hardy's novel *Tess of the D'Urbervilles* (1891) is a famous bearer of the name.

RELATED NAMES: **Terri, Tessie.**

Tessa (F) a short form of **Teresa,** usually given as a name in its own right. Famous modern bearers include the British athlete Tessa Sanderson.

RELATED NAMES: **Tess, Tessie, Terri.**

Tessie (F) a short form of **Tessa** or **Teresa,** sometimes given as a name in its own right. It is chiefly

associated with the 20th-century British entertainer Tessie O'Shea and her signature tune, 'Two Ton Tessie from Tennessee'.
RELATED NAMES: **Tess, Terri.**

Tex (M) from a nickname sometimes given to people from Texas in the USA, such as the US animator Tex Avery (whose real name was Frederick).

Thaddeus (M) a biblical name, possibly meaning 'gift of God' or 'given by God'. In the Bible, Thaddeus is one of Jesus Christ's apostles.
SHORT FORM: **Thad.**
RELATED NAMES: **Tad, Theodore.**

Thalia [THAY-li-a, THAL-i-a] (F) 'flourishing'. The name of the Greek muse of comedy.
ALTERNATIVE FORM: **Talia.**

Thea [THEE-a] (F) a short form of Dorothea ('gift of God'), sometimes given as a name in its own right.
RELATED NAMES: **Dorothy, Theodora, Theda, Dora, Dee, Dolly, Dodie.**

Theda (F) a short form of Theodora (or a similar name), sometimes given in its own right. It was made famous by the silent-film star Theda Bara (whose real name was Theodosia).

Thelma (F) a name coined by the British novelist Marie Corelli for the heroine of her novel *Thelma* (1887), possibly meaning 'wish, will'. It is borne by one of the title characters of the film *Thelma and Louise* (1991).

Thelonius (M) the Latin form of the German name *Till* or *Tillo*, borne by a 7th-century saint. The 20th-century US jazz musician Thelonious Monk bore the name in an unconventional spelling.

Theo (M) a short form of **Theodore** or any other name beginning with these letters, sometimes given in its own right. It has recently been popularized by the British footballer Theo Walcott.
RELATED NAMES: **Ted, Teddy.**

Theobald (M) 'brave people'. The name is borne by a character in E. M. Forster's novel *Howards End* (1910) who is usually called Tibby.
SHORT FORM: **Tibby.**
RELATED NAME: **Tybalt.**

Theodora (F) the feminine form of Theodore. The name was borne by a 6th-century Byzantine empress.
RELATED NAMES: **Dora, Dorothea, Thea, Theda, Dorothy, Dee, Dolly, Dodie.**

Theodore (M) 'gift of God'. The 20th-century US president Theodore Roosevelt was a famous bearer of the name.
RELATED NAMES: **Theo, Ted, Teddy, Thaddeus.**

Theodoric (M) 'ruler of the people'.

The name was borne in the 5th century by two kings of the Visigoths and a king of the Ostrogoths.
RELATED NAMES: **Derek, Dirk, Terry**.

Theophilus (M) 'loving God' or 'loved by God'. A biblical name, borne by a number of early saints. It was made famous in the late 20th century by the comic character Theophilus P. Wildebeest, a singing 'sex god' created by the British comedian Lenny Henry.
RELATED NAME: **Amadeus**.

Theresa (F) another spelling of **Teresa**.

Thirza (F) another form of **Tirzah** ('delight').
ALTERNATIVE FORM: **Thirzah**.

Thomas (M) 'twin'. A biblical name borne by one of the twelve apostles, known as 'Doubting Thomas' because he refused to believe in Christ's resurrection without proof. It was popularized in the 20th century by the Rev. W. Awdry's books for children about Thomas the Tank Engine.
FEMININE FORMS: **Thomasina, Tamsin**.
RELATED NAMES: **Tomas, Tom, Tommy**.

Thomasina (F) a feminine form of **Thomas**.

ALTERNATIVE FORMS: **Thomasine, Thomasin**.
RELATED NAMES: **Tamsin, Tammy**.

Thora (F) a feminine form of *Thor*, the name of the Norse god of thunder. Famous modern bearers include the British actress Thora Hird and the US actress Thora Birch.
ALTERNATIVE FORM: **Thyra**.

Thornton (M) from a surname and place name meaning 'thorn-bush settlement'. The name was borne by the 20th-century US writer Thornton Wilder.

Thyra (F) another form of **Thora** or **Tyra**, or a blend of the two names.

Tia (F) possibly a short form of various names ending with these letters, given as a name in its own right. It is also a Spanish or Portuguese word meaning 'aunt', as in the name of the liqueur Tia Maria.

Tiana (F) a short form of **Christiana** ('Christian'), sometimes given as a name in its own right. The name is borne by the British actress Tiana Benjamin.
ALTERNATIVE FORM: **Tianna**.
RELATED NAMES: **Tina, Christina, Christine, Christie, Christa, Kristen, Kirsten, Kirsty**.

Tiara (F) from the word *tiara*, meaning 'jewelled headdress'.

Tibby (M) short for **Theobald**.

Tiernan [TEER-nin] (M) 'little lord'. A popular Irish name that is also found as a surname.
ALTERNATIVE FORM: **Tiarnan**.

Tierney [TEER-nee] (M/F) 'lord'. An Irish boys' name, borne by a 6th-century saint, that is now also given to girls. It is more frequently found as a surname.

Tiffany (F) 'Epiphany (a Christian festival on 6 January)'. The name is also associated with Tiffany's, a famous US jewellery company, and with the film *Breakfast at Tiffany's* (1961), starring Audrey Hepburn.

Tilda (F) a short form of **Matilda**, sometimes given as a name in its own right. As a short form it is used by the British actress Tilda Swinton.
RELATED NAMES: **Tilly, Maud**.

Tilly (F) a short form of **Matilda**, sometimes given as a name in its own right.
RELATED NAMES: **Tilda, Maud**.

Tim (M) a short form of **Timothy**, sometimes given as a name in its own right. Famous bearers include the fictional character Tiny Tim in Charles Dickens' book *A Christmas Carol* (1843) and the British tennis player Tim Henman.
RELATED NAME: **Timmy**.

Timmy (M) short form of **Timothy**, sometimes given as a name in its own right. In Enid Blyton's 'Famous Five' books it is borne by the children's dog.
RELATED NAME: **Tim**.

Timothy (M) 'honouring God' or 'honoured by God'. The name of an early Christian to whom two of St Paul's epistles are addressed. The British actor Timothy West is a famous modern bearer.
RELATED NAMES: **Tim, Timmy**.

Tina (F) a short form of **Christina** ('Christian') or another name ending with these letters, often given as a name in its own right. The US singer Tina Turner was born Anna Mae Bullock in 1939.
RELATED NAMES: **Christine, Christiana, Tiana, Christie, Christa, Kristen, Kirsten, Kirsty**.

Tirzah (F) a biblical name meaning 'delight'. In the film *Ben-Hur* (1959) it is borne by the hero's sister, who is miraculously cured of leprosy.
ALTERNATIVE FORMS: **Tirza, Thirza, Thirzah**.

Tish (F) short for **Tisha, Letitia**, or **Patricia**.

Tisha (F) a short form of **Letitia** ('joy') or **Patricia** ('noble'), sometimes given as a name in its own right.
SHORT FORM: **Tish**.
RELATED NAMES: **Lettice, Trisha, Patty, Patsy, Patrice**.

Titus (M) from a Roman name,

possibly meaning 'honoured'. The name of an early Christian to whom one of St Paul's epistles is addressed. Famous bearers in literature include the title characters of Shakespeare's play *Titus Andronicus* and Mervyn Peake's *Titus Groan* (1946), the first novel of the *Gormenghast* trilogy.

Tobias (M) a biblical name meaning 'God is good'. The 18th-century British novelist Tobias Smollett was a famous bearer.
RELATED NAME: **Toby**.

Toby (M) another form of **Tobias**. It is the name of Punch's dog in the traditional 'Punch and Judy' puppet show. Famous human bearers include Sir Toby Belch (a comic character in Shakespeare's play *Twelfth Night*) and the British actor Toby Stephens.

Todd (M) from the surname, meaning 'fox'. The Irish-born actor Todd Carty is a famous modern bearer of the name.
ALTERNATIVE FORM: **Tod**.

Toinette (F) short for **Antoinette**.

Tolly (M) short for **Bartholomew** or **Ptolemy**.

Tom (M) a short form of **Thomas** or **Tommy**, often given as a name in its own right. As a short form it is used by the US actors Tom Cruise and Tom Hanks. The name occurs in the phrase 'every Tom, Dick, and Harry'

and is also borne by the cat in the 'Tom and Jerry' cartoons.
RELATED NAMES: **Tommy, Tomas**.

Tomas (M) the Irish or Scottish form of **Thomas**. It is also used in various countries of mainland Europe, such as Spain, and may be pronounced with the stress on the second syllable.

Tommy (M) a short form of **Thomas**, sometimes given as a name in its own right. Famous bearers include the British singer and actor Tommy Steele (whose full name is Thomas) and the title character of the rock opera *Tommy* (1969) by The Who, a boy who loses the ability to see, hear, and speak after witnessing a murder.
RELATED NAMES: **Tom, Tomas**.

Toni (F) a short form of **Antonia** or **Antoinette**, sometimes given as a name in its own right. Famous bearers include the US writer Toni Morrison, born Chloe Anthony Wofford, who won the Nobel Prize for literature in 1993.
RELATED NAMES: **Tonia, Antonella**.

Tonia (F) a short form of **Antonia**, sometimes given as a name in its own right.
ALTERNATIVE FORM: **Tonya**.
RELATED NAMES: **Toni, Antoinette, Antonella**.

Tony (M) a short form of **Anthony** or **Antonio**, sometimes given as a name in its own right. It is borne by the

British politician Tony Blair (whose full name is Anthony Charles Lynton Blair) and the US actor Tony Curtis (whose real name is Bernard Schwartz).
RELATED NAMES: **Anton, Antoine.**

Topsy (F) a name of uncertain origin. Famous fictional bearers include a black slave girl in Harriet Beecher Stowe's novel *Uncle Tom's Cabin* (1852) and one of the title characters of the 'Topsy and Tim' children's books by Jean and Gareth Adamson.

Tori (F) short for **Victoria.**
ALTERNATIVE FORM: **Tory.**

Toria (F) short for **Victoria.**

Torquil (M) 'Thor's cauldron'. From a Scandinavian name that entered the English-speaking world via Scotland.

Tracy (F/M) from a surname of French aristocratic origin. Originally given to boys, it became a very popular girls' name in the latter half of the 20th century, falling from favour in the 1980s and 1990s. The British comedian Tracey Ullman is a famous bearer.
ALTERNATIVE FORMS: **Tracey, Tracie** (F).

Travis (M) from the surname, meaning 'tollkeeper' or 'crossing'.

Trefor [TREV-or, TREV-a] (M) from a Welsh surname and place name meaning 'large settlement'.
ALTERNATIVE FORM: **Trevor.**

Trent (M) from the river name, meaning 'traveller' or 'trespasser', which is also found as a surname.

Trevelyan [tri-VEL-i-un] (M) from a Cornish surname and place name.

Trevor (M) the English form of **Trefor.** Famous modern bearers include the British television newsreader and presenter Trevor McDonald and the British footballer Trevor Francis.
SHORT FORM: **Trev.**

Trey (M) 'three'. The name is sometimes given to the third child of a family, or used as a nickname for a boy who bears the same name as his father and grandfather.

Tricia (F) another spelling of **Trisha.**

Trina (F) short for **Katrina** or **Catrina.**

Trinity (F) from the name used in Christianity to refer to the Father, Son, and Holy Ghost.

Trish (F) short for **Trisha** or **Patricia.**

Trisha (F) a short form of **Patricia** ('noble'), sometimes given as a name in its own right. The British television chat-show host Trisha Goddard is a famous bearer.
SHORT FORM: **Trish.**
ALTERNATIVE FORM: **Tricia.**

RELATED NAMES: **Tisha, Patty, Patsy, Patrice**.

Tristan (M) a name of uncertain origin, sometimes associated with a Latin word meaning 'sad'. It is borne in Celtic legend by the lover of Isolde. More recent fictional bearers include a character in James Herriot's vet stories, published in the 1970s, and the hero of Peter Carey's novel *The Unusual Life of Tristan Smith* (1994).

ALTERNATIVE FORM: **Tristram**.

Tristram (M) another form of **Tristan**, found in some versions of the Celtic legend. It is also the name of the narrator of Laurence Sterne's novel *Tristram Shandy* (1759–67).

Trixie (F) a short form of **Beatrix** ('blessed' or 'voyager'), sometimes given as a name in its own right.

Troy (M/F) from the surname (which comes from the French place name Troyes) or from the name of the ancient city of Troy. The name is borne by two successful Australian motorcycle racers, Troy Bayliss and Troy Corser.

Trudy (F) a short form of **Gertrude** ('strong with a spear') or **Ermintrude** ('wholly beloved'), sometimes given as a name in its own right.

ALTERNATIVE FORMS: **Trudi, Trudie**.

Truman (M) from the surname, meaning 'trusty man'. Famous modern bearers of the forename include the US writer Truman Capote and the central character of the film *The Truman Show* (1998).

ALTERNATIVE FORM: **Trueman**.

Tudor (M) 'ruler of the people'. A Welsh name that is most familiar as the surname of the English royal family in the 15th century. It is also a Romanian name that is another form of **Theodore**.

Turlough [TER-la] (M) 'instigator' or 'helper'. An Irish name borne in the late 17th and early 18th centuries by the blind harpist and composer Turlough O'Carolan.

ALTERNATIVE FORM: **Turlach**.

Ty (M) a short form of **Tycho, Tyler, Tyrone**, or **Tyson**, sometimes given as a name in its own right.

Tybalt [TIB-ult] (M) another form of **Theobald** ('brave people'). Shakespeare gave this form of the name to a character in his play *Romeo and Juliet*.

Tycho (M) 'hitting the mark'. The 16th-century Danish astronomer Tycho Brahe was a famous bearer of the name.

RELATED NAME: **Ty**.

Tyler (M/F) from the surname, meaning 'tiler'.

RELATED NAME: **Ty**.

Tyra (F) a feminine form of *Tyr*, the

name of the Norse god of war. The US celebrity Tyra Banks is a famous bearer of the name.
ALTERNATIVE FORM: **Thyra**.

Tyrone (M) from the name of the Irish county. Famous bearers include the 20th-century US actor Tyrone Power.
RELATED NAME: Ty.

Tyson (M) from the surname, meaning 'son of Denise' or 'hot-tempered', which is chiefly associated with the US boxer Mike Tyson.
RELATED NAME: Ty.

U

Ulric (M) 'wolf power', or another form of the German name *Ulrich* meaning 'wealth and power'.
FEMININE FORM: **Ulrica**.

Ulrica (F) the feminine form of Ulric. In the Scandinavian form *Ulrika* (meaning 'wealth and power') it is borne by the television personality Ulrika Jonsson.

Ulysses (M) the Latin name of the Greek hero Odysseus, whose story is told in Homer's *Odyssey*, on which James Joyce's novel *Ulysses* (1922) is loosely based. The 19th-century US president Ulysses S. Grant was a famous bearer of the name.

Uma [oo-ma] (F) an Indian name meaning 'flax', which is sometimes given to the wife of Shiva. The name is borne by the US actress Uma Thurman.

Umar (M) another form of the Arabic name **Omar** ('prosperous').

Una [yoo-na, oo-na] (F) 'lamb' or 'one'. A name of Gaelic origin.

Famous bearers include the British actress Una Stubbs.
ALTERNATIVE FORM: **Oona**.
RELATED NAMES: **Juno, Unity**.

Undine [UN-deen] (F) 'little wave' or 'of the waves'. The name of a water nymph in German mythology.

Unity (F) from the word *unity*, meaning 'oneness', or another form of **Una**. The British socialite Unity Mitford was notorious for her association with prominent Nazis in the years before the Second World War.
RELATED NAME: **Juno**.

Uri (M) a Jewish name meaning 'light'. The best-known modern bearer of the name is the illusionist Uri Geller.

Uriah (M) a biblical name meaning 'God is light'. In the Bible, Uriah is a Hittite warrior whose wife, Bathsheba, commits adultery with King David. Charles Dickens gave the name to an obsequious and cunning clerk in his novel *David Copperfield* (1850).
RELATED NAME: **Uriel**.

Uriel (M) a biblical name meaning 'God is light'.

RELATED NAME: Uriah.

Ursula (F) 'little bear'. Famous bearers of the name include a 4th-century saint and, more recently, the Swiss-born film star Ursula Andress.

Usha [oo-sha] (F) an Indian name meaning 'dawn', made famous by a character in the BBC radio soap opera *The Archers*.

V

Val (M/F) a short form of **Valentine** or **Valerie**, sometimes given as a name in its own right. Famous male bearers include the Irish singer Val Doonican and the US actor Val Kilmer.

Valda (F) a feminine form of **Waldo** ('power, rule') or a compound of **Val** and the name-ending *-da*.

Valentine (M/F) 'healthy, strong'. The name was borne by St Valentine, a 3rd-century male martyr whose feast day (14 February) is traditionally associated with love.
ALTERNATIVE FORM: **Valentina** (F).
RELATED NAMES: **Val, Valerie** (F).

Valerie (F) 'healthy, strong'. From a Roman family name. Famous modern bearers include the British television presenter Valerie Singleton.
RELATED NAMES: **Val, Valentine**.

Van (M) short for **Ivan** or **Evan**.

Vance (M) from the surname, meaning 'person who lives in a fen'.

Vanessa (F) a name coined in the early 18th century by Jonathan Swift for his friend Esther Vanhomrigh. In more recent times it has been borne by the British actress Vanessa Redgrave.
SHORT FORM: **Nessie**.
RELATED NAME: **Nessa**.

Vashti (F) a biblical name, possibly meaning 'beautiful', borne by a Persian queen.

Vasu (M) 'bright' or 'excellent'. An Indian name given to various gods.

Vaughan (M) from the Welsh surname, meaning 'small'.
ALTERNATIVE FORM: **Vaughn**.

Velma (F) a name of uncertain origin, possibly another form of **Wilhelmina** ('resolute protector') or a blend of **Val** and **Thelma**.

Venetia (F) from the Latin name for the Italian city of Venice. It was popularized as a forename in the 19th century by Benjamin Disraeli's novel *Venetia* (1837).

Venus (F) 'beauty, delight'. The name of the Roman goddess of love. The

US tennis player Venus Williams is a famous bearer of the name.

Vera [VEER-a] (F) 'faith' or 'true'. The British singer Vera Lynn popularized the name in the 1940s.

Vere (M) from a surname of French aristocratic origin, which comes from a place name meaning 'alder'.

Verena (F) a name of uncertain origin, possibly another form of **Vera**. St Verena, born in Egypt, went to Switzerland as a nurse in the 3rd century.
ALTERNATIVE FORMS: **Verina, Verona**.

Vergil (M) another spelling of **Virgil**.

Verity (F) 'truth'. The British television producer Verity Lambert is a famous bearer of the name.
RELATED NAME: **Alethea**.

Verna (F) a name of uncertain origin, sometimes associated with the word *vernal* meaning 'of the spring'. Alternatively, it may be a feminine form of **Vernon**, a short form of **Laverna**, or another form of **Verena** or **Verona**.

Vernon (M) from a surname of French aristocratic origin, which comes from a place name meaning 'alder grove'. It is borne by the young hero of DBC Pierre's novel *Vernon God Little* (2003).
SHORT FORM: **Vern**.
FEMININE FORM: **Verna**.

Verona (F) from the name of the Italian city. It is borne by the British actress Verona Joseph.

Veronica (F) 'true image'. According to a traditional story, an image of Christ's features was left on the cloth used by St Veronica to wipe his face as he made his way to his crucifixion. Alternatively, the name may be another form of **Berenice** ('bringer of victory'). It was popularized in the 20th century by the US film star Veronica Lake (whose real name was Constance).
RELATED NAME: **Ronni**.

Vesta (F) the name of the Roman goddess of the hearth and its fire. It may also be associated with the vestal virgins who served the goddess and looked after the fire. Famous bearers of the name include the British music-hall entertainer Vesta Tilley (born Matilda Powles).

Vi (F) short for various names beginning with these letters, especially **Violet**.

Vicky (F) a short form of **Victoria**, sometimes given as a name in its own right. Vicky Pollard, an overweight teenage delinquent, is one of the stock characters of the television comedy series *Little Britain*.
ALTERNATIVE FORMS: **Vicki, Vickie, Vikki**.

Victor (M) 'conqueror'. Famous 20th-century bearers of the name include the US actor Victor Mature and the British dance-band leader Victor Silvester.

SHORT FORM: Vic.

FEMININE FORM: Victoria.

Victoria (F) 'victory'. Alternatively, the name may be regarded as a feminine form of **Victor**. It was little used in the UK before the reign of Queen Victoria in the 19th century, after which it became increasingly popular. The British comedian Victoria Wood and the British singer Victoria Beckham are famous modern bearers of the name.

SHORT FORMS: Tori, Toria.

RELATED NAME: Vicky.

Vijay (M) an Indian name meaning 'victory'.

FEMININE FORM: Vijaya.

Vijaya (F) the feminine form of Vijay.

Vikki (F) another spelling of Vicky.

Vikram (M) 'stride' or 'valour'. An Indian name sometimes given to the god Vishnu. Famous modern bearers include the Indian writer Vikram Seth.

Vinay (M) an Indian name meaning 'guidance' or 'leading asunder'.

Vince (M) a short form of Vincent, sometimes given as a name in its own right. It was popularized in the 1980s by the character of this name

played by Paul Nicholas in the television sitcom *Just Good Friends*.

Vincent (M) 'conquering'. The name was borne by various saints, including the 17th-century French priest St Vincent de Paul. The 19th-century Dutch painter Vincent Van Gogh is the subject of the song 'Vincent' (1971) by the US singer and songwriter Don McLean. The short form is used by the British footballer and actor Vinnie Jones.

SHORT FORM: Vinnie.

RELATED NAME: Vince.

Vinnie (M/F) short for Vincent or Lavinia.

ALTERNATIVE FORM: Vinny.

Viola (F) 'violet'. Shakespeare gave the name to one of the principal characters of his play *Twelfth Night*.

Violet (F) from the flower name. It was particularly popular in the late 19th and early 20th centuries.

SHORT FORM: Vi.

Virgil (M) from the Roman name *Vergilius*, borne in the 1st century BC by the Roman poet known as Virgil. In the case of the 8th-century Irish monk St Virgil of Salzburg, it is another form of **Fergal**. Other famous bearers include the puppet astronaut Virgil Tracy in *Thunderbirds*, a children's television series of the 1960s.

ALTERNATIVE FORM: Vergil.

Virginia (F) 'virgin'. The American

state of Virginia was named in honour of Elizabeth I, who was known as the 'Virgin Queen'. Famous modern bearers include the British novelist Virginia Woolf and the British tennis player Virginia Wade.
SHORT FORM: **Ginny**.
RELATED NAME: **Gina**.

Vishnu (M) 'all-pervasive'. An Indian name borne by an important Hindu god.

Vita (F) 'life'. In the case of the 20th-century British writer Vita Sackville-West, probably the best-known bearer of the name, it was short for **Victoria**.

Vivian (F/M) 'alive'. Originally a boys' name, it is now more often given to girls. Famous male bearers include the 20th-century British explorer Sir Vivian Fuchs and the anarchic punk Vyvyan (played by Adrian Edmondson) in the British television comedy series *The Young Ones*.
SHORT FORM: **Viv**.
ALTERNATIVE FORMS: **Vyvyan, Vivien** (F).

Vivien (F) another form of **Vivian**, of French origin, now given only to girls. Famous bearers include the 20th-century British actress Vivien Leigh (whose name was originally spelt Vivian).
SHORT FORM: **Viv**.
ALTERNATIVE FORM: **Vivienne**.

W

Wade (M) from the surname, meaning 'ford'.

Waldo (M) 'power, rule'. Famous bearers of the name include the 19th-century US writer Ralph Waldo Emerson.
FEMININE FORM: **Valda**.

Walid (M) an Arabic name meaning 'newborn baby'.

Wallace (M) from the surname, meaning 'foreign'. It is borne by a cheese-loving inventor who lives with his dog Gromit in a series of animated films of the late 20th and early 21st centuries.
SHORT FORM: **Wally**.

Wallis (M/F) another form of **Wallace** that is sometimes given to girls. It was the middle name of the US divorcee known as Wallis Simpson, who married the former Edward VIII after his abdication and became the Duchess of Windsor.

Walter (M) 'army ruler'. Famous bearers of the name include the 16th-century navigator Sir Walter Raleigh and the 20th-century film producer Walt Disney.
SHORT FORMS: **Walt, Wally**.

Wanda (F) a name of uncertain origin, popularized in the late 19th century by the British writer Ouida's novel *Wanda* (1883). More recently it has featured in the comedy film *A Fish Called Wanda* (1988), borne by a human jewel thief as well as the title character.

Warren (M) from the surname, meaning 'guard' or from the French place name La Varenne. The US actor Warren Beatty and the British actor Warren Mitchell are famous bearers of the name.

Warwick [WORR-ik] (M) from the surname and place name, meaning 'farm by a weir'.

Washington (M) from the surname of the first US president, George Washington, which ultimately comes from an English place name. The forename was borne by the 19th-century US writer Washington Irving.

Wasim (M) an Arabic name meaning 'handsome'.

Wayne (M) from the surname, which was originally given to a driver or maker of carts and is now chiefly associated with the 20th-century US actor John Wayne. The forename was particularly popular in the 1970s but had fallen from favour by the 1990s, when it was borne by the comic character Wayne Slob in Harry Enfield's television series.

Wenda (F) a blend of **Wendy** and **Wanda**.

Wendell (M) from the surname, which ultimately comes from the name of a medieval European people. The 19th-century US writer Oliver Wendell Holmes and his lawyer son were famous bearers.

Wendy (F) a name coined in the early 20th century by J. M. Barrie for the fictional character Wendy Darling in his children's story *Peter Pan*. It is also used as a short form of **Gwendolen**. Famous real-life bearers include the British actresses Wendy Craig and Wendy Richard.

Wentworth (M) from a surname and place name meaning 'winter enclosure'. The US actor Wentworth Miller is a famous bearer of the name.

Wesley (M) from the surname, which ultimately comes from a place name meaning 'western meadow' and is chiefly associated with the brothers John and Charles Wesley, who founded the Methodist Church in the 18th century. Famous modern bearers of the forename include the US actor Wesley Snipes and the US film director Wes Craven.
SHORT FORM: **Wes**.

Weston (M) from a surname and place name meaning 'western settlement'.

Whitney (F/M) from the surname, which ultimately comes from a place name meaning 'white island'. The best-known bearer of the name is the US singer and actress Whitney Houston.

Wilbert (M) 'resolute and illustrious'. The name was borne by the Rev. Wilbert Awdry, a 20th-century British clergyman and writer of children's books featuring Thomas the Tank Engine and his friends.

Wilbur (M) 'resolute and strong'. The African-born novelist Wilbur Smith is a famous bearer of the name.

Wilfred (M) 'desiring peace'. The name was particularly popular in the early 20th century, when it was given to the British radio personality Wilfred Pickles and the British actor Wilfrid Hyde-White.
SHORT FORM: **Wilf**.
ALTERNATIVE FORM: **Wilfrid**.

Wilhelmina (F) a feminine form of **William**, of German origin.

RELATED NAMES: **Mina, Minnie, Wilma, Willa, Billie.**

Wilkie (M) from a surname that originated as a short form of **William**. The 19th-century British writer Wilkie Collins was a famous bearer of the name.
RELATED NAMES: **Will, Billy, Liam, Gwilym.**

Will (M) a short form of **William** or **Willard**, sometimes given as a name in its own right. It is borne by Will Parry, the young hero of Philip Pullman's trilogy *His Dark Materials* (1995–2000), and by the British singer Will Young (whose full name is William).
FEMININE FORMS: **Willa, Billie.**
RELATED NAMES: **Billy, Liam, Gwilym, Wilkie.**

Willa (F) a short form of **Wilhelmina** (or another name beginning with *Wil-*) or a feminine form of **Will**. The 20th-century US writer Willa Cather was a famous bearer of the name.
RELATED NAMES: **Billie, Wilma, Mina, Minnie.**

Willard (M) from the surname, meaning 'resolute and brave'. It is the full name of the US actor known as Will Smith.
RELATED NAME: **Will.**

William (M) 'resolute protector'. The name has had many royal bearers, from William the Conqueror in the 11th century to Prince William in the 20th century. It may also be associated with the *Just William* stories of Richmal Crompton, about a boy who is always getting into trouble.
SHORT FORMS: **Willy, Willie, Bill, Wills.**
FEMININE FORMS: **Wilhelmina, Wilma, Mina, Minnie, Willa, Billie.**
RELATED NAMES: **Will, Billy, Liam, Gwilym, Wilkie.**

Willis (M) from a surname meaning 'of Will'. The 20th-century British dramatist Willis Hall was a famous bearer of the name.

Willoughby (M) from a surname and place name meaning 'willow settlement'.

Willow (F) from the name of the tree, possibly influenced by the word *willowy*, meaning 'slender and graceful'.

Wilma (F) a short form of **Wilhelmina**. It is chiefly associated with Wilma Flintstone, wife of Fred, in the US cartoon series *The Flintstones*.
RELATED NAMES: **Willa, Billie, Mina, Minnie.**

Windsor (M) from the surname and place name, both of which are associated with the British royal family. The British actor Windsor Davies is a famous bearer of the forename.

Winifred (F) another form of a Welsh

name meaning 'blessed reconciliation' (as in the case of the 7th-century martyr St Winifred) or of an Old English name meaning 'friend of peace'.
SHORT FORM: Win.
RELATED NAMES: Winnie, Freda.

Winnie (F/M) a short form of **Winifred** or **Winston**, sometimes given as a name in its own right, especially to girls. Famous bearers include the South African political activist Winnie Mandela (female) and the fictional bear Winnie-the-Pooh (male), who features in the children's stories and poems of A. A. Milne.
RELATED NAME: Freda.

Winona (F) 'firstborn daughter'. A name of American Indian origin, borne by a legendary princess. The city of Winona in Minnesota was named after the princess, and the US actress Winona Ryder was named after the city.

Winston (M) from a surname and place name. The forename is chiefly associated with the 20th-century British statesman Sir Winston Churchill. It is also borne by Winston Smith, the hero of George Orwell's novel *Nineteen Eighty-Four* (1949).
RELATED NAME: Winnie.

Winton (M) from a surname and place name with various meanings.

Wolf (M) from the name of the animal.

ALTERNATIVE FORM: Wolfe.

Woodrow (M) from a surname and place name meaning 'row of houses by a wood'. It was the middle name of the 20th-century US president known as Woodrow Wilson.
RELATED NAME: Woody.

Woody (M) a short form of **Woodrow**, sometimes given as a name in its own right. Famous bearers include the 20th-century US folk singer Woody Guthrie (whose full name was Woodrow) and the US actor, screenwriter, and film director Woody Allen (born Allen Stewart Konigsberg in 1935).

Wyatt (M) from the surname, meaning 'brave warrior'. The forename is chiefly associated with the US lawman and gunfighter Wyatt Earp.

Wyn (M/F) another form of **Wynn** or of the Welsh boys' name **Gwyn** ('fair').

Wyndham (M) from the surname, which comes from the English place name Wymondham. It was the middle name of the 20th-century British writer and artist known as Wyndham Lewis.

Wynn (M/F) from the surname, meaning 'friend'.
ALTERNATIVE FORMS: Wynne, Wyn.

Wystan (M) 'battle stone'. The name was borne by a 9th-century saint and by the 20th-century British poet known as W. H. Auden.

X

Xandra [ZAN-dra] (F) another spelling of **Zandra** ('defender of men').

Xander [ZAN-da] (M) a short form of **Alexander** ('defender of men'), sometimes given as a name in its own right.
ALTERNATIVE FORM: **Zander**.
RELATED NAMES: **Alec, Alex, Lex, Lexie, Alistair, Sasha**.

Xanthe [ZANTH-ee] (F) 'yellow'. The name is borne by various characters in Greek mythology.

Xavier [ZAY-vi-a, ZAV-i-a] (M) from the surname of the 16th-century Spanish missionary St Francis Xavier, which comes from a place name meaning 'the new house'.

Xena [ZEE-na] (F) 'stranger, foreigner'. The name has recently been popularized by the US television series *Xena: Warrior Princess*.
ALTERNATIVE FORM: **Zena**.

Xenia [ZEE-ni-a] (F) 'hospitality'.
ALTERNATIVE FORM: **Zenia**.

Y

Yael [ya-EL] (F) a Jewish name meaning 'wild goat'.
ALTERNATIVE FORM: **Jael**.

Yale (M) from a surname and place name meaning 'fertile upland', of Welsh origin. The surname was borne by the benefactor of Yale University in Connecticut and by the founder of the company that manufactures Yale locks.

Yarrow (F) from the name of a plant used in herbal medicine.

Yasir (M) an Arabic name meaning 'rich'.

Yasmin (F) another form of **Jasmine**. The original Persian form of the name, it was popularized in the 1980s by the British model Yasmin Le Bon, whose father is Iranian.
ALTERNATIVE FORM: **Yasmine**.
RELATED NAME: **Jessamine**.

Yehudi [yi-HOO-dee] (M) 'Jew'. A Hebrew name made famous by the 20th-century violinist Yehudi Menuhin.

Yentl (F) a Jewish name meaning 'kind' or 'noble'. It was popularized by a play and film with this title, based on a short story by Isaac Bashevis Singer about a Jewish girl who disguises herself as a boy.

Yitzhak (M) a Jewish form of **Isaac** (possibly meaning 'laughter').
RELATED NAME: **Zak**.

Yolanda (F) a name of uncertain origin, possibly another form of **Iolanthe** ('violet flower').
SHORT FORM: **Yola**.
ALTERNATIVE FORM: **Yolande**.

Yoram (M) a Jewish name meaning 'exalted by God'.

Yorath (M) another form of the Welsh name **Iorwerth** ('handsome lord').
RELATED NAME: **Iolo**.

Ysabel (F) another spelling of **Isabel**.

Yusra (F) an Arabic name meaning 'prosperity'.

Yusuf (M) the Arabic form of **Joseph** ('God will add').
RELATED NAMES: **Joe, Joey, Jose**.

Yves [eev] (M) 'yew'. Of French origin, the name has been popularized in English-speaking countries by the French fashion designer Yves Saint Laurent.
ALTERNATIVE FORM: **Yvon**.
FEMININE FORMS: **Yvette, Yvonne**.
RELATED NAME: **Ivo**.

Yvette (F) a feminine form of **Yves**.
ALTERNATIVE FORM: **Evette**.

Yvonne (F) a feminine form of **Yves**. The Canadian-born actress Yvonne De Carlo was a famous bearer of the name.
ALTERNATIVE FORM: **Evonne**.

Z

Zachary (M) another form of Zechariah. Famous bearers include the 19th-century US president Zachary Taylor and the 20th-century US actor Zachary Scott. In the alternative form Zacharias, the name is borne in the Authorized Version of the Bible by the father of John the Baptist.
ALTERNATIVE FORMS: Zacharias, Zachariah, Zakaria.
RELATED NAME: Zak.

Zadie (F) another form of Sadie ('princess'), recently popularized by the British writer Zadie Smith.
RELATED NAMES: Sarah, Sally, Zara.

Zahir (M) an Arabic name meaning 'shining'.

Zahra (F) an Arabic name meaning 'flower'.
ALTERNATIVE FORMS: Zahrah, Zara.

Zak (M) a short form of Zachary or Isaac (possibly meaning 'laughter'), sometimes given as a name in its own right.
ALTERNATIVE FORMS: Zach, Zack, Zac.

RELATED NAMES: Zechariah, Yitzhak.

Zander (M) another spelling of Xander ('defender of men').

Zandra (F) a short form of Alexandra ('defender of men'), given as a name in its own right. Its best-known bearer is the 20th-century British fashion designer Zandra Rhodes.
ALTERNATIVE FORM: Xandra.
RELATED NAMES: Alex, Lexie, Sandy, Sandra, Sasha.

Zane (M) from a surname of uncertain origin. It was the middle name of the 20th-century US novelist known as Zane Grey.

Zara (F) another form of Sara ('princess') or Zahra ('flower'). The British equestrian Zara Phillips, daughter of Princess Anne, is a famous bearer of the name.
RELATED NAMES: Sadie, Sally, Zadie.

Zaynab (F) another spelling of Zeinab.

Zeb (M) a short form of Zebedee (or

another name beginning with these letters), sometimes given as a name in its own right.

Zebedee (M) 'gift of God'. A biblical name, borne by the father of Jesus Christ's apostles James and John. More recently it has been associated with a bouncing character in the children's television series *The Magic Roundabout* (1965–77).
RELATED NAME: **Zeb**.

Zechariah (M) 'God has remembered'. The name of a biblical prophet and the book of the Bible that tells his story. In some versions of the Bible it is also used (instead of Zacharias) for the father of John the Baptist.
RELATED NAMES: **Zachary, Zak**.

Zeinab (F) from the Arabic name of a fragrant flower. Famous bearers of the name include the daughter and granddaughter of Muhammad and, more recently, the television news presenter Zeinab Badawi.
ALTERNATIVE FORM: **Zaynab**.

Zeke (M) a short form of Ezekiel ('God strengthens'), sometimes given as a name in its own right.

Zelda (F) a Jewish name meaning 'luck, happiness' or a short form of Griselda ('grey warrior') given as a name in its own right. It was made famous in the 1920s by Zelda Fitzgerald, the glamorous but mentally unstable wife of the US writer F. Scott Fitzgerald.

Zena (F) another spelling of Xena ('stranger, foreigner') or a short form of Zenobia ('life of Zeus') given as a name in its own right.
ALTERNATIVE FORM: **Zina**.

Zenia (F) another spelling of Xenia ('hospitality').

Zenobia (F) 'life of Zeus'. The name was borne in the 3rd century by a beautiful and powerful queen of Palmyra in Syria.
RELATED NAME: **Zena**.

Zephaniah [zef-a-NYE-a] (M) 'hidden by God'. The name of a biblical prophet and the book of the Bible containing his sayings. It has recently been popularized as the surname of the poet Benjamin Zephaniah.

Zeta (F) a name of uncertain origin, possibly another spelling of Zita. It is chiefly associated with the Welsh-born actress Catherine Zeta-Jones, who gained it from her grandmother.

Zillah (F) a biblical name meaning 'shade'.
ALTERNATIVE FORM: **Zilla**.

Zina (F) another spelling of Zena or a short form of various European names beginning with *Zin-* or ending with *-sina*.

Zinnia (F) from the flower name.

Zipporah (F) 'bird'. A biblical name, borne by the wife of Moses.

Zita (F) 'girl'. The name was borne in the 13th century by a devout and conscientious Italian servant who became St Zita, patron saint of servants.
ALTERNATIVE FORM: **Zeta**.

Zoe (F) 'life'. The name was particularly popular in the late 20th century. Famous modern bearers include the actress Zoë Wanamaker.
ALTERNATIVE FORMS: **Zoë, Zoey**.

Zola (F) an African name meaning 'quiet, tranquil' or a blend of **Zoe** and **Lola**. It may also be given in honour of the 19th-century French novelist Émile Zola. The South African runner Zola Budd is a famous bearer of the name.

Zora (F) a name of uncertain origin, possibly meaning 'dawn' or from the biblical place name Zorah. It was borne by the 20th-century US writer Zora Neale Hurston.

Zuleika [ZOO-LAY-ka, ZOO-LYE-ka, ZOO-LEE-ka] (F) a name of uncertain origin, possibly meaning 'brilliant beauty'. Famous bearers include the wife of the biblical character Potiphar (an Egyptian official), who tries and fails to seduce Joseph, and the beautiful heroine of Max Beerbohm's novel *Zuleika Dobson* (1911), whose rejected admirers commit suicide.

Appendix:
The most popular names in the UK

The material in these tables comes from the National Statistics website (www.statistics.gov.uk), the website of the General Register Office for Scotland (www.gro-scotland.gov.uk), and the website of the Northern Ireland Statistics and Research Agency (www.nisra.gov.uk). Crown copyright material is reproduced with the permission of the Controller of HMSO under the terms of the Click-Use Licence.

Top 50 names for boys in England and Wales, 1974-2006

	1974	1984	1995	2000	2006
1	Paul	Christopher	Jack	Jack	Jack
2	Mark	James	Daniel	Thomas	Thomas
3	David	David	Thomas	James	Joshua
4	Andrew	Daniel	James	Joshua	Oliver
5	Richard	Michael	Joshua	Daniel	Harry
6	Christopher	Matthew	Matthew	Harry	James
7	James	Andrew	Ryan	Samuel	William
8	Simon	Richard	Luke	Joseph	Samuel
9	Michael	Paul	Samuel	Matthew	Daniel
10	Matthew	Mark	Jordan	Callum	Charlie
11	Stephen	Thomas	Joseph	Luke	Benjamin
12	Lee	Adam	Liam	William	Joseph
13	John	Robert	Alexander	Lewis	Callum
14	Robert	John	Benjamin	Oliver	George
15	Darren	Lee	Michael	Ryan	Jake
16	Daniel	Benjamin	Adam	Benjamin	Alfie

	1974	1984	1995	2000	2006
17	Steven	Steven	Connor	George	Luke
18	Jason	Jonathan	William	Liam	Matthew
19	Nicholas	Craig	Jake	Jordan	Ethan
20	Jonathan	Stephen	Christopher	Adam	Lewis
21	Ian	Simon	George	Alexander	Jacob
22	Neil	Nicholas	Harry	Jake	Mohammed
23	Peter	Peter	Callum	Connor	Dylan
24	Stuart	Anthony	Lewis	Cameron	Alexander
25	Anthony	Alexander	Oliver	Nathan	Ryan
26	Martin	Gary	Kieran	Kieran	Adam
27	Kevin	Ian	Andrew	Mohammed	Tyler
28	Craig	Ryan	Robert	Jamie	Harvey
29	Philip	Luke	Nathan	Jacob	Max
30	Gary	Jamie	David	Michael	Cameron
31	Scott	Stuart	Jamie	Ben	Liam
32	Wayne	Philip	Aaron	Ethan	Jamie
33	Timothy	Darren	Bradley	Charlie	Leo
34	Benjamin	William	Ashley	Bradley	Owen
35	Adam	Gareth	Jacob	Brandon	Connor
36	Alan	Martin	Jonathan	Aaron	Harrison
37	Dean	Kevin	Mohammed	Max	Nathan
38	Adrian	Scott	Kyle	Dylan	Ben
39	Carl	Dean	John	Kyle	Henry
40	Thomas	Joseph	Sam	Reece	Archie
41	William	Jason	Ben	Robert	Edward
42	Graham	Neil	Scott	Christopher	Michael
43	Alexander	Samuel	Charles	David	Aaron
44	Colin	Carl	Sean	Edward	Muhammad
45	Jamie	Ben	Edward	Charles	Kyle
46	Gareth	Sean	Cameron	Owen	Noah
47	Justin	Timothy	Nicholas	Louis	Oscar
48	Barry	Oliver	Reece	Alex	Lucas
49	Christian	Ashley	Charlie	Joe	Rhys
50	Karl	Wayne	Dominic	Rhys	Bradley

Top 50 names for girls in England and Wales, 1974-2006

	1974	1984	1995	2000	2006
1	Sarah	Sarah	Jessica	Chloe	Olivia
2	Claire	Laura	Lauren	Emily	Grace
3	Nicola	Gemma	Rebecca	Megan	Jessica
4	Emma	Emma	Sophie	Charlotte	Ruby
5	Lisa	Rebecca	Charlotte	Jessica	Emily
6	Joanne	Claire	Hannah	Lauren	Sophie
7	Michelle	Victoria	Amy	Sophie	Chloe
8	Helen	Samantha	Emily	Olivia	Lucy
9	Samantha	Rachel	Chloe	Hannah	Lily
10	Karen	Amy	Emma	Lucy	Ellie
11	Amanda	Jennifer	Shannon	Georgia	Ella
12	Rachel	Nicola	Laura	Rebecca	Charlotte
13	Louise	Katie	Bethany	Bethany	Katie
14	Julie	Lisa	Megan	Amy	Mia
15	Clare	Kelly	Katie	Ellie	Hannah
16	Rebecca	Natalie	Lucy	Katie	Amelia
17	Sharon	Louise	Sarah	Emma	Megan
18	Victoria	Michelle	Alice	Abigail	Amy
19	Caroline	Hayley	Jade	Molly	Isabella
20	Susan	Hannah	Danielle	Grace	Millie
21	Alison	Helen	Abigail	Courtney	Evie
22	Catherine	Charlotte	Olivia	Shannon	Abigail
23	Elizabeth	Joanne	Rachel	Caitlin	Freya
24	Deborah	Lucy	Eleanor	Eleanor	Molly
25	Donna	Elizabeth	Samantha	Jade	Daisy
26	Tracey	Leanne	Elizabeth	Ella	Holly
27	Tracy	Danielle	Georgia	Leah	Emma
28	Angela	Donna	Victoria	Alice	Erin
29	Jane	Katherine	Holly	Holly	Isabelle
30	Zoe	Clare	Zoe	Laura	Poppy
31	Kerry	Stephanie	Natasha	Anna	Jasmine
32	Melanie	Stacey	Paige	Jasmine	Leah

	1974	1984	1995	2000	2006
33	Sally	Lauren	Nicole	Sarah	Keira
34	Jennifer	Joanna	Georgina	Elizabeth	Phoebe
35	Dawn	Kerry	Chelsea	Amelia	Caitlin
36	Andrea	Emily	Stephanie	Rachel	Rebecca
37	Suzanne	Catherine	Alexandra	Amber	Georgia
38	Lucy	Sophie	Natalie	Phoebe	Lauren
39	Joanna	Anna	Jodie	Natasha	Madison
40	Anna	Jessica	Ellie	Niamh	Amber
41	Charlotte	Zoe	Grace	Zoe	Elizabeth
42	Paula	Kirsty	Gemma	Paige	Eleanor
43	Katherine	Kimberley	Kirsty	Nicole	Bethany
44	Maria	Kate	Abbie	Abbie	Isabel
45	Marie	Jenna	Amber	Mia	Paige
46	Fiona	Caroline	Katherine	Imogen	Scarlett
47	Kelly	Natasha	Molly	Lily	Alice
48	Natalie	Rachael	Melissa	Alexandra	Imogen
49	Kathryn	Amanda	Kayleigh	Chelsea	Sophia
50	Jacqueline	Kathryn	Jennifer	Daisy	Anna

Top 20 names for boys and girls in Scotland and Northern Ireland, 2006

	Boys, Scotland	Girls, Scotland	Boys, N Ireland	Girls, N Ireland
1	Jack	Sophie	Jack	Katie
2	Lewis	Emma	Matthew	Grace
3	Callum	Erin	Ryan	Emma
4	Ryan	Katie	James	Sophie
5	James	Lucy	Daniel	Ellie
6	Cameron	Chloe	Adam	Lucy
7	Jamie	Ellie	Joshua	Sarah
8	Daniel	Amy	Callum	Hannah
9	Matthew	Olivia	Ben	Jessica
10	Kyle	Emily	Ethan	Erin
11	Adam	Hannah	Jamie	Niamh
12	Ben	Rebecca	Conor	Caitlin
13	Aaron	Jessica	Luke	Chloe
14	Andrew	Grace	Thomas	Amy
15	Logan	Megan	Dylan	Leah
16	Connor	Leah	Sean	Aoife
17	Alexander	Rachel	Michael	Rebecca
18	Dylan	Aimee	Aaron	Emily
19	Liam	Isla	Jake	Aimee
20	Thomas	Sarah	Calum	Anna